Microsoft AJAX Library Essentials

Client-side ASP.NET AJAX 1.0 Explained

A practical tutorial to using Microsoft AJAX Library
to enhance the user experience of your ASP.NET
Web Applications

Bogdan Brinzarea

Cristian Darie

BIRMINGHAM - MUMBAI

Microsoft AJAX Library Essentials
Client-side ASP.NET AJAX 1.0 Explained

First published: August 2007

Production Reference: 2200807

Published by Packt Publishing Ltd.
32 Lincoln Road
Olton
Birmingham, B27 6PA, UK.

ISBN 978-1-847190-98-7

www.packtpub.com

Cover Image by www.visionwt.com

Credits

Authors

Bogdan Brinzarea

Cristian Darie

Reviewers

Ruben Cordoba

Cosmin Mihai Gheorghita

Development Editor

Douglas Paterson

Technical Editor

Rajlaxmi Nanda

Editorial Manager

Dipali Chittar

Project Manager

Patricia Weir

Project Coordinator

Abhijeet Deobhakta

Indexer

Bhushan Pangaonkar

Proofreaders

Chris Smith

Martin Brooks

Production Coordinator

Manjiri Nadkarni

Cover Designer

Manjiri Nadkarni

About the Authors

Bogdan Brinzarea-Iamandi has a strong background in Computer Science holding Master and Bachelor Degrees at the Automatic Control and Computers Faculty of the Politehnica University of Bucharest, Romania, and also an Auditor diploma at the Computer Science department at Ecole Polytechnique, Paris, France. His main interests cover a wide area from embedded programming, distributed and mobile computing, and new web technologies.

Currently, he is employed as Supervisor within the Alternative Channels Sector team of the IT Division in Banca Romaneasca, a Member of National Bank of Greece. He is Project Manager for Internet Banking and he coordinates other projects related to new technologies and applications to be implemented in the banking area.

This is Bogdan's second book on AJAX, following the popular *AJAX and PHP: Building Responsive Web Applications*, also published by Packt.

Cristian Darie is a software engineer with experience in a wide range of modern technologies, and the author of numerous technical books. Cristian currently lives in Bucharest, Romania, studying distributed application architectures for his PhD. He's getting involved with various commercial and research projects, and when not planning to buy Google, he enjoys his bit of social life. If you want to say "hi" you can reach Cristian through his personal website at `http://www.cristiandarie.ro`.

About the Reviewers

Ruben Cordoba graduated from Merida University (Spain) and has a Bachelor Degree in Technical Engineering of Computer Systems. Programming and web development are his passions. He has loved computers from the moment his dad presented him his first computer, an AMSTRAD CPC464 with green screen, at the age of six. When he is not programming, Ruben likes walking his dog along the beach, getting inspired with new ideas to code. He lives in the South of Spain and works as a web programmer.

Cosmin Mihai Gheorghita is working as a computer programmer for a small and dynamic Romanian company. His skills range from low-level programming using microcontrollers to high-level web development. Although he likes to experiment with hot technologies such as Ruby On Rails, he has specialized in .NET technologies with an emphasis on C# and ASP.NET.

Table of Contents

Preface	**1**
Chapter 1: AJAX and ASP.NET	**7**
The Big Picture	**8**
AJAX and Web 2.0	10
Building Websites Since 1990	**11**
HTTP and HTML	11
ASP.NET and Other Server-Side Technologies	13
JavaScript and Other Client-Side Technologies	14
What's Missing?	15
The World of AJAX	**15**
What is AJAX Made Of?	17
Uses and Misuses of AJAX	18
Introducing ASP.NET AJAX	20
Resources and Tools	21
Setting Up Your Environment	**22**
Installing IIS	22
Installing Visual Web Developer	25
Creating a Folder for Your Project	25
Preparing the Atlas Application in Windows Vista	26
Preparing the Atlas Web Application in Windows XP	27
Hello World!	**28**
Time for Action—Quickstart AJAX	31
What Just Happened?	35
Summary	**43**
Chapter 2: AJAX Foundations	**45**
JavaScript and the Document Object Model	**45**
Time for Action—Playing with JavaScript and the DOM	48
What Just Happened	50

JavaScript Events and the DOM	**51**
Time for Action—Using JavaScript Events and the DOM	53
What Just Happened?	54
Even More DOM	**56**
Time for Action—Even More DOM	57
What Just Happened?	59
JavaScript, DOM, and CSS	**61**
Time for Action—Working with CSS and JavaScript	61
What Just Happened?	64
The XMLHttpRequest Object	**65**
Creating the XMLHttpRequest Object	65
Initiating Server Requests	69
Handling the Server Response	72
Time for Action—Making Asynchronous Calls with XMLHttpRequest	74
What Just Happened?	77
Summary	**80**
Chapter 3: Object-Oriented JavaScript	**81**
Concepts of Object-Oriented Programming	**81**
Objects and Classes	82
Encapsulation	83
Inheritance	83
Polymorphism	84
Object-Oriented JavaScript	**84**
JavaScript Functions	85
Functions as Variables	86
Anonymous Functions	88
Inner Functions and JavaScript Closures	89
JavaScript Classes	90
Class Diagrams	93
C# and JavaScript Classes	93
Referencing External Functions	96
Thinking of Objects as Associative Arrays	96
Creating Object Members on the Fly	98
Private Members	99
Prototypes	100
The JavaScript Execution Context	101
var x, this.x, and x	102
Using the Right Context	103
Inheritance using Closures and Prototypes	105
Inheritance Using Closures	105
Inheritance Using Prototyping	108
Introducing JSON	**110**
Summary	**112**

Chapter 4: Introducing the Microsoft AJAX Library   113

Microsoft AJAX Library Components   **113**

Asynchronous Communication   **116**

  Client Asynchronous Communication   117

  Server Asynchronous Communication   118

Working with WebRequest   **119**

  Time for Action—WebRequest   120

  What Just Happened?   125

More WebRequests   **129**

  Time for Action—More WebRequest   130

  What Just Happened?   132

Summary   **133**

Chapter 5: OOP with the Microsoft AJAX Library   135

The New Features   **136**

JavaScript Base Classes Extensions   **136**

  Time for Action: Bubble Sort and Base Classes Extensions   137

  What Just Happened?   140

Classes in Microsoft AJAX Library   **142**

  The Type, Namespaces, and Events   143

    Time for Action—Creating and Using the Person Class   144

    What Just Happened?   148

  Inheritance   154

    Time for Action—Implementing Inheritance using Microsoft   156

    What Just Happened?   161

  AJAX Library

  Enumerations   165

  Interfaces   166

    Ti me for action—Inheritance and Interfaces   167

    What Just Happened?   173

  OOP Recommendations   175

Summary   **175**

Chapter 6: Creating Client Components   177

DOM Elements and Events   **177**

Components, Behaviors, and Controls   **180**

  Creating Components   182

  Disposing of Components   183

  Sys.Application and Client Page Life-Cycle Events   184

    The **init** Event   186

    The **load** Event   186

    The **pageLoad()** Method   187

    The **pageUnload()** Method   188

    The **unload** Event   188

Behaviors	188
Controls	190
Quicksteps for Creating Custom Client Components	191
Summary	**192**
Chapter 7: Case Study: Timer and EnhancedTextBox	**193**
The Timer Component	**193**
The EnhancedTextBox Behavior	**194**
Creating Timer and EnhancedTextBox	**196**
Time for Action—Creating Custom Client Components	197
What Just Happened?	210
Using the Components	**216**
Summary	**217**
Chapter 8: Debugging Tools and Techniques	**219**
AJAX Debugging Overview	**220**
Debugging and Tracing with Microsoft AJAX Library	**220**
MicrosoftAjax.debug.js	222
Anonymous Functions vs. Pseudo-Named Functions	222
Parameters Validation	224
Debugging in Internet Explorer	**225**
Web Development Helper	228
Internet Explorer Developer Toolbar	228
Other tools	229
Debugging in Firefox	**230**
Firebug	230
Venkman JavaScript Debugger	231
Web Developer	233
Fiddler	**233**
Testing	**234**
Summary	**234**
Appendix A: Microsoft AJAX Library Reference	**235**
Conventions	**235**
Function Class	**238**
emptyMethod() Method	238
_validateParams() Method	238
createDelegate() Method	240
createCallback() Method	241
Type Class	242
JavaScript Base Type Extensions	**242**
Array Class	243
Boolean Class	245
Date Class	245

Error Class   248
  create() Method   248
Number Class   251
Object Class   252
RegExp Class   252
String Class   252
Sys Namespace   **254**
Sys.Application Class   255
Sys.ApplicationLoadEventArgs Class   256
Sys.Browser Class   256
Sys.CancelEventArgs Class   257
Sys.Component Class   257
Sys.CultureInfo Class   258
Sys.Debug Class   258
Sys.EventArgs Class   259
Sys.EventHandlerList Class   259
Sys.IContainer Interface   260
Sys.IDisposable Interface   260
Sys.INotifyDisposing Interface   260
Sys.INotifyPropertyChange Interface   261
Sys.PropertyChangedEventArgs Class   261
Sys.ScriptLoader Class   262
Sys.ScriptLoaderTask Class   263
Sys.StringBuilder Class   263
Sys.UI Namespace   **264**
Sys.UI.Behavior Class   264
Sys.UI.Bounds Class   265
Sys.UI.Control Class   265
Sys.UI.DomElement Class   266
  getElementById() Method ($get)   266
  addCssClass() Method   266
  containsCssClass() Method   267
  removeCssClass() Method   267
  toggleCssClass() Method   267
  getLocation() Method   268
  getBounds() Method   268
  setLocation() Method   268
Sys.UI.DomEvent Class   269
Sys.UI.Key Class   270
  addHandler() Method ($addHandler)   270
  addHandlers() Method ($addHandlers)   271
  clearHandlers() Method ($clearHandlers)   271
  preventDefault() Method   272

removeHandler() Method   272
stopPropagation() Method   272
Sys.UI.MouseButton Enumeration   273
Sys.UI.Point Class   273
Sys.UI.VisibilityMode Enumeration   273
Sys.Net Namespace   **274**
Sys.Net.NetworkRequestEventArgs Class   274
Sys.Net.WebRequest Class   275
Sys.Net.WebRequestExecutor Class   276
Sys.Net.WebRequestManager Class   277
Sys.Net.XmlHttpExecutor Class   278
Sys.Serialization Namespace   **279**
Sys.Serialization.JavaScriptSerializer Class   279
serialize() Method   279
deserialize() Method   280
Index   **281**

Preface

AJAX is a complex phenomenon that means different things to different people. Computer users appreciate that their favorite websites are now friendlier and feel more responsive. Web developers learn new skills that empower them to create sleek web applications with little effort. Indeed, everything sounds good about AJAX!

At its roots, AJAX is a mix of technologies that let you get rid of the evil page reload, which represents the dead time when navigating from one page to another. While this may be regarded as a minor feature, the elimination of page reloads opened the way for implementing more complex features into websites, such as real-time, server-supported data validation, drag and drop, and other tasks that were traditionally associated only with desktop applications. The central technology in the AJAX mix is JavaScript, which has been key to the success of AJAX: JavaScript is a lightweight language, it's loaded quickly by the web browser, and it's supported by all modern web browsers. No additional plug-ins or tools are required from the user to load an AJAX web application.

Microsoft created the **ASP.NET AJAX Framework** to build on the features offered by JavaScript, integrating the amazing power of AJAX into the world of ASP.NET. Available as a separate download from `http://ajax.asp.net/`, and integrated into the upcoming Visual Studio "Orcas" Edition, the ASP.NET AJAX Framework includes a wealth of server-side and client-side features that allow creating powerful web applications quickly.

The ASP.NET AJAX Framework is composed of a client-side JavaScript library named the **Microsoft AJAX Library**, and a set of server-side ASP.NET controls built on top of this library, named the **Microsoft AJAX Extensions**. This book covers the Microsoft AJAX Library, which can be a significant challenge for the typical server-side ASP.NET developer — the target of this book. Why is that so? For starters, in order to successfully use the Microsoft AJAX Library, one needs to have decent exposure to JavaScript, and an understanding of how objects work in JavaScript. This book addresses these topics in Chapters 2 and 3. If you aren't a JavaScript wizard yet, you'll find that JavaScript is quite different than the typical .NET environment, but we're certain that you'll end up liking it. You also need to understand the environment created by the library, which implements the typical features of the .NET platform into JavaScript, such as namespaces, interfaces, and so on.

To become a good ASP.NET AJAX Framework developer you'll need, obviously, to learn how to work with the ASP.NET AJAX Extensions as well. You can do so before or after reading this book. In both cases, this book will help you truly understand how the client-side part of the framework functions, how to work with it, and how to extend it.

We hope you'll find this book useful and relevant to your projects. For the latest details and updates regarding this book, please visit the support page maintained by Bogdan Brinzarea and Cristian Darie at http://www.cristiandarie.ro/asp-ajax/.

What This Book Covers

Chapter 1: AJAX and ASP.NET is an initial incursion into the world of AJAX and the vast possibilities it opens up for web developers and companies, to offer a better experience to their users. In this chapter you'll learn about the world of AJAX and Web 2.0, you'll set up your development environment, and you'll even build your first AJAX-enabled web page.

Chapter 2: AJAX Foundations guides you through the foundation technologies used to implement AJAX features, such as JavaScript, DOM, Cascading Style Sheets (CSS), and the XMLHttpRequest object.

Chapter 3: Object-Oriented JavaScript teaches you how objects *really* work in JavaScript. After a quick definition for terms such as encapsulation, inheritance, and polymorphism, you'll learn about JavaScript anonymous functions and closures, JavaScript prototypes, the JavaScript execution context and scope, how to implement inheritance using closures and prototypes, how to read class diagrams and implement them using JavaScript code, and more.

Chapter 4: Introducing the Microsoft AJAX Library is the first chapter where you actually work with the Microsoft AJAX Library. You learn what the library is made of, how it is structured, and what its main components do. At the end of the chapter you re-create the quickstart exercise from Chapter 1, but this time using the Microsoft AJAX Library to perform the asynchronous server call.

Chapter 5: OOP with the Microsoft AJAX Library presents the features in Microsoft AJAX Library that extend JavaScript with features of the .NET world, such as namespaces, interfaces, a more powerful inheritance paradigm, extended base classes, properties, events, enumerations, and more.

Chapter 6: Creating Client Components teaches you how to create client components using the Microsoft AJAX Library, which implies working with (and extending) elements of the page, registering events, creating controls and behaviors, and understanding the page life cycle.

Chapter 7: Case Study: Timer and EnhancedTextBox walks you through an exercise that implements the theory you had learned in the book. You create two client-side components, `Timer` and `EnhancedTextBox`, which are complex enough to offer a realistic view on creating components with the Microsoft AJAX Library.

Chapter 8: Debugging Tools and Techniques is a short overview of the major tools that you can use to debug your Microsoft AJAX Library projects, using Mozilla Firefox and Microsoft Internet Explorer.

Appendix A: Microsoft AJAX Library Reference is a quick reference and a visual guideline to the Microsoft AJAX Library namespaces and classes, which complements the official documentation at `http://ajax.asp.net/docs/ClientReference/`.

What You Need for This Book

To follow this book you need to have a Windows-based machine that can run a web server and Microsoft Visual Web Developer 2005 Express Edition. The installation and setup instructions for your development environment are described in Chapter 1.

Who is This Book for

This book has been written for ASP.NET developers entering the world of the ASP.NET AJAX Framework, and for existing ASP.NET AJAX developers looking for a more detailed tutorial on the client-side of the framework: the Microsoft AJAX Library.

Conventions

In this book, you will find a number of styles of text that distinguish between different kinds of information. Here are some examples of these styles, and an explanation of their meaning.

There are three styles for code. Code words in text are shown as follows: "The `Response.ContentType` property corresponds to the `Content-Type` HTTP header."

A block of code will be set as follows:

```
// set the response content type
Response.ContentType = "text/xml";
// output the XML header
Response.Write("<?xml version=\"1.0\" encoding=
                              \"UTF-8\" standalone=\"yes\"?>");
Response.Write("<response>");
```

When we wish to draw your attention to a particular part of a code block, the relevant lines or items will be made bold:

```
<html>
  <head>
    <script type="text/javascript" src="file.js"></script>
  </head>
</html>
```

Any command-line input and output is written as follows:

```
cd C:\Windows\Microsoft.NET\Framework\v2.0.50727

aspnet_regiis.exe -i
```

New terms and **important words** are introduced in a bold-type font. Words that you see on the screen, in menus or dialog boxes for example, appear in our text like this: "When the user clicks one of the **Style** buttons, the JavaScript DOM is used to assign those styles to the elements of the table."

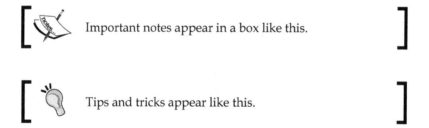

Important notes appear in a box like this.

Tips and tricks appear like this.

Reader Feedback

Feedback from our readers is always welcome. Let us know what you think about this book, what you liked or may have disliked. Reader feedback is important for us to develop titles that you really get the most out of.

To send us general feedback, simply drop an email to feedback@packtpub.com, making sure to mention the book title in the subject of your message.

If there is a book that you need and would like to see us publish, please send us a note in the **SUGGEST A TITLE** form on www.packtpub.com or email suggest@packtpub.com.

If there is a topic that you have expertise in and you are interested in either writing or contributing to a book, see our author guide on www.packtpub.com/authors.

Customer Support

Now that you are the proud owner of a Packt book, we have a number of things to help you to get the most from your purchase.

Downloading the Example Code for the Book

Visit http://www.packtpub.com/support, and select this book from the list of titles to download any example code or extra resources for this book. The files available for download will then be displayed.

The downloadable files contain instructions on how to use them.

Errata

Although we have taken every care to ensure the accuracy of our contents, mistakes do happen. If you find a mistake in one of our books—maybe a mistake in text or code—we would be grateful if you would report this to us. By doing this you can save other readers from frustration, and help to improve subsequent versions of this book. If you find any errata, report them by visiting http://www.packtpub.com/support, selecting your book, clicking on the **Submit Errata** link, and entering the details of your errata. Once your errata are verified, your submission will be accepted and the errata added to the list of existing errata. The existing errata can be viewed by selecting your title from http://www.packtpub.com/support.

Questions

You can contact us at questions@packtpub.com if you are having a problem with some aspect of the book, and we will do our best to address it.

1
AJAX and ASP.NET

"Computer, draw a robot!" said my young cousin to the first computer he had ever seen. (Since I had instructed it not to listen to strangers, the computer wasn't receptive to this command.) If you're like me, your first thought would be *"how silly"* or *"how funny"*—but this is a mistake. We're being educated to accommodate computers, to compensate for the lack of ability of computers to understand humans, but in an ideal world that spoken command should have been enough to have the computer please my cousin.

This book doesn't aim to teach you how to create software applications that intelligently interact with children—we're still far from that point. However, we'll help you make a small but important step in that direction. We'll teach you how to use web development technologies available today—AJAX and ASP.NET AJAX in particular—to enhance web users' experience of your web site, by creating more usable and friendly web interfaces. As far as this chapter is concerned, we'll discuss the following topics:

- **The Big Picture**. Here we'll answer a question we're often asked: "Why bother improving our applications' user interfaces and features, when the existing ones perform satisfactorily?"

- **Building Websites Since 1990**. What are the fundamental principles of the Web, and what are the important technologies that make it work? You probably know most of this, but we hope you'll welcome this quick refresher.

- **The World of AJAX**. As you will learn (if you don't already know), AJAX is a powerful tool that you can use to improve your web interfaces. However, it's important to understand when you should use it, and when you should probably not. We'll also discuss the basic principles of AJAX, and refer to online resources and tools that can help you along the way.

- **Setting Up Your Environment**. In this book you'll find plenty of code—and you'll probably be curious to execute it, and see it in action. We've taken care of that by including step-by-step instructions with every exercise. To avoid any potential problems following the exercises, in this section we walk you through the installation and configuration process for the software you need.

- **Hello World!** After reading so much pure theory, and installing many software packages (and we all know how *boring* software installation can be), you'll probably be eager to write some code, so at the end of this chapter, you'll write your first AJAX application.

Let's get started. We hope your journey through this book will be a pleasant and useful one!

The Big Picture

The story about Cristian's 7-years old cousin—which happened back in 1990—is still relevant today, regarding the way people instinctively work with computers. The ability of technology to be user-friendly has evolved very much in the past years, but there's still a long way until we have really intelligent computers that self-adapt to our needs. Until then, people need to *learn* how to work with computers—some to the extent that they end up loving a black screen with a tiny command prompt on it!

We will be very practical and concise in this book, but before getting back to your favorite mission—writing code—it's worth taking a little step back, just to remember what we are doing and why we are doing it. We love technology to the sound made by each key stroke, so it's very easy to forget that the very reason technology exists is to serve people and make their lives at home more entertaining, and at work more efficient.

The computer-working habits of many are driven by software with user interfaces that allow for intuitive (and enjoyable) human interaction. Not coincidentally, successful companies are typically one step ahead of their competition in offering their users simple and *natural* ways of achieving their goals. This probably explains the popularity of the mouse, of fancy features such as **drag and drop**, and of that simple text box that searches all the Web for you in just 0.1 seconds (or so it says).

Understanding the way people's brains work would be the key to building the ultimate software application. While we're far from that point, what we do understand is that end users need intuitive user interfaces; they don't really care what operating system they're running as long as the functionality they get is what they *want*. This is a very important detail to keep in mind, as programmers typically tend to think and speak in technical terms when interacting with end users. If you disagree, try to remember how many times you've said the word "database" when talking to a non-technical person.

The behavior of any computer software that interacts with humans is now even more important than it used to be, because nowadays the computer user base varies much more than in the past, when the users were technically sound as well. Now you need to display good looking reports to Cindy, the sales department manager, and you need to provide easy-to-use data entry forms to Dave, the sales person.

By observing people's needs and habits while working with computer systems, the term **software usability** was born—referring to the *art* of meeting users' interface expectations, understanding the nature of their work, and building software applications accordingly. AJAX in general, and the ASP.NET AJAX Framework in particular, are modern tools that web developers can use to develop user-friendly Web Applications. As with any other tool, however, they can be used improperly, complicating the user experience, neglecting users with disabilities, or lowering search engine performance.

This being a programming book, our strong focus will regard the technical aspects of Microsoft AJAX Library. However, as a responsible web developer, you should not lose sight of the complementary aspects that affect the success of a web application. If you haven't already, we strongly recommend that you check at least some of these resources:

- *Don't Make Me Think: A Common Sense Approach to Web Usability*, second edition, by Steve Krug (New Riders Press, 2005)
- *Prioritizing Web Usability*, by Jakob Nielsen and Hoa Loranger (New Riders Press, 2006)
- *Designing Interfaces: Patterns for Effective Interaction Design*, by Jenifer Tidwell (O'Reilly, 2005)
- *Web Accessibility: Web Standards and Regulatory Compliance*, by Andrew Kirkpatrick, Richard Rutter, Christian Heilmann, Jim Thatcher, and Cynthia Waddell (Friends of ED, 2006)
- *Ambient Findability*, by Peter Morville (O'Reilly, 2005)
- *Bulletproof Web Design*, second edition, by Dan Cederholm (New Riders Press, 2007)
- *Professional Search Engine Optimization with ASP.NET: A Developer's Guide to SEO*, by Cristian Darie and Jaimie Sirovich (Wrox Press, 2007)

Historically, building user-friendly software has always been easier with desktop applications than with web applications, simply because the Web lacked the technical tools to implement more complex features. Indeed, the Web was designed as a means of delivering simple documents formed of text, images, and links. However, as the Internet gets more mature, the technologies it supports become increasingly potent.

Many technologies have been developed—and are still being developed—to add flashy lights, accessibility, and power to web applications. Notable examples include **Java applets**, **Flash**, and **Silverlight**, which execute inside web browsers that have specific plugins installed. AJAX and ASP.NET AJAX have similar purpose, but on a different scale. They offer support for implementing lightweight rich internet applications without requiring additional plugins, while using a simpler programming model.

AJAX and Web 2.0

These days it's increasingly harder to discuss AJAX without mentioning Web 2.0 (`http://en.wikipedia.org/wiki/Web_2`). What is Web 2.0? Some say it is simply a marketing buzzword without any special meaning, while others use this term to describe the new open, interactive web that facilitates online information sharing and collaboration.

How did it start? In the words of Tim O'Reilly, who coined the term, Web 2.0 was born in 2004 after "a brainstorming session between O'Reilly and Medialive International". As a result, a series of Web 2.0 conferences was born, and the term ended up gaining huge popularity.

Even today, we can find controversies about the definition of "Web 2.0", but the version number is an obvious allusion to the recent changes of the World Wide Web. The initial goal of the Web addressed the delivery of static content in the form of text and images. The new generation of web applications tends to offer a richer user experience, much closer to that of desktop applications, while using live data from the Internet.

Initially, Web 2.0 was associated with the **Semantic Web** (`http://en.wikipedia. org/wiki/Semantic_web`). The Semantic Web is envisioned to be the next step in the Web's evolution, based on online social-networking applications, using tag-based *folksonomies* (user-generated tags for data categorization). W3C director Tim-Berners Lee stated that *"people keep asking what Web 2.0 is. I think maybe when you've got an overlay of scalable vector graphics - everything rippling and folding and looking misty - on Web 2.0 and access to a semantic Web integrated across a huge space of data, you'll have access to an unbelievable data resource"*.

Even if the services offered by Web 2.0 are far away from those aimed by the Semantic Web, where machines are able to understand and extract meanings from the content they offer, Web 2.0 still represents a step forward. In the world of Web 2.0 AJAX plays an essential role, offering the technological support for implementing rich and responsive Web interfaces.

Building Websites Since 1990

Before getting into the details of ASP.NET AJAX, let's take the inevitable history lesson, to make sure we've got our definitions straight. We promise to keep this *short*. If you're a web development veteran, feel free to skip ahead to "The World of AJAX" section.

Although the history of the Internet is a bit longer, 1991 is the year when **Hypertext Transfer Protocol** (**HTTP**), which is still used to transfer data over the Internet, was invented. In its first few initial versions, it didn't do much more than opening and closing connections. The later versions of HTTP (version 1.0 in 1996 and version 1.1 in 1999) became the protocols that we all know and use.

HTTP and HTML

HTTP is supported by all web browsers, and it does very well the job it was conceived for—retrieving simple web content. Whenever you request a web page using your favorite web browser, the HTTP protocol is assumed. So, for example, when you type www.msn.com in the location bar of your web browser, it will assume by default that you meant http://www.msn.com.

The standard document type of the Web is **Hypertext Markup Language (HTML)**, and it is built of markup that web browsers *understand*, *parse*, and *display*. HTML is a language that describes documents' formatting and content, which is basically composed of static text and images. HTML wasn't designed for building complex web applications with interactive content or user-friendly interfaces. When you need to get to another HTML page via HTTP, you need to initiate a full page reload, and the HTML page you requested must exist at the mentioned location, as a static document, prior to the request. It's obvious that these restrictions don't really encourage building anything interesting.

Nevertheless, HTTP and HTML are still very successful technologies that both web servers and web clients (browsers) understand. They are the foundation of the Web as we know it today. Figure 1-1 shows a simple transaction where a user requests a web page from the Internet using the HTTP protocol:

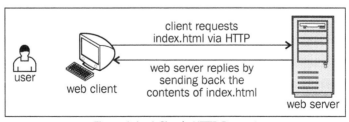

Figure 1-1. A Simple HTTP Request

Three points for you to keep in mind here:

1. HTTP transactions always happen between a *web client* (the software making the request, such as a web browser) and a *web server* (the software responding to the request, such as Microsoft's **IIS** [Internet Information Services]). *From now on in this book, when saying 'client', we refer to the web client, and when saying 'server', we refer to the web server.*

2. The *user* is the person using the client.

3. Even though HTTP (and its secure version, HTTPS) is arguably the most important protocol used on the Internet, it is not the only one. Web servers use different protocols to accomplish various tasks, usually unrelated to simple web browsing. The protocol that we'll use most frequently in this book is HTTP, and when we say 'web request' we'll assume a request using HTTP protocol, unless another protocol is mentioned explicitly.

The HTTP-HTML combination is very limited in what it can do *by itself*—it only enables users to retrieve static content (HTML pages) from the Internet. To complement the lack of features, several technologies have been developed.

All the web requests from now on in this book will use the HTTP protocol for transferring the data, but the data itself can be built dynamically on the web server (for example, using information from a database), and this data can contain more than plain HTML allowing the client to perform some functionality rather than simply display static pages.

The technologies that enable the Web to act smarter are grouped in the following two main categories:

-   **Client-side technologies** enable the web client to do more interesting things than displaying static documents. Usually these technologies complement HTML rather than replacing it entirely.

-   **Server-side technologies** are those that enable the server to store logic and build web pages on the fly. They usually have support for implementing complex logical, object-oriented programming, working with databases, and so on.

ASP.NET and Other Server-Side Technologies

ASP.NET is Microsoft's server-side web development technology, offering a solid development platform. It has many competitors, such as PHP, Java Server Pages (JSP), Perl, ColdFusion, Ruby on Rails, and others, each of them having their own sets of weaknesses and strengths.

ASP.NET is part of the .NET Framework. Since .NET's initial release Microsoft's marketing team have come up with more definitions for it, but for our purposes, the .NET Framework is the core technology that allows developing and executing ASP.NET Web Applications.

Figure 1-2 shows a request for a ASP.NET page called `Default.aspx`. This time, instead of sending back the contents of `Default.aspx`, the server executes `Default.aspx`, and sends back the results. These results must still be in the form of HTML, or in another format that the client understands.

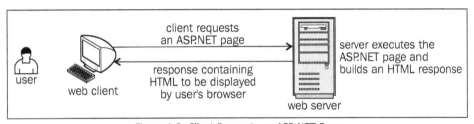

client requests
an ASP.NET page

response containing
HTML to be displayed
by user's browser

user

web client

server executes the
ASP.NET page and
builds an HTML response

web server

Figure 1-2. Client Requests an ASP.NET Page

To write the server-side code for ASP.NET web pages, you can use a number of programming langages, C# and VB.NET being the most popular. In this book we'll use C#, but if you're a VB.NET fan you should be able to easily translate the code. Since both C# and VB.NET work using the base functionality packaged in the .NET Framework, the major difference between these languages is the syntax.

> Since you're reading this book, you're probably already familiar with ASP.NET. Should you need further guidance, you can check out Cristian's *Build Your Own ASP.NET 2.0 Web Site Using C# & VB* (Sitepoint, 2006).

However, even with ASP.NET that can build custom-made database-driven responses, the browser still displays a static, boring, and not very smart web document. The need for smarter and more powerful functionality on the web client generated a separate set of technologies, called client-side technologies. Today's browsers know how to parse more than simple HTML. Let's see how.

JavaScript and Other Client-Side Technologies

The various client-side technologies differ in many ways, starting with how they get loaded and executed by the web client (web browser). **JavaScript** is a scripting language, whose code is written in plain text and can be embedded into HTML pages to empower them. When a client requests an HTML page, that HTML page may contain JavaScript. JavaScript is supported by all modern web browsers without requiring users to install new components.

JavaScript is a language in its own right (theoretically it isn't tied to web development), it's supported by most web browsers under any platform, and it has object-oriented capabilities. However, JavaScript's OOP support doesn't follow the same paradigm you're used to from typical ASP.NET coding—but more on this later. JavaScript is not a compiled language so it's not suited for intensive calculations or writing device drivers, and it must arrive in one piece at the client to be interpreted. This doesn't make it suited for writing sensitive business logic (this wouldn't be a recommended practice anyway), but it does a good job when used in web pages.

With JavaScript, developers could finally build web pages with snow falling over them (remember the days?), with client-side form validation so that the user won't cause a whole page reload (incidentally losing all typed data) if he or she forgot to enter all the required fields (such as password, or credit card number), or if the email address had an incorrect format. However, despite its potential, JavaScript was never used consistently to make the web experience truly user-friendly, like a desktop application.

Other popular technologies that perform functionality at the client side are Java applets and Macromedia Flash. **Java applets** are written in the popular and powerful Java language, and are executed through a **Java Virtual Machine** that needs to be installed separately on the system. Java applets are certainly the way to go for more complex projects, but they have lost the popularity they once had over web applications because they consume many system resources. Sometimes they even need long startup times, and are generally too heavy and powerful for the small requirements of simple web applications.

Macromedia Flash has very powerful tools for creating animations and graphical effects, and it's the de-facto standard for delivering such kind of programs via the Web. Flash also requires the client to install a browser *plug-in*. Flash-based technologies become increasingly powerful, and new ones keep appearing.

At the time of writing this book Microsoft is preparing for the launch of **Silverlight**, a competitor to both Java applets and Flash. Silverlight applications execute inside the web browser though a lightweight version of the .NET Framework supported through browser plugins.

What's Missing?

With all these options for developing powerful features inside web browsers, why would anyone want anything new? What's been missing?

As pointed out at the beginning of this chapter, technology exists to serve market needs. And part of the market wants more powerful functionality to web clients without using Flash, Java applets, or other technologies that are considered either too flashy or heavy-weight for certain purposes. A typical example is that of interactive form validation, where the data typed by the visitor must be checked against some validation rules coded on the server for compliancy.

For such scenarios, developers have usually created websites and web applications using HTML, JavaScript, and ASP.NET (or another server-side technology). The typical request with this scenario is shown in Figure 1-3, which shows an HTTP request, and a response made up of HTML and JavaScript built programmatically with ASP.NET.

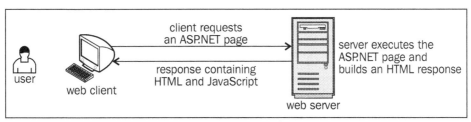

Figure 1-3. HTTP, HTML, ASP.NET, and JavaScript in Action

The hidden problem with this scenario is that each time the client needs new data from the server, a new HTTP request must be made to reload the page, freezing the user's activity. The page **reload** is the problem in the present day scenario, and AJAX comes to our rescue.

The World of AJAX

AJAX is an acronym for **Asynchronous JavaScript and XML**. If you think it doesn't say much, we agree. Simply put, AJAX can be read "empowered JavaScript", because it essentially offers a technique for client-side JavaScript to make background server calls and retrieve additional data as needed, updating certain portions of the page without causing full page reloads. The next figure offers a visual representation of what happens when a typical AJAX-enabled web page is requested by a visitor.

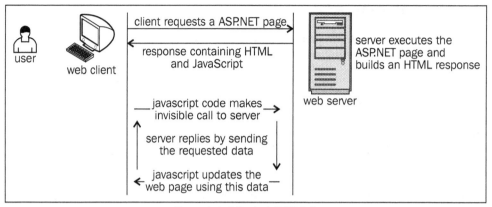

Figure 1-4. A Typical AJAX Call

When put into perspective, AJAX is about reaching a better balance between client functionality and server functionality when executing the action requested by the user. Up until now, client-side functionality and server-side functionality were regarded as separate bits of functionality that work one at a time to respond to user's actions. AJAX comes with the solution to balance the load between the client and the server by allowing them to communicate in the background *while the user is working on the page.*

To explain with a simple example, consider web registration forms where the user is asked to write some data (such as name, e-mail address, password, credit card number, etc) that has to be validated before being used by the server-side code of your application. There are three important ways to implement this:

1. Let the user type all the required data, let him or her *submit* the page, and perform the validation on the server. If the validation doesn't succeed, the server sends back the form, asking the visitor to correct the invalid entries. In this scenario the user experiences a *dead time* after submitting the form, while waiting for the new page to load.

2. Do the validation at the client side, using JavaScript. This way, the user is told about invalid data , and he or she can correct the invalid entires, before submitting the form. However this technique only works for very simple validation that doesn't require additional data from the server while the user is filling the form in. Also, it doesn't work with proprietary or secret validation algorithms that can't be transferred to the client in the form of JavaScript code.

3. Use AJAX form validation so that the web application can validate the entered data by making server calls in the background, while the user keeps typing. For example, after the user types the first letter of the city, the web browser calls the server to load the list of cities that start with that letter, without interrupting the user's current activity.

The situations where AJAX can make a difference are endless. Here are just a few of them:

- **Windows Local Live** (`http://local.live.com`): Microsoft maps service equivalent to other similar services offered by Google (Google Maps – `http://maps.google.com`) and Yahoo (Yahoo Maps – `http://maps.yahoo.com`).

- **Flickr** (`http://flickr.com/`): "the best way to store, search, sort and share your photos".

- **PageFlakes** (`http://pageflakes.com`): "your personalized start page with news, photos, music, bookmarks, blogs, weather and much more".

- **Google Suggest** (`http://www.google.com/webhp?complete=1`): a Google query autocompletion feature that helps you with your Google searches. Similar functionality is offered by **Yahoo! Instant Search**, accessible at `http://instant.search.yahoo.com/`.

- **GMail** (`http://www.gmail.com`): a very popular service by now and doesn't need any introduction. Other web-based email services such as **Yahoo! Mail** and **Hotmail** have followed this trend and offer AJAX-based interfaces.

- **Digg** (`http://www.digg.com`): This is a hugely popular social bookmarking website featuring community-powered content.

So AJAX is about creating more versatile and interactive web applications by enabling web pages to make asynchronous calls to the server transparently while the user is working. AJAX is a tool that web developers can use to create smarter web applications that behave better than traditional web applications when interacting with humans.

What is AJAX Made Of?

The technologies AJAX is made of are already implemented in all modern web browsers, such as **Mozilla Firefox**, **Internet Explorer**, **Opera**, or **Safari**, so the client doesn't need to install any extra modules to run an AJAX website. AJAX is made up of the following:

- JavaScript is the essential ingredient of AJAX, allowing you to build the client-side functionality. In your JavaScript functions you'll make heavy use of the **Document Object Model** (**DOM**) to manipulate parts of the HTML page.

- The **XMLHttpRequest** object enables JavaScript to access the server asynchronously, so that the user can continue working, while functionality is performed in the background. Accessing the server just involves a simple HTTP request for a file or script located on the server. HTTP requests are easy to make and don't cause any firewall-related problems.

- Except for the simplest applications, a server-side technology is required to handle requests that come from the JavaScript client. In this book, we'll use ASP.NET to perform the server-side part of the job.

None of the AJAX components is new, or revolutionary (or even evolutionary) as the current buzz around AJAX might suggest. The newest AJAX component is XMLHttpRequest, which was released by Microsoft in 1998. The name "Ajax" was born in 2005, in Jesse James Garret's article at http://www.adaptivepath.com/publications/essays/archives/000385.php, and gained much popularity when used by Google in many of its applications. You can read more on the history of AJAX at http://en.wikipedia.org/wiki/AJAX.

What's new with AJAX is that, for the first time, there is enough energy in the market to encourage standardization and define a clear direction of evolution. As a consequence, many AJAX frameworks are being developed, and many AJAX-enabled websites have appeared. Microsoft through its ASP.NET AJAX project is pushing AJAX development as well.

For client-server communication, the JavaScript client code and the ASP.NET server-side code need a way to *pass data* and *understand* that data. Passing the data is the simple part. The client script accessing the server (using the XMLHttpRequest object) can send name-value pairs using GET or POST. It's very simple to read these values with any server script.

The server script simply sends back the response via HTTP, but unlike with a usual website, the response will be in a format that can be simply parsed by the JavaScript code on the client. The two popular formats are XML and **JavaScript Object Notation (JSON)**, both of which will be introduced in Chapter 3.

This book assumes that you are already familiar with the AJAX ingredients, except maybe the XMLHttpRequest object, which is less popular. However, to make sure that we're all on the same level, we'll have a look together at how these pieces work, and how they work together, in Chapter 2. Until then, for the remainder of this chapter we'll focus on the big picture, and we will write an AJAX program for the joy of the most impatient readers.

Uses and Misuses of AJAX

As noted earlier, AJAX can improve your visitors' experience with your web site, but it can also worsen it when used inappropriately. In the vast majority of cases, AJAX is best used in addition to the traditional web development paradigms, rather than changing or replacing them.

For example, unless your application has really special requirements, it's wise to let your users navigate your content using the good, old hyperlinks. Web browsers have a long history of dealing with content navigation, and web users have a long history of using browsers' navigational features.

Let's quickly review the potential benefits AJAX can bring to your projects:

- It makes it possible to create better and more responsive web applications.

- It encourages the development of patterns and frameworks, such as ASP.NET AJAX, that help developers avoid re-inventing the wheel when performing common tasks.

- It makes use of existing technologies and features supported by all modern web browsers.

- It makes use of many existing developer skills.

Potential problems with AJAX are:

- Using AJAX for the wrong purposes. Increased awareness of usability, accessibility, web standards and search engine optimization will help you make better decisions when designing and implementing web sites.

- You can't easily allow for bookmarking AJAX-enabled pages. Typically AJAX applications run inside a web page whose URL doesn't change in response to user actions, in which case you can only bookmark the entry page. It is possible to enable bookmarking by dynamically adding page anchors using your JavaScript code, such as in `http://www.example.com/my-ajax-app.html#Page2`. You also need to create supporting code that loads and saves the state of your application through the anchor parameter.

- The **Back** and **Forward** buttons in browsers don't produce the same result as with classic web sites, unless your AJAX application is programmed to support loading and saving states.

- Search engines cannot index content dynamically generated by JavaScript in an AJAX application, because they don't execute any JavaScript code when indexing the web site. If search engine optimization is important for your web site, you shouldn't use AJAX for content delivery and navigation.

- JavaScript can be disabled at the client side, which makes the AJAX application non-functional.

To enable AJAX page bookmarking and the Back and Forward browser buttons, you can use frameworks such as Really Simple History by Brad Neuberg (`http://codinginparadise.org/projects/dhtml_history/README.html`), or Nikhil Kothari's UpdateHistory control for ASP.NET AJAX (`http://www.nikhilk.net/UpdateControls.aspx`).

Following the popularity of AJAX, a large numbers of AJAX-enabled frameworks and toolkits have been developed, including common features and offering great, tested features. Max Kiesler (`http://www.maxkiesler.com/`) has put a list of such products on his weblog, but in reality there are many more. Some are server-agnostic, while others are specifically created for ASP.NET, Java, PHP, Coldfusion, Flash and Perl backends. Among the most popular server-agnostic toolkits are **Dojo** (`http://dojotoolkit.org`), **Prototype** (`http://prototype.conio.net`), and **script.aculo.us** (`http://script.aculo.us`).

As far as ASP.NET developers are concerned, their main choice—strongly promoted by Microsoft—is ASP.NET AJAX. Another popular choice is **Ajax.NET Professional**—developed by Michael Schwartz (`http://www.ajaxpro.info`).

Introducing ASP.NET AJAX

ASP.NET AJAX (`http://ajax.asp.net/`), initially known only by its code name, Atlas, is a powerful AJAX framework written by Microsoft for ASP.NET developers. ASP.NET AJAX includes a wealth of tested functionality allowing you to build solid, cross-browser AJAX-based interfaces.

ASP.NET AJAX is a complex framework which includes AJAX-enabled ASP.NET server controls, as well as a very powerful client-side library. The native integration with Visual Studio .NET 2005 allows the developer to build rich internet applications (RIA) that are built upon the .NET 2.0, .NET 3.0, and .NET 3.5 frameworks without forcing the end user to have anything installed on the client.

The world of ASP.NET AJAX is composed of:

1. **Microsoft AJAX Library**. This is a powerful client-side Javascript library that offers a common API for all modern browsers, and supports any backend web technology. In theory at least, you can use the Microsoft AJAX Library with a PHP or Java server script. In practice, the Microsoft AJAX Library is really meant to be used togehter with its server-side companion from the ASP.NET AJAX Extensions. Keep an eye on Jay Kimble's Java integration project for Microsoft AJAX Library at `http://www.codeplex.com/dtajax/`, and on the PHP integration at `http://www.codeplex.com/phpmsajax`.

2. **ASP.NET AJAX Extensions** includes the Microsoft AJAX Library, and also a set of server-side AJAX-enabled controls that integrate well with that library (`ScriptManager`, `UpdatePanel`, `Timer`, `UpdateProgress`, and `AsyncPostbackTrigger`). At installation the product integrates with Visual Studio 2005 so that you can access its controls through the Visual Studio Toolbox, and will be included into the next version of Visual Studio, which at the time of writing this book is code-named Orcas.

3. The **ASP.NET AJAX Control Toolkit** is a set of free, shared source controls and components that help you get the most value from the ASP.NET AJAX Extensions. At the time of writing this book, the control toolkit is still under development, and it isn't part of the 1.0 release of ASP.NET AJAX. However, it will ship together with Visual Studio "Orcas".

This book is dedicated to the first of these three parts of ASP.NET AJAX. We'll cover the Microsoft AJAX Library in detail, and by end of it you'll be able to masterfully use its features at their full potential.

The Microsoft AJAX Library is the kind of technology that's easy to start with, but as you dwelve into its details, you'll notice that its complexity requires a longer learning curve than you may expect. In our opinion, there aren't any real shortcuts to this process: you need to understand the foundations of this framework very well before you can be efficient with it.

Understanding the Microsoft AJAX Library also requires a good knowledge of JavaScript and its object-oriented model. In theory, working with an API only requires knowledge of that API's publicly exposed features. In practice however, dealing with a JavaScript framework—especially one that is young and sometimes imperfect—frequently requires an understanding of the details of its inner workings. Sooner or later, you'll be tempted to open the source code of the Microsoft AJAX Library. This is not something that you'd expect from a C# library, but we're dealing with a different kind of "monster" here.

The first part of this book will cover the basics of AJAX with JavaScript and ASP.NET, without involving the Microsoft AJAX Library. You will find that you can implement simple AJAX features by hand, simply coding the necessary asynchronous server calls yourself. Then we'll set the ground for ASP.NET AJAX by teaching the more advanced features of JavaScript, such as prototypes and closures.

If you already understand the theory of JavaScript and its interaction with ASP.NET, feel free to skip to Chapter 4. However, we advise you to look at Chapters 2 and 3 so that we're on the same level when we meet again in Chapter 4.

Resources and Tools

Finally, here are a few places that may help you in your journey into the exciting world of AJAX. For starters, here are a few useful generic AJAX resources:

- http://www.ajaxian.com is the AJAX website of Ben Galbraith and Dion Almaer, the authors of *Pragmatic Ajax* (Pragmatic Bookshelf, 2006).
- http://ajaxpatterns.org is an informative website about AJAX design patterns, and the home page of *Ajax Design Patterns* by Michael Mahemoff (O'Reilly, 2006).

- `http://www.fiftyfoureleven.com/resources/programming/ xmlhttprequest` is a comprehensive collection of articles about AJAX.
- `http://www.sitepoint.com/subcat/javascript` is Sitepoint's AJAX home, featuring some excellent articles.
- `http://developer.mozilla.org/en/docs/AJAX` is Mozilla's page on AJAX.
- `http://en.wikipedia.org/wiki/Ajax` is the Wikipedia page on AJAX.

This list is by no means complete. If you need more online resources, search engines will surely be available for help. For specific information on ASP.NET AJAX and related technologies, we recommend that you visit the following resources from time to time—ideally by subscribing to their RSS or Atom feeds:

Blogger or Resource Name	URL
Atlas team	`http://weblogs.asp.net/atlas-team/`
Dino Esposito	`http://weblogs.asp.net/despos/`
Eilon Lipton	`http://weblogs.asp.net/leftslipper/`
Alessandro Galo	`http://aspadvice.com/blogs/garbin/`
Jay Kimble	`http://codebetter.com/blogs/jay.kimble/`
Luis Abreu	`http://msmvps.com/blogs/luisabreu/`
Nikhil Kothari	`http://www.nikhilk.net/`
Steve Marx	`http://smarx.com/`

Setting Up Your Environment

In the next few pages we'll guide you through installing the following softwares, which you'll need for this book:

1. IIS (Internet Information Services), which is the Web Server used to serve ASP.NET pages.
2. Visual Web Developer 2005 Express Edition, which is the tool that you'll be using to develop your ASP.NET applications.
3. The ASP.NET AJAX Framework.

Installing IIS

To run ASP.NET web applications, you can use either Visual Web Developer's integrated Web server (Cassini), or you can use IIS. Theoretically, the most important difference between the two environments are the credentials under which the code runs. Cassini runs with the credentials of the logged in user, while IIS uses a special system account named ASPNET.

If you really want to, you can also run ASP.NET pages using Apache, although we've not tested this configuration for the purposes of this book. Read more details at `http://weblogs.asp.net/israelio/archive/2005/09/11/424852.aspx`.

The two major benefits of using Cassini are:

- Cassini works on systems that don't ship with IIS, such as Windows XP Home Edition.

- Cassini can be used in case you don't want to use your main IIS Web Server for development purposes.

Even if these advantages don't convince you, we still recommend using IIS because your application would end up running under an IIS server anyway, so the development environment would more closely resemble the production environment.

IIS is delivered with most versions of server-capable Windows operating systems, including Windows Vista Business, Windows XP Professional, Windows XP Media Center Edition, Windows 2000 Professional, Server, Advanced Server, and Windows Server 2003, but it's not installed automatically in all versions, which is why it may not be present on your computer.

IIS isn't available in Windows XP Home Edition, Windows Vista Home Basic, or Windows Vista Home Premium— if you run one of these, you'll need to rely on Cassini.

 The main development tool we'll use in this book is Visual Web Developer 2005, which works best with IIS 6, which ships with Windows XP. Windows Vista, on the other hand, includes IIS 7, whose default settings aren't very friendly with Visual Web Developer 2005. This explains that you have more configuration work to do before you'll be able to run and debug your ASP.NET Web Applications under Windows Vista properly.

To install IIS, simply follow these steps:

1. In the **Control Panel**, select **Programs and Features** (in Windows Vista), or **Add or Remove Programs** (in Windows XP).

2. Choose **Turn Windows features on or off** (in Windows Vista), or **Add/Remove Windows Components** (in Windows XP). The list of components will become visible within a few seconds.

3. In the list of components, check **Internet Information Services**. If running Windows XP, expand the node and make sure that the IIS Frontpage Extensions node is checked.

In Windows Vista, also select the following options (also see Figure 1-4).

1. **Web Management Tools | IIS 6 Management Compatibility** node, and its **IIS Metabase and IIS 6 configuration compatibility** sub-node. (IIS 6 Management Compatbility is required by Visual Web Developer 2005 when connecting to your web site through FrontPage Extensions.)

2. **World Wide Web Services | Application Development Features | ASP. NET** node.

3. Select the **World Wide Web Services | Security | Windows Authentication** node, which is necessary if you want to run applications in debug mode.

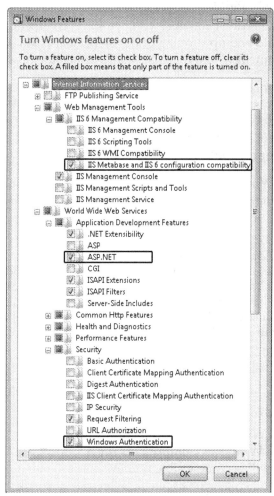

Figure 1-5. Configuring IIS 7 Options in Windows Vista

4. Click **Next** or **OK**. Windows may prompt you to insert the Windows CD or DVD.

To administer IIS, you use the **Internet Information Services (IIS) Manager** tool (in Windows Vista) or the **Internet Information Services** tool (in Windows XP) that you can find in the **Administrative Tools** menu of the **Control Panel**.

Installing Visual Web Developer

Install Visual Web Developer 2005 Express Edition following these simple steps:

1. Go to `http://msdn.microsoft.com/vstudio/express/vwd/`.

2. Click the **Download** link. You'll download a file named `vwdsetup.exe`.

3. Execute the downloaded file.

4. Accept the default options. At one point you'll be asked about installing Microsoft MSDN 2005 Express Edition, which is the product's documentation. Installing it will do no harm, but you need to be patient, because it's quite big.

5. Install the Visual Web Developer Service Pack 1. If you use Windows Vista, you should install the Service Pack 1 for Windows Vista.

6. The final step involves configuring ASP.NET with IIS. If you'll be using Cassini or IIS 7, this step is not needed. Start a command-line console (Start | Run | cmd), and type the following commands:

```
cd C:\Windows\Microsoft.NET\Framework\v2.0.50727
aspnet_regiis.exe -i
```

Creating a Folder for Your Project

To keep your hard drive tidy, let's create a folder that we'll be using for every exercise in this book. Create a folder named `Atlas` in an easily accessible place of your hard drive. I'll assume you're creating it as `C:\Atlas`.

Now we need to configure this folder as an IIS virtual directory so that it doesn't interfere with other applications you may have on your machine. After preparing the Atlas Web Application, the `http://localhost/Atlas/` application will be loaded from the `C:\Atlas` physical folder. If you can't use IIS, then skip to the "Hello World!" section, a bit later in this chapter.

Because of the interface differences between the IIS 5/6 and IIS 7, separate installation instructions are provided for Windows XP and Windows Vista.

Preparing the Atlas Application in Windows Vista

If you're running Windows Vista and IIS 7, follow these steps to prepare your `Atlas` folder.

1. Open the IIS Manager tool from the **Administrative Tools** section of the **Control Panel**.

2. Find the **Default Web Site** in the **Connections** tab, and make sure it's started. If its status is **Stopped**, right-click on it and select **Start**.

3. Right-click **Default Web Site**, and select **Add Application** from the context menu.

4. Choose **Atlas** for the alias name, and **C:\Atlas** for its "physical" path. Then click **Select...**, choose **Classic .NET AppPool**, and click **OK**. (If you don't choose the Classic .NET AppPool, you won't be able to debug the project using Visual Web Developer 2005.) In the end, the **Add Application** dialog should look like Figure 1-6.

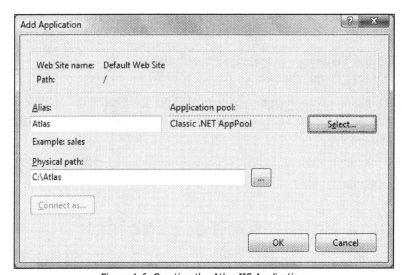

Figure 1-6. Creating the Atlas IIS Application

5. After clicking **OK** to close the **Add Application** dialog, the **Atlas** virtual directory will show up as a child node under **Default Web Site**. Select the **Atlas** node, double-click the **Authentication** icon, and enable **Windows Authentication**.

6. Close the IIS Manager.

Preparing the Atlas Web Application in Windows XP

If you're running Windows XP, follow these steps to prepare your Atlas folder

1. Open the **Internet Information Services** tool from the **Administrative Tools** section of the **Control Panel**. Then expand the node for your local computer, then expand the **Web Sites** node, as shown in Figure 1-7.

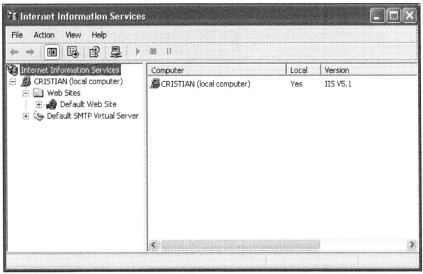

Figure 1-7. Internet Information Services Tool in Windows XP

2. Make sure that the **Default Web Site** is running. If its status is **Stopped**, right-click on it and select **Start**:

3. Right-click **Default Web Site**, and select **New | Virtual Directory**.

4. In the wizard that shows up, first click **Next**, then type **Atlas** for the name of the Virtual Directory. Then click **Next**.

5. Type the full path for the "physical" folder where you'll save the examples from this book. If you created the folder as suggested, then the path whould be **C:\Atlas**.

6. In the next screen, check **Read and Run scripts (such as ASP)**, and click **Next**.

7. Click **Finish** to close the wizard, then close the Internet Information Services applet.

Hello World!

ASP.NET AJAX is a powerful and exciting framework which comes with lot of built-in features, but in order to make the most out of it, it's best to take a disciplined approach and learn the basics first. Chapter 2 and Chapter 3 will teach you the foundations, and how to implement basic AJAX features with ASP.NET without using the ASP.NET AJAX Framework. You'll start using the Microsoft AJAX Library in Chapter 4.

This chapter ends with an exercise where we'll build a simple AJAX application with ASP.NET, named **Quickstart**. This application doesn't make use of any of the components of the Microsoft ASP.NET AJAX Framework. Instead, it uses simple JavaScript and C# code.

Going through this exercise is optional. The exercise is for the most impatient readers willing to start coding as soon as possible, but it assumes you're already familiar with JavaScript, ASP.NET, and XML. If this is not the case, or if at any time you feel this exercise is too challenging, feel free to skip to Chapter 2.

Quickstart is a simple AJAX form-validation application where the user is requested to type his or her name, and the server keeps verifying if it recognizes the typed name while the user is writing. Figure 1-8 shows the initial page, `Quickstart.html`, loaded by the user.

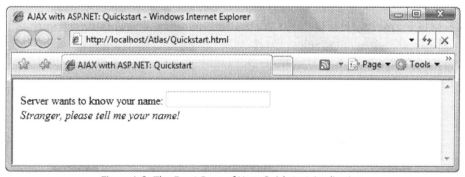

Figure 1-8. The Front Page of Your Quickstart Application

While the user is typing, the server is being called asynchronously, at regular intervals, to validate the current user input. The server is called automatically, approximately once per second, which explains why we don't need a button (such as a **Send** button) to notify when we're done typing. (This method may not be appropriate for real log-in mechanisms but it's very good to demonstrate the basic AJAX functionality).

Depending on the entered name, the message from the server may differ; see an example in Figure 1-9.

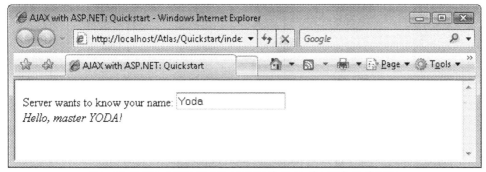

Figure 1-9. User Receives a Prompt Reply From the Web Application

Check out this example online at `http://www.cristiandarie.ro/asp-ajax/Quickstart.html`. Maybe at first sight there's nothing extraordinary going on there. We've kept this first example simple on purpose, to make things easier to understand. What's special about this application is that the displayed message comes automatically from the server, without interrupting the user's actions. (The messages are displayed as the user types a name.) The page doesn't get reloaded to display the new data, even though a server call needs to be made to get that data. This wasn't a simple task to accomplish using non-AJAX web development techniques. The application consists of the following three files:

- `Quickstart.html` is the initial HTML file the user requests.
- `Quickstart.js` is a file containing JavaScript code that is loaded on the client along with `Quickstart.html`. This file will handle making the asynchronous requests to the server, when server-side functionality is needed.
- `Quickstart.aspx` is an ASP.NET page residing on the server that gets called by the JavaScript code in `Quickstart.js` file from the client.

Figure 1-10 shows the actions that happen when running this application:

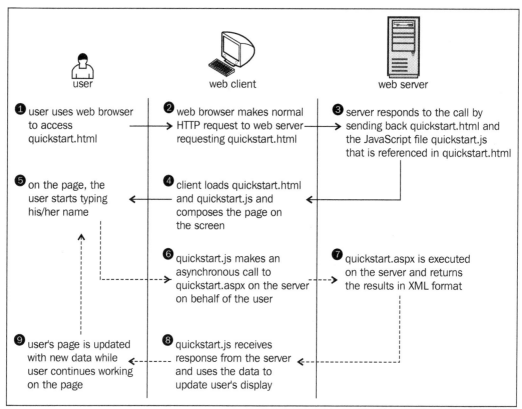

Figure 1-10. Diagram Explaining the Inner Works of Your Quickstart Application

Steps 1 through 5 are a typical HTTP request. After making the request, the user needs to wait until the page gets loaded. With typical (non-AJAX) web applications, such a page reload happens every time the client needs to get new data from the server.

Steps 5 through 9 demonstrate an AJAX-type call—more specifically, a sequence of asynchronous HTTP requests. The server is accessed in the background using the XMLHttpRequest object. During this period the user can continue to use the page normally, as if it were a normal desktop application. No page refresh or reload is experienced in order to retrieve data from the server and update the web page with that data.

Now it's time to implement this code on your machine. Before moving on, ensure you've prepared your working environment as shown earlier in this chapter.

All the exercises in this book assume that you've installed software on your machine as shown earlier in this chapter. If you set up your environment differently you may need to implement various changes, such as using different folder names, and so on.

Time for Action—Quickstart AJAX

1. Open Visual Web Developer, and select **File | Open Web Site**.

2. Select the **Local IIS** location, and the Atlas application, as shown in Figure 1-11. Then click OK.

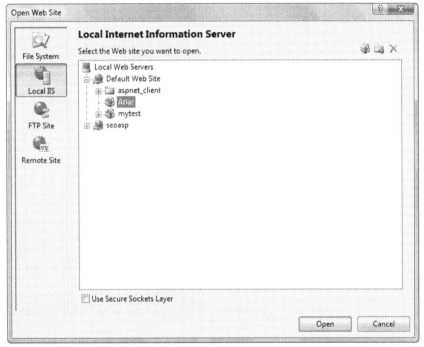

Figure 1-11. Loading the Atlas Application in Visual Web Developer

 If you don't have IIS, or intend to use Cassini for any reason, set the **Location** type to **File System**, and type C:\Atlas\ for the location.

3. Right-click the root node in Solution Explorer, and select **Add New Item**. Choose the **HTML Page** template, and type Quickstart.html for the name. Then click **Add**.

4. Modify the HTML code generated for you like this:

```
<!DOCTYPE html PUBLIC "-//W3C//DTD XHTML 1.0 Transitional//EN"
"http://www.w3.org/TR/xhtml1/DTD/xhtml1-transitional.dtd">
<html xmlns="http://www.w3.org/1999/xhtml">
  <head>
    <title>AJAX with ASP.NET: Quickstart</title>
    <script type="text/javascript" src="Quickstart.js"></script>
  </head>
  <body onload="process()">
    <div>
      Server wants to know your name:
      <input type="text" id="myName" />
    </div>
    <div id="divMessage" />
  </body>
</html>
```

5. Right-click the root node in Solution Explorer, then click **Add New Item**, and add a file named Quickstart.js using the JScript File template. Then type the following code:

```
// stores a reference to an XMLHttpRequest instance
var xmlHttp = createXmlHttpRequestObject();

// retrieves the XMLHttpRequest object
function createXmlHttpRequestObject()
{
  // will store the reference to the XMLHttpRequest object
  var xmlHttp;
  // this should work for all browsers except IE6 and older
  try
  {
    // try to create XMLHttpRequest object
    xmlHttp = new XMLHttpRequest();
  }
  catch(e)
  {
    // assume IE6 or older
    xmlHttp = new ActiveXObject("Microsoft.XMLHTTP");
  }
  // return the created object or display an error message
  if (!xmlHttp)
    alert("Error creating the XMLHttpRequest object.");
  else
    return xmlHttp;
}
```

```
// make asynchronous HTTP request using the XMLHttpRequest object
function process()
{
  // proceed only if the xmlHttp object isn't busy
  if (xmlHttp.readyState == 4 || xmlHttp.readyState == 0)
  {
    // retrieve the name typed by the user on the form
    name = encodeURIComponent(document.getElementById("myName").
                                                           value);
    // execute the Quickstart.aspx page from the server
    xmlHttp.open("GET", "Quickstart.aspx?name=" + name, true);
    // define the method to handle server responses
    xmlHttp.onreadystatechange = handleServerResponse;
    // make the server request
    xmlHttp.send(null);
  }
  else
    // if the connection is busy, try again after one second
    setTimeout("process()", 1000);
}

// executed automatically when a message is received from server
function handleServerResponse()
{
  // move forward only if the transaction has completed
  if (xmlHttp.readyState == 4)
  {
    // status of 200 indicates success
    if (xmlHttp.status == 200)
    {
      // extract the XML retrieved from the server
      xmlResponse = xmlHttp.responseXML;
      // obtain the root element of the XML structure
      xmlDocumentElement = xmlResponse.documentElement;
      // get the text message from the first child of the document
      helloMessage = xmlDocumentElement.firstChild.data;
      // display the data received from the server
      document.getElementById("divMessage").innerHTML =
        "<i>" + helloMessage + "</i>";
      // restart sequence
      setTimeout("process()", 1000);
    }
    // a HTTP status different than 200 signals an error
    else
    {
      alert("There was a problem accessing the server: " +
                                        xmlHttp.statusText);
```

```
      }
    }
  }
```

6. Create a new file named `Quickstart.aspx` in your project using the Web Form template. Choose **Visual C#** for the language, and make sure both the **Place code in separate file** and **Select master page** checkboxes are unchecked. While using code-behind files is a good idea in most cases, this time we don't want to complicate things unnecessarily.

7. Delete the template code generated by Visual Web Developer for you, and type the following code in `Quickstart.aspx`:

```csharp
<script runat="server" language="C#">
  protected void Page_Load()
  {
    // declare the names that are recognized by the server
    string[] names = new string[] { "CRISTIAN", "BOGDAN", "YODA" };

    // retrieve the current name sent by the client
    string currentUser = Request.QueryString["name"] + "";

    // set the response content type
    Response.ContentType = "text/xml";

    // output the XML header
    Response.Write("<?xml version=\"1.0\" encoding=\"UTF-8\"
                                        standalone=\"yes\"?>");
    Response.Write("<response>");

    // if the name is empty...
    if (currentUser.Length == 0)
    {
      Response.Write("Stranger, please tell me your name!");
    }
    // if the typed name is in the names array
    else if (Array.IndexOf(names, currentUser.ToUpper().Trim()) >= 0)
    {
      Response.Write("Hello, master " + currentUser + "!");
    }
    // if the name is neither empty or recognized
    else
    {
      Response.Write(currentUser + ", I don't know you!");
    }

    // output the XML document
    Response.Write("</response>");
```

```
    // flush the response stream
    Response.Flush();
  }
</script>
```

8. Double-click `Quickstart.html` in Solution Explorer, and press *F5* to execute the project in debug mode (You can also execute the project without debugging, by hitting *CTRL+F5*). Visual Web Developer will offer to enable debugging by creating a `Web.config` file with the appropriate settings for you, as shown in Figure 1-12. Click **OK**.

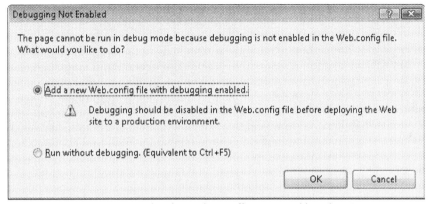

Figure 1-12. Visual Web Developer Offering to Enable Debugging

9. A browser window will load `http://localhost/Atlas/Quickstart.html`, which should look like shown earlier in Figures 1-9 and 1-10.

> Should you encounter any problems running the application, check whether you correctly followed the installation and configuration procedures. Most errors happen because of small problems such as typos. In Chapter 2 you'll learn how to implement error handling in your JavaScript and ASP.NET code.

What Just Happened?

Here comes the fun part—understanding what happens in that code. (Remember that we'll discuss the technical details in the following chapters.)

Let's start with the file the user first interacts with, `Quickstart.html`. This file references the mysterious JavaScript file called `Quickstart.js`, and builds a very simple web interface for the client.

In the following code snippet from `Quickstart.html`, notice the elements highlighted in bold:

```
<body onload="process()">
  <div>
    Server wants to know your name:
    <input type="text" id="myName" />
  </div>
  <div id="divMessage" />
</body>
```

When the page loads, a function from `Quickstart.js` called `process()` is executed. This somehow causes the `<div>` element to be populated with a message from the server. Before seeing what happens inside the `process()` function, let's see what happens at the server side.

The server is represented by a page called `Quickstart.aspx`. This page receives the name typed by the visitor, and it replies with an XML message. You may want to have another look at Figure 1-10, which describes the process. This XML message `Quickstart.aspx` sends back to the client consists of a `<response>` element that packages the response message:

```
<?xml version="1.0" encoding="UTF-8" standalone="yes"?>
<response>
   ... message the server wants to transmit to the client ...
</response>
```

If the user name received from the client is empty, the message will be, **"Stranger, please tell me your name!"**. If the name is **Cristian**, **Bogdan**, or **Yoda**, the server responds with **"Hello, master <user name>!"**. If the name is anything else, the message will be **"<user name>, I don't know you!"**. So if **Mickey Mouse** types his name, the server will send back the following XML structure:

```
<?xml version="1.0" encoding="UTF-8" standalone="yes"?>
<response>
  Mickey Mouse, I don't know you!
</response>
```

If you want to test this actually happens, it's quite simple. The advantage of sending parameters from the client via GET is that it's very simple to emulate such a request using your web browser, since GET simply means that you append the parameters as name/value pairs in the URL query string. So to simulate the server request done by the client when the user types Yoda, simply load `http://localhost/Atlas/Quickstart.aspx?name=Yoda` into your web browser. You should get the XML response shown in Figure 1-13.

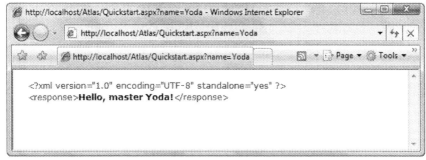

Figure 1-13: The XML Data Generated by Quickstart.aspx

The `Quickstart.aspx` page contains a simple script that contains the `Page_Load()` method, which executes by default when the script is accessed. `Page_Load()` starts by declaring the array of strings that will be the names "known" by the server:

```
protected void Page_Load()
{
   // declare the names that are recognized by the server
   string[] names = new string[] { "CRISTIAN", "BOGDAN", "YODA" };
```

Next, the `Page_Load()` method contains the entire server logic behind this example. It retrieves the name sent by the client:

```
// retrieve the current name sent by the client
string currentUser = Request.QueryString["name"] + "";
```

The value of the `name` query string parameter is read using `Request.QueryString["name"]`. This returns null when `name` doesn't exist in the query string, and we use a little trick—appending an empty string to it—to avoid errors when this happens. (In production code, when performance is a factor, you may prefer to use different error-avoiding techniques.)

Next, we set the content type of the response to `text/xml`, and we start building the XML response by opening the `<response>` element:

```
// set the response content type
Response.ContentType = "text/xml";
// output the XML header
Response.Write("<?xml version=\"1.0\" encoding=
                              \"UTF-8\" standalone=\"yes\"?>");
Response.Write("<response>");
```

The `Response.ContentType` property corresponds to the `Content-Type` HTTP header. We use it to set the content type to `text/xml`, which is appropriate when the page sends back an XML structure. `Response.Write()` is used to send content to the output. The first bits we output are the XML document definition, and the `<response>` document element.

We continue by writing the message itself to the output. If the name is an empty string, the message will be "Stranger, please tell me your name!"

```
// if the name is empty...
if (currentUser.Length == 0)
{
  Response.Write("Stranger, please tell me your name!");
}
```

If the name is one of those in the names array, the message will be a bit more friendly:

```
// if the typed name is in the names array
else if (Array.IndexOf(names, currentUser.ToUpper().Trim()) >= 0)
{
  Response.Write("Hello, master " + currentUser + "!");
}
```

Here's the code that outputs the text in case the name isn't recognized:

```
// if the name is neither empty or recognized
else
{
  Response.Write(currentUser + ", I don't know you!");
}
```

Finally, we close the `<response>` element, and flush the response stream:

```
// output the XML document
Response.Write("</response>");

// flush the response stream
Response.Flush();
}
```

This XML message outputted by the server (`Quickstart.aspx`) is read at the client by the `handleServerResponse()` function in `Quickstart.js`. More specifically, the following lines of code extract the **Hello, master Yoda!** message, assuming the reader has typed **Yoda** in the text box:

```
// extract the XML retrieved from the server
xmlResponse = xmlHttp.responseXML;
// obtain the document element (the root element) of
the XML structure
xmlDocumentElement = xmlResponse.documentElement;
// get the text message, which is in the first child of
the document element
helloMessage = xmlDocumentElement.firstChild.data;
```

Here, `xmlHttp` is the `XMLHttpRequest` object used to call the server page `Quickstart.aspx` from the client. Its `responseXML` property extracts the retrieved XML document. XML structures are hierarchical by nature, and the root element of an XML document is called the **document element**. In this case, the document element is the `<response>` element, which contains a single child, which is the text message we're interested in. Once the text message is retrieved, it's displayed on the client's page by using the DOM to access the `<divMessage>` element in `Quickstart.html`:

```
// update the client display using the data received
from the server
document.getElementById("divMessage").innerHTML = helloMessage;
```

`document` is a default object in JavaScript that allows you to manipulate the elements in the HTML code of your page.

The rest of the code in `Quickstart.js` deals with making the request to the server to obtain the XML message. The `createXmlHttpRequestObject()` function creates and returns an instance of the `XMLHttpRequest` object. This function is longer than it could be because we need to make it cross-browser compatible — we'll discuss the details in Chapter 2. For now, it's important to know what it does. The `XMLHttpRequest` instance, called `xmlHttp`, is used in `process()` to make the asynchronous server request:

```
// make asynchronous HTTP request using the XMLHttpRequest object
function process()
{
  // proceed only if the xmlHttp object isn't busy
  if (xmlHttp.readyState == 4 || xmlHttp.readyState == 0)
  {
    // retrieve the name typed by the user on the form
    name = encodeURIComponent(document.getElementById("myName").
                                                             value);
    // execute the Quickstart.aspx page from the server
    xmlHttp.open("GET", "Quickstart.aspx?name=" + name, true);
    // define the method to handle server responses
    xmlHttp.onreadystatechange = handleServerResponse;
    // make the server request
    xmlHttp.send(null);
  }
  else
    // if the connection is busy, try again after one second
    setTimeout("process()", 1000);
}
```

What you see here is, actually, the heart of AJAX—the code that makes the asynchronous call to the server.

You may wonder why it is it so important to call the server asynchronously. Asynchronous requests, by their nature, don't freeze processing (and with it the user experience) from when the call is made until the response is received. Asynchronous processing is implemented by *event-driven* architectures, a good example being the way graphical user interface code is built. Without events, you'd probably need to check continuously if the user has clicked a button or resized a window. Using events, the button notifies the application automatically when it has been clicked, and you can take the necessary actions in the event handler function. With AJAX, this theory applies when making a server request—you are automatically notified when the response comes back.

If you're curious to see how the application would work using a synchronous request, change the third parameter of xmlHttp.open() to false, and then call handleServerResponse() as shown below. If you try this, the input box where you're supposed to write your name will freeze when the server is contacted (although the delay may not noticeable when testing this on the local machine).

```
// function calls the server using the XMLHttpRequest object
function process()
{
  // retrieve the name typed by the user on the form
  name = encodeURIComponent(document.getElementById("myName").value);
  // execute the Quickstart.aspx page from the server
  xmlHttp.open("GET", "Quickstart.aspx?name=" + name, false);
  // synchronous server request (freezes processing until completed)
  xmlHttp.send(null);
  // read the response
  handleServerResponse();
}
```

The process() function is supposed to initiate a new server request using the XMLHttpRequest object. However, this is only possible if the XMLHttpRequest object isn't busy making another request. In our case, this can happen if it takes more than one second for the server to reply, which could happen if the Internet connection is very slow. So process() starts by verifying that it is clear to initiate a new request. Chapter 2 will show more details about the various possible states of the request, but for now, it's enough to know that a state of 0 or 4 means the connection is available to make a new request. (It's not possible to perform more that one request through a single XMLHttpRequest object at any given time.)

```
// make asynchronous HTTP request using the XMLHttpRequest object
function process()
{
  // proceed only if the xmlHttp object isn't busy
  if (xmlHttp.readyState == 4 || xmlHttp.readyState == 0)
  {
```

So, if the connection is busy, we use `setTimeout()` to retry after one second (the function's second argument specifies the number of milliseconds to wait before executing the piece of code specified by the first argument:

```
// if the connection is busy, try again after one second
setTimeout("process()", 1000);
```

If the line is clear, you can safely make a new request. The lines of code that prepare the server request but don't commit it:

```
// execute the Quickstart.aspx page from the server
xmlHttp.open("GET", "Quickstart.aspx?name=" + name, true);
```

The first parameter specifies the method used to send the user name to the server, and you can choose between GET and POST (you will learn more about them in Chapter 2). The second parameter is the server page you want to access; when the first parameter is GET, you send the parameters as name/value pairs in the query string. The third parameter is true if you want the call to be made asynchronously. When making asynchronous calls, you don't wait for a response. Instead, you define another function to be called *automatically* when the state of the request changes:

```
// define the method to handle server responses
xmlHttp.onreadystatechange = handleServerResponse;
```

Once you've set this option, you can rest calm — the handleServerResponse() function will be executed by the system when anything happens to your request. After everything is set up, you initiate the request by calling the XMLHttpRequest object's send method:

```
// make the server request
xmlHttp.send(null);
}
```

Let's now look at the handleServerResponse() function:

```
// executed automatically when a message is received from the server
function handleServerResponse()
{
  // move forward only if the transaction has completed
  if (xmlHttp.readyState == 4)
  {
```

```
// status of 200 indicates the transaction completed successfully
if (xmlHttp.status == 200)
{
```

The `handleServerResponse()` function is called multiple times, whenever the status of the request changes. The data received from the server can be read only if `xmlHttp.readyState` is 4 (which happens when the response was fully received from the server), and the HTTP status code is 200, signaling that there were no problems during the HTTP request. We'll learn more about these concepts in chapter 2. For now, suffice to say that when they are met, you can read the server response, which you can use to display an appropriate message to the user.

After the response is received and used, the process is restarted using the `setTimeout()` function, which will cause the `process()` function to be executed after one second (although that it's not necessary, even with AJAX, to have repetitive tasks in your client-side code):

```
// restart sequence
setTimeout("process()", 1000);
```

Finally, let's reiterate what happens after the user loads the page (you can refer to Figure 1-6 for a visual representation):

1. The user loads `Quickstart.html` (this corresponds to steps 1–4 in Figure 1-10).

2. The user starts (or continues) typing his or her name (this corresponds to step 5 in Figure 1-10.

3. When the `process()` method in `Quickstart.js` is executed, it calls a server script named `Quickstart.aspx` asynchronously. The text entered by the user is passed on the call as a query string parameter (via GET). The `handeServerResponse()` function is designed to handle request state changes.

4. `Quickstart.aspx` executes on the server. It composes an XML document that encapsulates the message the server wants to transmit to the client.

5. The `handleServerResponse()` method on the client is executed multiple times as the state of the request changes. It's called for the last time when the response has been successfully received. The XML is read; the message is extracted and displayed on the page.

6. The user display is updated with the new message from the server, but the user can continue typing without any interruptions. After a delay of one second, the process is restarted from step 2.

Summary

This chapter was a quick introduction to the world of AJAX. In order to proceed with learning how to build AJAX applications, it's important to understand why and where they are useful. As with any other technology, AJAX isn't the answer to all problems, but it offers means to solve some of them.

AJAX combines client-side and server-side functionality to enhance the user experience of your site. The `XMLHttpRequest` object is the key element that enables the client-side JavaScript code to call a page on the server asynchronously. This chapter was intentionally short and probably has left you with many questions — that's good! Be prepared for a whole book dedicated to answering questions and demonstrating lots of interesting functionality!

2
AJAX Foundations

It is said that one picture is worth a thousand words. And so is a well-written piece of code, we would say. In this chapter you will get plenty of both, while learning the foundations of client-side AJAX development.

Hopefully, the first chapter has developed your interest in AJAX well enough that you will endure the second chapter with lots of theory to be learned. On the other hand, if you found the first exercise too challenging, be assured that this time we will advance a bit slower. We will learn the theory in parts by going through many short examples. In this chapter, we will meet client AJAX technologies, which include:

- JavaScript
- The Document Object Model (DOM)
- Cascading Style Sheets (CSS)
- The XMLHttpRequest object

You will learn how to make these components work together smoothly, and form a strong foundation for your future AJAX applications.

JavaScript and the Document Object Model

JavaScript is the heart of AJAX. JavaScript is a programming language supported by all modern web browsers, with a similar syntax to the good old C language. JavaScript is a *parsed language* (not compiled), and it has some **Object-Oriented Programming** (**OOP**) capabilities. JavaScript was initially designed for writing simple scripts to implement (or complement) a web application's client-side functionality, but powerful frameworks—such as the Microsoft AJAX Library, prototype, script. aculo.us, Dojo, and many others—have been recently developed upon the features introduced by newer versions of the language. A brief history and description of the language can be found at http://en.wikipedia.org/wiki/JavaScript.

Because the JavaScript programs are parsed, their code must arrive unaltered at the client for execution. This is a strength and weakness at the same time, and you need to keep it in mind when developing your JavaScript code. You can find very good introductions to JavaScript at the following web links:

- `http://www.echoecho.com/javascript.htm`
- `http://www.webteacher.com/javascript/`
- `http://www.w3schools.com/js/default.asp`

Part of JavaScript's power on the client resides in its ability to manipulate the parent HTML document, and it does that through the Document Object Model (DOM) interface. The DOM is a standard that allows for the programmatic representation and manipulation of hierarchical structures such as HTML and XML. It is available with a multitude of languages and technologies, including JavaScript, Java, PHP, C#, C++, and so on.

When developing AJAX applications you need to use JavaScript's DOM to read, parse, alter, and create HTML elements of the web page. To learn more about the DOM, we recommend you check out the following tutorials:

`http://www.quirksmode.org/dom/intro.html`
`http://www.javascriptkit.com/javatutors/dom.shtml`

You can play a nice DOM game at `http://www.topxml.com/learning/games/b/default.asp`. A comprehensive reference of the JavaScript DOM can be found at `http://krook.org/jsdom/`. The Mozilla reference for the JavaScript DOM is available at `http://www.mozilla.org/docs/dom/reference/javascript.html`.

In the first example of this chapter, you will use the DOM to write a piece of text on the web page. When adding JavaScript code to an HTML file, one option is to write the JavaScript code in a `<script>` element within the `<body>` element. Take the following HTML file for example, which executes a simple JavaScript script when loaded. Notice the `document` object, which is a default DOM object in JavaScript that represents the HTML page.

Here we use its `write()` method to add content to the page. The code will display "Hello, world!" on the page unless you execute it between 10 PM and 5 AM, in which case it will display "You should go to sleep".

```
<!DOCTYPE html PUBLIC "-//W3C//DTD XHTML 1.0 Transitional//EN"
"http://www.w3.org/TR/xhtml1/DTD/xhtml1-transitional.dtd">
<html xmlns="http://www.w3.org/1999/xhtml">
  <head>
    <title>AJAX Tutorial: JavaScript and DOM</title>
```

```
<script type="text/javascript">
  // declaring new variables
  var date = new Date();
  var hour = date.getHours();
  // demonstrating the if statement
  if (hour >= 22 || hour <= 5)
    document.write("You should go to sleep.");
  else
    document.write("Hello, world!");
</script>
</head>
<body>
</body>
</html>
```

The `document.write()` commands generate output that is added to the `<body>` element of the page when the script executes. The content that you generate becomes part of the HTML code of the page, so you can add HTML elements in there if you want (ideally you'd avoid creating elements dynamically whenever possible, however).

Writing compliant markup maximizes the chances that your pages will work fine with most existing and future web browsers. A useful article about following web standards can be found at `http://www.w3.org/QA/2002/04/Web-Quality`. A good article explaining the document type declaration (`DOCTYPE`) can be found at `http://www.alistapart.com/stories/doctype/`.

We advise you try to write well-formed and valid HTML code whenever possible. When creating static pages, or pages that are dynamically created on the server, you can check their compliancy using the W3C Markup Validator Service at `http://validator.w3.org/`. However, the service can't be used to check pages with elements generated by JavaScript. The validator service, just like web search engines, doesn't execute the JavaScript code on the page, so it can't see any content that is generated dynamically.

The debate on standards seems to be an endless one, with one group of people being very passionate about strictly following the standards, while others are just interested in their pages looking good on a certain set of browsers. At the moment of writing, the front pages of Google and other important companies do not output compliant HTML. The examples in this book contain valid HTML code, with the exception of a few cases where we broke the rules a little bit in order to make the code easier to understand. A real fact is that very few online websites follow the standards, for various reasons.

You will usually prefer to write the JavaScript code in a separate .js file that is referenced from the .html file, instead of writing the JavaScript code in the .html file itself. This allows you to keep the HTML code clean and have all the JavaScript code organized in a single place. You can reference a JavaScript file in HTML code by adding a child element called `<script>` to the `<head>` element, like this:

```
<html>
  <head>
    <script type="text/javascript" src="file.js"></script>
  </head>
</html>
```

 Even if you don't have anything between the `<script>` and `</script>` tags, don't be tempted to use the short form:`<script type="text/javascript" src="file.js" />`. This causes problems with Internet Explorer 6, which doesn't load the JavaScript file any more. (This problem doesn't affect tags used to reference other kinds of files, such as CSS files, for example.)

Let's do a short exercise.

Time for Action—Playing with JavaScript and the DOM

1. Open Visual Web Developer, and load the http://localhost/Atlas web site that you created in Chapter 1.

2. Right-click the project's root in Solution Explorer, and select **Add New Item**. Select the **HTML Page** template, type JavaScriptDom.html for the name, click **Add**, and then modify it like this:

```
<!DOCTYPE html PUBLIC "-//W3C//DTD XHTML 1.0 Transitional//EN"
"http://www.w3.org/TR/xhtml1/DTD/xhtml1-transitional.dtd">
<html xmlns="http://www.w3.org/1999/xhtml" >
<head>
  <title>AJAX Tutorial: JavaScript and DOM</title>
  <script type="text/javascript" src="JavaScriptDom.js"></script>
</head>
<body>
  What's up?
</body>
</html>
```

 Visual Web Developer will warn you that including text directly in the `<body>` element isn't compliant with the XHTML 1.0 Transitional standard. This is one of the examples where we break the rules a little bit for the purpose of keeping the exercise simple.

3. Add a new file to the project, using the **JScript File** template, named `JavaScriptDom.js`. Add the following code to the file:

```
// declaring new variables
var date = new Date();
var hour = date.getHours();

// simple conditional content output
if (hour >= 22 || hour <= 5)
  document.write("Goodnight, world!");
else
  document.write("Hello, world!");
```

 Be very careful while writing this code, because JavaScript is case sensitive. Even a small typo will usually make the code non-functional. In case you run into trouble, please see Chapter 8 for details about debugging your JavaScript code.

4. Select **File | Save All** (or press *Ctrl + Shift + S*) to save your changes.

5. Load `http://localhost/Atlas/JavaScriptDom.html` in your web browser, and assuming it's not late enough, expect to see the message as shown in Figure 2-1 (if it's past 10 PM, the message would be a bit different). You can see the page online at `http://www.cristiandarie.ro/asp-ajax/JavaScriptDom.html`.

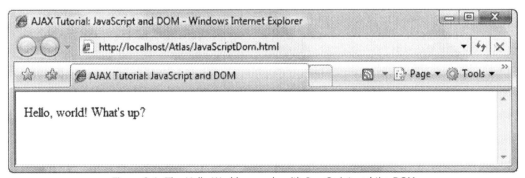

Figure 2-1. The Hello World example with JavaScript and the DOM

While `JavaScriptDom.html` is open in Visual Web Developer, you can press *Ctrl + F5* to have it load automatically in your web browser. Pressing *F5* would execute the project with debugging enabled, which would work as well, but at this moment debugging is not necessary because you have no ASP.NET code to debug. When you execute your project with debugging for the first time, Visual Web Developer will offer to set up the appropriate `Web.config` options for your project, to enable debugging. Confirm this action.

Also, if you are using Windows Vista and IIS 7 and want to be able to debug an ASP.NET application, you need to configure IIS as explained in Chapter 1, and set your web application to use **Classic .NET AppPool** instead of **Default AppPool**.

What Just Happened

The code is very simple indeed and hence it doesn't need detailed explanations. Here are the main ideas you need to be aware of:

- JavaScript doesn't require you to declare the variables, so in theory you can avoid the `var` keywords. This isn't a recommended practice though.

- The JavaScript code in `JavaScriptDom.js` executes automatically when you load the HTML file. You can, however, group the code in JavaScript functions, which only execute when called explicitly.

- The code in the JavaScript file is executed when the file is referenced. In our exercise, the file is referenced in the `<head>` section, which explains why **Hello World!** appears before **What's Up?**.

- The text generated by your JavaScript code isn't visible to clients that don't execute JavaScript code, such as search engine spiders. If search engine optimization is a concern, keep in mind to never output indexable content only using JavaScript.

- Because there is no server-side ASP.NET code involved, you can load the file in your web browser directly from the disk, instead of accessing it through an HTTP web server. In that case the URL will be `file:///C:/Atlas/JavaScriptDom.html`. When loading an HTML page with JavaScript code from a local location (`file://`) rather than through a web server (`http://`), Internet Explorer will ask for confirmation to execute the JavaScript code with higher privileges, as shown in Figure 2-2. (We will learn more about security later in this chapter.)

Figure 2-2. Internet Explorer asks for permission to execute local JavaScript code

One of the problems of the presented example is that we don't control the place where the JavaScript code displays its output. The code executes right in the place where it's referenced, which in this case is before the <body> element. If you wanted to have the "Hello World!" message displayed after "What's up", you would need to move the script file reference inside <body>, like this:

```
<body>
  What's up?
  <script type="text/javascript" src="JavaScriptDom.js"></script>
</body>
```

Needless to say, you don't want to move JavaScript file references around depending on what needs to be displayed. Except for the most simple of cases, having just JavaScript code that executes unconditionally when the HTML page loads is not enough. You will usually want to have more control over when and how portions of JavaScript code execute, and the solution consists in using JavaScript *functions*, and executing these *functions* when certain *events* (such as a button click) on the HTML page are triggered.

JavaScript Events and the DOM

In the next exercise, we will create a simple HTML structure from JavaScript code using the DOM. When creating a web page that has dynamically generated parts, you first need to create its *template* (which contains the static parts), and use **placeholders** for the dynamic parts. The placeholders must be uniquely identifiable HTML elements (elements with the ID attribute set).

The typical elements used as placeholders are <div> and <span>, due to their generic usage purpose. In practice they're typically used in conjunction with CSS to customize the appearance of the displayed content. The <div> and <span> elements are nicely (and briefly) described at http://en.wikipedia.org/wiki/Span_and_div.

Take a look at the following HTML document:

```
<!DOCTYPE html PUBLIC "-//W3C//DTD XHTML 1.1//EN" "http://www.w3.org/
TR/xhtml11/DTD/xhtml11.dtd">
<html>
  <head>
    <title>AJAX Tutorial: JavaScript Events and DOM</title>
  </head>
  <body>
    <p>
      Hello dude! Here's a cool list of colors for you:
    </p>
    <ul>
      <li>Black</li>
      <li>Orange</li>
      <li>Pink</li>
    </ul>
  </body>
</html>
```

Suppose that you want to have the `<ul>` element and its children — which are highlighted in the code snippet — generated dynamically using JavaScript and DOM. The first step is to create a placeholder in their place. This placeholder must have an id, so that it can be then identified by your JavaScript code. If the `<div>` element is used as a placeholder, then your page would look like this:

```
<!DOCTYPE html PUBLIC "-//W3C//DTD XHTML 1.1//EN" "http://www.w3.org/
TR/xhtml11/DTD/xhtml11.dtd">
<html>
  <head>
    <title>AJAX Tutorial: JavaScript Events and DOM</title>
  </head>
  <body>
    <p>
      Hello dude! Here's a cool list of colors for you:
    </p>
    <div id="myDivElement"/>
  </body>
</html>
```

Your goals for the next exercise are:

- Access the named `<div>` element programmatically from a JavaScript function.
- Have the JavaScript code execute *after* the HTML page loads, so that it can access the `<div>` element. HTML elements in `<body>` aren't accessible from

JavaScript code that executes in the `<head>` element, so we can't use the same technique as in the previous exercise. Now we will execute the JavaScript code from the `<body>` element's `onload` event.

• Group the JavaScript code in a function for easier code handling.

 If you've run the previous exercise in debug mode using Visual Web Developer, remember to stop debugging (**Debug | Stop Debugging**) before proceeding to the next exercise. Visual Web Developer doesn't allow you to add files and perform various changes to a project that is being debugged.

Time for Action—Using JavaScript Events and the DOM

1. In the same `http://localhost/Atlas/` application, add a new **HTML Page** named `JavaScriptEvents.html`, and add the following code to it:

```
<!DOCTYPE html PUBLIC "-//W3C//DTD XHTML 1.0 Transitional//EN"
"http://www.w3.org/TR/xhtml1/DTD/xhtml1-transitional.dtd">
<html xmlns="http://www.w3.org/1999/xhtml">
  <head>
    <title>AJAX Tutorial: JavaScript Events and
DOM</title>
    <script type="text/javascript" src="JavaScriptEvents.js">
    </script>
  </head>
  <body onload="process()">
    <p>
      Hello dude! Here's a cool list of colors for you:
    </p>
    <div id="myDivElement" />
  </body>
</html>
```

2. Add a new **JScript File** called `JavaScriptEvents.js`, with the following contents:

```
function process()
{
  // create the HTML code
  var string;
  string = "<ul>"
        + "<li>Black</li>"
        + "<li>Orange</li>"
        + "<li>Pink</li>"
        + "</ul>";
  // obtain a reference to the <div> element on the page
  myDiv = document.getElementById("myDivElement");
```

```
    // add content to the <div> element
    myDiv.innerHTML = string;
}
```

3. Save your files, then load `http://localhost/Atlas/JavaScriptEvents`
   `.html` in a web browser. You should see a window like the one in Figure 2-3.
   You can see the page online at `http://www.cristiandarie.ro/asp-ajax/`
   `JavaScriptEvents.html`.

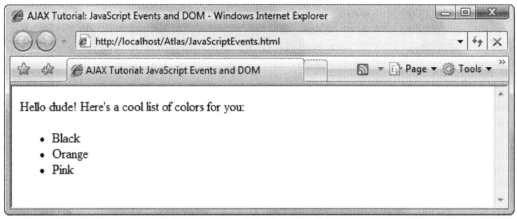

Figure 2-3. JavaScript Events and DOM

What Just Happened?

The code is pretty simple. In the HTML code, the important details are highlighted in
the following code snippet:

```
<!DOCTYPE html PUBLIC "-//W3C//DTD XHTML 1.1//EN" "http://www.w3.org/
TR/xhtml11/DTD/xhtml11.dtd">
<html>
  <head>
    <title>AJAX Tutorial: JavaScript Events and DOM</title>
    <script type="text/javascript" src="JavaScriptEvents.js">
    </script>
  </head>
  <body onload="process()">
    <p>
      Hello dude! Here's a cool list of colors for you:
    </p>
    <div id="myDivElement" />
  </body>
</html>
```

Everything starts by referencing the JavaScript source file using the <script> element. The JavaScript file contains a function called process(), which is used as an event-handler function for the body's onload event. Note that the JavaScript file is loaded at the time the <head> element is parsed by the browser, but none of the code is executed because it is included in the process() function. Functions are executed only when called explicitly.

 You can find a very useful introduction to JavaScript events at http://www.quirksmode.org/js/introevents.html, which is continued with more details about the different events supported by various web browsers at http://www.quirksmode.org/js/events_events.html.

The onload event of <body> fires after the HTML file is fully loaded, and it executes the process() function. The onload event is fired after the whole page has been loaded by the browser, so at the time process() executes, it has access to the elements inside <body>, including the <div> element we want to populate. The function starts by creating the HTML code we want to add to the <div> element:

```
function process()
{
  // Create the HTML code
  var string;
  string = "<ul>"
          + "<li>Black</li>"
          + "<li>Orange</li>"
          + "<li>Pink</li>"
          + "</ul>";
```

Next, we obtained a reference to <myDivElement>, using the getElementById() function of the document object. Remember that document is a default DOM object in JavaScript, referencing the body of your HTML document:

```
// obtain a reference to the <div> element on the page
myDiv = document.getElementById("myDivElement");
```

 Note that JavaScript allows you to use either single quotes or double quotes for string variables. The previous line of code can be successfully written like this:

```
myDiv = document.getElementById("myDivElement");
```

In the case of JavaScript, both choices are equally good, as long as you are consistent about using only one of them. If you use both notations in the same script you risk ending up with parse errors. In this book, we will use double quotes in JavaScript programs.

Finally, we populated `<myDivElement>` by adding the HTML code you built in the `string` variable:

```
    // add content to the <div> element
    myDiv.innerHTML = string;
}
```

In this example, you have used the `innerHTML` property of the DOM to add the composed HTML to your document.

 The `innerHTML` property that we used in this exercise isn't part of the W3C standard, and many recommend against using it. We generally recommend against using it in production code when you have decent alternatives. However, this property is still very frequently used—especially when creating code prototypes—because of its ease of use and speed.

Even More DOM

In the previous exercise, you have created the list of elements by joining strings to compose a simple HTML structure, and used the `innerHTML` property of the `<div>` element to add that structure to your page. We used this technique because it was the easiest way to demonstrate how to use page events, and you can successfully use it for similar purposes in your own development. However, using `innerHTML` is not the most elegant way to get things done.

This time we'll take a look at how to use standards-compliant DOM functions to generate HTML output. The structure we want to create is similar to that from the previous exercise, except this time we also generate the paragraph and the "Hello dude..." dynamically:

```
<div id="myDivElement">
  <p>
    Hello dude! Here's a cool list of colors for you:
  </p>
  <ul>
    <li>Black</li>
    <li>Orange</li>
    <li>Pink</li>
  </ul>
</div>
```

A DOM document is a hierarchical structure of elements, where each element can have one or more attributes. In this HTML fragment, the single element with an attribute is `<div>`, which has an attribute called `id` with the value `myDivElement`.

The root node that you can access through the document object is <body>. When implementing this HTML document, you will end up with a structure such as the one in Figure 2-4.

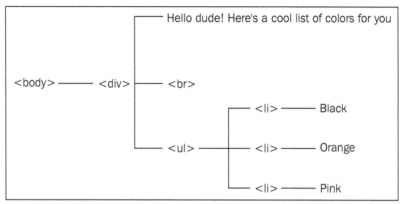

Figure 2-4. A Hierarchy of HTML Elements

In the previous figure, you have seen an HTML structure formed of <body>, <div>, <p>, <ul>, and <li> elements, and four text nodes ("**Hello...**", "**Black**", "**Orange**", "**Pink**"). In the next exercise, you will create this structure using the DOM functions createElement(), createTextNode(), and appendChild().

Time for Action—Even More DOM

1. Make sure your project isn't running in debug mode, and create a new HTML file called DomStandard.html, and add the following code to it:

```
<!DOCTYPE html PUBLIC "-//W3C//DTD XHTML 1.0 Transitional//EN"
"http://www.w3.org/TR/xhtml1/DTD/xhtml1-transitional.dtd">
<html xmlns="http://www.w3.org/1999/xhtml" >
  <head>
    <title>AJAX Tutorial: More JavaScript and DOM</title>
    <script type="text/javascript" src="DomStandard.js"></script>
  </head>
<body onload="process()">
    <div id="myDivElement" />
  </body>
</html>
```

2. Add a new JScript file to your project called `DomStandard.js`, and type the following code:

```
function process()
{
  // create the <p> element
  oP = document.createElement("p");
  // create the "Hello..." text node
  oHelloText = document.createTextNode
    ("Hello dude! Here's a cool list of colors for you:");
  // add the text node as a child element of <p>
  oP.appendChild(oHelloText);

  // create the <ul> element
  oUl = document.createElement("ul")

  // create the first <li> element and add a text node to it
  oLiBlack = document.createElement("li");
  oBlackText = document.createTextNode("Black");
  oLiBlack.appendChild(oBlackText);

  // create the second <li> element and add a text node to it
  oLiOrange = document.createElement("li");
  oOrangeText = document.createTextNode("Orange");
  oLiOrange.appendChild(oOrangeText);

  // create the third <li> element and add a text node to it
  oLiPink = document.createElement("li");
  oPinkText = document.createTextNode("Pink");
  oLiPink.appendChild(oPinkText);

  // add the <ui> elements as children of the <ul> element
  oUl.appendChild(oLiBlack);
  oUl.appendChild(oLiOrange);
  oUl.appendChild(oLiPink);

  // obtain a reference to the <div> element on the page
  myDiv = document.getElementById("myDivElement");

  // add the <p> and <ul> elements to the <div> element
  myDiv.appendChild(oP);
  myDiv.appendChild(oUl);
}
```

3. Load `DomStandard.html` in a web browser. The result should look like Figure 2-5. The example can be viewed online at http://www. cristiandarie.ro/asp-ajax/DomStandard.html.

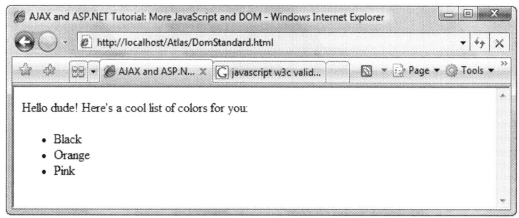

Figure 2-5. Even More JavaScript and DOM

 JavaScript is case sensitive, and when writing long code listings it's very easy to make mistakes. Please see Chapter 8 for details about debugging your JavaScript code.

What Just Happened?

Well, what just happened is exactly what happened after the previous exercise, but this time with much more code, as you can see by having a look at the `process()` function. Although there are many lines of code, the functionality is pretty simple, and it follows a cleaner coding practice that—in theory at least—generates code that is easier to maintain in the long run.

It's pretty clear using the DOM to create HTML structures may not always be your best option. However, in more complex projects—such as most real-world ones are—this coding technique can actually make your life easier, for the following reasons:

- It's fairly easy to programmatically create dynamic HTML structures, such as building elements in `for` loops, because you're not concerned about text formatting but about building the hierarchical structure.

- As a consequence, you don't need, for example, to manually add closing tags. When you add a 'ui' element, the DOM will take care to generate the `<ui>` tag and an associated closing `</ui>` tag for you.

- You can treat the nodes as if they were independent nodes, and decide later how to build the hierarchy. Again, the DOM takes care of the implementation details; you just need to tell it what you want.

Note that if you use the "View Source" feature of your web browser, or if you save the page to disk, you will find the original HTML page, instead of the final form of the page that was generated using JavaScript. If you want to browse the final results as displayed by your browser, you can use the DOM Inspector tool that ships with Firefox, accessible through **Tools | DOM Inspector** (*Ctrl + Shift + I*). Figure 2-6 shows how **DOM Inspector** sees the page we've just created.

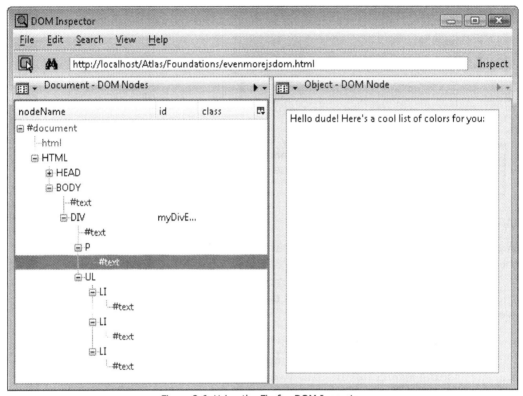

Figure 2-6. Using the Firefox DOM Inspector

The DOM functions used in this exercise are perhaps the most frequently used, but obviously there are many more—we'll bore you with some additional theory later in the book. To learn about the insidious details of DOM, including the implementation differences between various web browsers, we recommend that you bookmark the tutorial at http://www.howtocreate.co.uk/tutorials/javascript/dombasics—you'll find it useful, sooner or later.

JavaScript, DOM, and CSS

CSS (Cascading Style Sheets) is certainly a familiar term to you. CSS is a powerful language used to describe the appearance of the elements of a web page. CSS definitions can be stored in one or more files with the `.css` extension, allowing web designers to detach the CSS styling definitions from the HTML document structure. If the job is done right and CSS is used consistently in a website, CSS will allow you to make visual changes to the entire site (or parts of the site) with very little effort, just by editing the CSS file.

While *technically* it's not necessary to know CSS when implementing AJAX, in practice it's very desirable to be at least educated in CSS basics, even if the HTML and CSS design is created by someone else. CSS is a vast subject; there are many books and tutorials on CSS, including those you can find at `http://www.w3.org/Style/CSS/learning` and `http://www.csstutorial.net/`. The Wikipedia page on CSS (`http://en.wikipedia.org/wiki/Cascading_Style_Sheets`) contains useful material on the history of CSS, and its current state and limitations.

We will go through a simple exercise to demonstrate a few techniques of using CSS with JavaScript, which is the most relevant scenario in the context of AJAX development. In the following exercise, you will draw a nice table, and you will have two buttons named **Set Style 1** and **Set Style 2**. These buttons will change the table's colors and appearance by just switching the current styles. See Figure 2-7 to get a feeling about what you're about to create, or visit it online at `http://www.cristiandarie.ro/asp-ajax/JavaScriptCSS.html`.

Time for Action—Working with CSS and JavaScript

1. Add a new HTML file to your project named `JavaScriptCSS.html`, and modify it like this:

```
<!DOCTYPE html PUBLIC "-//W3C//DTD XHTML 1.0 Transitional//EN"
"http://www.w3.org/TR/xhtml1/DTD/xhtml1-transitional.dtd">
<html xmlns="http://www.w3.org/1999/xhtml" >
  <head>
    <title>AJAX Tutorial: JavaScript and CSS</title>
    <script type="text/javascript" src="JavaScriptCSS.js"></
script>
    <link href="TableStyles.css" type="text/css"
rel="stylesheet"/>
  </head>
  <body>
    <table id="table">
      <tr>
        <th id="tableHead">
```

```
                  Product Name
                </th>
              </tr>
              <tr>
                <td id="tableFirstLine">
                  Airplane
                </td>
              </tr>
              <tr>
                <td id="tableSecondLine">
                  Big car
                </td>
              </tr>
            </table>
            <p>
                <input type="button" value="Style 1"
        onclick="setStyle1();"/>
                <input type="button" value="Style 2"
        onclick="setStyle2();"/>
            </p>
          </body>
        </html>
```

2. Create a JScript file named `JavaScriptCSS.js` and write the following code in it:

```
// Change table style to style 1
function setStyle1()
{
  // obtain references to HTML elements
  oTable = document.getElementById("table");
  oTableHead = document.getElementById("tableHead");
  oTableFirstLine = document.getElementById("tableFirstLine");
  oTableSecondLine = document.getElementById("tableSecondLine");

  // set styles
  oTable.className = "Table1";
  oTableHead.className = "TableHead1";
  oTableFirstLine.className = "TableContent1";
  oTableSecondLine.className = "TableContent1";
}

// Change table style to style 2
function setStyle2()
{
  // obtain references to HTML elements
```

```
oTable = document.getElementById("table");
oTableHead = document.getElementById("tableHead");
oTableFirstLine = document.getElementById("tableFirstLine");
oTableSecondLine = document.getElementById("tableSecondLine");

// set styles
oTable.className = "Table2";
oTableHead.className = "TableHead2";
oTableFirstLine.className = "TableContent2";
oTableSecondLine.className = "TableContent2";
}
```

3. Finally, add a CSS file named `TableStyles.css`, using Visual Web Developer's **Style Sheet** template, and add the following definitions to it:

```
.Table1
{
  border: #339966 1px solid;
  background-color: #ccff66;
}
.TableHead1
{
  font-family: Verdana, Arial;
  font-weight: bold;
  font-size: 10pt;
}
.TableContent1
{  font-family: Verdana, Arial;
  font-size: 10pt;
}
.Table2
{
  border: #006699 1px solid;
  background-color: #ccffff;
}
.TableHead2
{
  font-family: Verdana, Arial;
  font-weight: bold;
  font-size: 10pt;
}
.TableContent2
{
  font-family: Verdana, Arial;
  font-size: 10pt;
}
```

4. Load `http://localhost/Atlas/JavaScriptCSS.html` in your web browser, and test that your buttons work as they should:

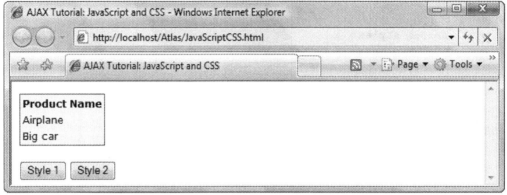

Figure 2-7. Table with CSS and JavaScript

What Just Happened?

Your `TableStyles.css` file contains two sets of styles that can be applied to the table in `JavaScriptCSS.html`. When the user clicks one of the **Style** buttons, the JavaScript DOM is used to assign those styles to the elements of the table.

In the first part of the `SetStyle` methods, we use the `getElementById()` function to obtain references to the HTML elements that we want to apply CSS styles to:

```
// obtain references to HTML elements
oTable = document.getElementById("table");
oTableHead = document.getElementById("tableHead");
oTableFirstLine = document.getElementById("tableFirstLine");
oTableSecondLine = document.getElementById("tableSecondLine");
```

 As with many other web development tasks, manipulating CSS can be the subject of significant inconsistencies between different browsers. For example, in the previous code snippet, try to rename the object names to be the same as their associated HTML elements (such as renaming `oTable` to `table`) to see Internet Explorer stop working. Internet Explorer doesn't like it if there's already an object with that ID in the HTML file.

After initializing these objects, the safe way that works with all browsers to set the elements' CSS style is to use their `className` property:

```
// set styles
oTable.className = "Table1";
oTableHead.className = "TableHead1";
oTableFirstLine.className = "TableContent1";
oTableSecondLine.className = "TableContent1";
```

The XMLHttpRequest Object

XMLHttpRequest is the object that enables the JavaScript code to make asynchronous HTTP server requests. This allows you to initiate HTTP requests and receive responses from the server in the background, without requiring the user to submit the page to the server. This feature, combined with the possibility to manipulate the web page using DOM and CSS, allows you to implement responsive functionality and visual effects backed with live data from the server, without the user experiencing any visual interruptions.

The XMLHttpRequest object was initially implemented by Microsoft in 1999 as an ActiveX object in Internet Explorer, and eventually became *de facto* standard for all the browsers, being supported as a native object by all modern web browsers except Internet Explorer 6.

Note that even if XMLHttpRequest has become a *de facto* standard in the web browsers, it is not yet a W3C standard. Similar functionality is proposed by the W3C DOM Level 3 Load and Save specification standard, which hasn't been implemented yet by web browsers.

The typical sequence of operations when working with XMLHttpRequest is as follows:

1. Create an instance of the XMLHttpRequest object.
2. Use the XMLHttpRequest object to make an asynchronous call to a server page, defining a callback function that will be executed automatically when the server response is received.
3. Read the server's response in the callback function.
4. Update the web page using the data received from the server.
5. Go to step 2.

Let's now see how to do these steps with real code.

Creating the XMLHttpRequest Object

The XMLHttpRequest object is implemented in different ways by the browsers. In Internet Explorer 6 and older, XMLHttpRequest is implemented as an ActiveX control, and you instantiate it like this:

```
xmlhttp = new ActiveXObject("Microsoft.XMLHttp");
```

For the other web browsers—including Firefox, Opera and Safari, and Internet Explorer 7, XMLHttpRequest is a native object, so you create instances of it like this:

```
xmlhttp = new XMLHttpRequest();
```

The ActiveX XMLHttp library comes in many more flavors and versions that you could imagine. Each piece of Microsoft software, including Internet Explorer and MDAC, came with new versions of this ActiveX control, each having its own name. Microsoft.XMLHttp is the oldest and is supported on all Windows machines, but the newer versions have performance improvements.

It is possible to write JavaScript code that automatically detects the latest XMLHttp version installed on the visitor's machine, if he or she is using Internet Explorer 6 or older. The technique is described in *AJAX and PHP: Building Responsive Web Applications* (Packt, 2006), but we will not insist on it here because the feature is included in the Microsoft AJAX Library.

The following JavaScript function creates an XMLHttpRequest instance by using the native object if available, or the Microsoft.XMLHttp ActiveX control for visitors that use Internet Explorer 6 or older:

```
// creates an XMLHttpRequest instance
function createXmlHttpRequestObject()
{
  // xmlHttp will store the reference to the XMLHttpRequest object
  var xmlHttp;
  // try to instantiate the native XMLHttpRequest object
  try
  {
    // create an XMLHttpRequest object
    xmlHttp = new XMLHttpRequest();
  }
  catch(e)
  {
    // assume IE6 or older
    try
    {
      xmlHttp = new ActiveXObject("Microsoft.XMLHttp");
    }
    catch(e) { }
  }
  // return the created object or display an error message
  if (!xmlHttp)
    alert("Error creating the XMLHttpRequest object.");
  else
    return xmlHttp;
}
```

This function uses the JavaScript `try`/`catch` construct, which is a powerful exception-handling technique that was initially implemented in OOP (Object-Oriented Programming) languages. Basically, when an error happens at run time in the JavaScript code, an *exception* is thrown. The exception is an object that contains the details of the error. Using the `try`/`catch` syntax, you can *catch* the exception and handle it locally, so that the error won't be propagated to the user's browser.

The `try`/`catch` syntax is as follows:

```
try
{
  // code that might generate an exception
}
catch (e)
{
  // code that executes if an exception was thrown in the try block
  // (exception details are available through the e parameter)
}
```

You place any code that might generate errors inside the `try` block. If an error happens, the execution is passed immediately to the `catch` block. If no error happens inside the `try` block, then the code in the `catch` block never executes.

Run-time exceptions propagate from the point they were raised, up through the call stack of your program. The **call stack** is the list of methods that are being executed. So if a function `A()` calls a function `B()` which at its turn calls a function called `C()`, then the call stack will be formed of these three methods. If an exception happens in `C()`, you can handle it using a `try`/`catch` block right there. If the exception isn't caught and handled in `C()`, it propagates, to `B()`, and so on. The final layer is the web browser. If your code generates an exception that you don't handle, the exception will end up getting caught by the web browser, which may display an unpleasant error message to your visitor.

The way you handle each exception depends very much on the situation at hand. Sometimes you will simply ignore the error, other times you will flag it somehow in the code, or you will display an error message to your visitor. In this book you will meet all kinds of scenarios.

In our particular case, when we want to create an `XMLHttpRequest` object, we will first try to create the object as if it was a native browser object, like this:

```
// try to instantiate the native XMLHttpRequest object
try
{
  // create an XMLHttpRequest object
  xmlHttp = new XMLHttpRequest();
}
```

Internet Explorer 7, Mozilla, Opera, Safari, and other browsers will execute this piece of code just fine, and no error will be generated, because XMLHttpRequest is a supported natively. However, Internet Explorer 6 and its older versions won't recognize the XMLHttpRequest object, an exception will be generated, and the execution will be passed to the catch block. For Internet Explorer 6 and older versions, the XMLHttpRequest object needs to be created as an ActiveX control:

```
catch(e)
{
  // assume IE6 or older
  try
  {
    xmlHttp = new ActiveXObject("Microsoft.XMLHttp");
  }
  catch(e) { }
}
```

Every JavaScript programmer seems to have his or her own technique for creating the XMLHttpRequest object, and surprisingly enough, all techniques work just fine. The implementation we presented uses try and catch to instantiate the object, because it (reasonably) guarantees the best chance of working well with future browsers, while doing proper error checking without consuming too many lines of code.

Alternatively, you could, for example, check whether your browser supports XMLHttpRequest before trying to instantiate it, using the typeof function:

```
if (typeof XMLHttpRequest != "undefined")
{
  xmlHttp = new XMLHttpRequest();
}
```

Using typeof can often prove to be very helpful. In our particular case, using typeof doesn't eliminate the need to guard against errors using try/catch, so you would just end up typing more lines of code.

Another technique is to use a JavaScript feature called **object detection**. This feature allows you to check whether a particular object is supported by the browser, and works like this:

```
if (window.XMLHttpRequest)
{
  xmlHttp = new XMLHttpRequest();
}
```

At the end of our createXmlHttpRequestObject function, we test that after all the efforts, we have ended up obtaining a valid XMLHttpRequest instance:

```
// return the created object or display an error message
if (!xmlHttp)
```

```
        alert("Error creating the XMLHttpRequest object.");
    else
        return xmlHttp;
```

 Here we used the reverse effect of JavaScript's object detection feature, which in our opinion is even nicer than the feature itself. Object detection says that JavaScript will evaluate a valid object instance, such as xmlHttp, to true. The negation of this expression, (!xmlHttp), returns true not only if xmlHttp is false, but also if it is null or undefined.

Initiating Server Requests

After creating the XMLHttpRequest object you can do lots of interesting things with it. Although it has different ways of being instantiated, all the instances of XMLHttpRequest are supposed to share the same API (Application Programming Interface) and support the same functionality. This API is formed of the following methods and properties:

Method/Property	Description
abort	Stops the current request.
getAllResponseHeaders()	Returns the response headers as a string.
getResponseHeader("headerLabel")	Returns a single response header as a string.
open("method", "URL"[, asyncFlag[, "userName"[, "password"]]])	Initializes the request parameters.
send(content)	Performs the HTTP request.
setRequestHeader ("label", "value")	Sets an HTTP request header.
onreadystatechange	Used to set the callback function that handles request state changes.
readyState	Returns the status of the request: 0 = uninitialized 1 = loading 2 = loaded 3 = interactive 4 = complete
responseText	Returns the server response as a string.
responseXml	Returns the server response as an XML document that can be manipulated using JavaScript's DOM functions.
status	Returns the status code of the request.
statusText	Returns the status message of the request.

The methods you will use with every server request are open() and send(). The open() method configures a request by setting various parameters, and send() sends the request to the server. When the request is made asynchronously, before calling send you will also need to set the onreadystatechange property with the callback method to be executed when the status of the request changes, thus enabling the AJAX mechanism.

The open() method is used for initializing a request. It has two required parameters and a few optional ones. The open() method doesn't initiate a connection to the server; it is only used to set the connection options. The first parameter specifies the method used to send data to the server page, such as GET, POST, or PUT. The second parameter is URL, which specifies where you want to send the request. The URL can be complete or relative. If the URL doesn't specify a resource accessible via HTTP, the first parameter is ignored.

The third parameter of open, called async, specifies whether the request should be handled asynchronously; true means that your code processing carries on after the send() method returns without waiting for a response from the server; false means that the script waits for a response before continuing processing, freezing the web page functionality. To enable asynchronous processing (which is the heart of the AJAX mechanism), you will need to set async to true, and handle the onreadystatechange event to process the response from the server.

When using GET to pass parameters, you send the parameters using the URL's query string, as in http://localhost/ajax/test.aspx?param1=x&param2=y. This server request passes two parameters to the server—a parameter called param1 with the value x, and a parameter called param2 with the value y:

```
// call the server to execute the server side operation
xmlHttp.open("GET", "http://localhost/ajax/test.
aspx?param1=x&param2=y", true);
xmlHttp.onreadystatechange = handleRequestStateChange;
xmlHttp.send(null);
```

When using POST, you send the query string as a parameter of the send() method, instead of joining it on to the base URL, like this:

```
// call the server page to execute the server side operation
xmlHttp.open("POST", "http://localhost/ajax/test.aspx", true);
xmlHttp.onreadystatechange = handleRequestStateChange;
xmlHttp.send("param1=x&param2=y");
```

The two code samples should have the same effects. In practice, there are a few differences between POST and GET that you should know about:

- Using GET can help with debugging because you can simulate GET requests with a web browser, so you can easily see with your own eyes what your server script generates.

- The POST method is required when sending data larger than 512 bytes, which cannot be handled by GET.

- GET is meant to be used for retrieving data from the server, while POST is meant to submit changes. In the real world, it's good to obey by these rules, otherwise strange things can happen. For example, search engines send GET requests to read data from the Web, but they never POST any data. If you use GET to submit changes, and a search engine becomes aware of the address of the server script, that search engine could start modifying your data—and you certainly don't want that!

The minimal implementation of a function named process() that makes asynchronous server calls using GET looks like this:

```
function process()
{
  // call the server to execute the server side operation
  xmlHttp.open("GET", "ServerScript.aspx", true);
  xmlHttp.onreadystatechange = handleRequestStateChange;
  xmlHttp.send(null);
}
```

This method has the following potential problems:

- process() may be executed even if xmlHttp doesn't contain a valid XMLHttpRequest instance. This may happen if, for example, the user's browser doesn't support XMLHttpRequest. This would cause an unhandled exception to happen. Our other efforts to handle errors don't help very much if we aren't consistent and do something about the process function as well.

- process() isn't protected against other kinds of errors that could happen. For example, as you will see later in this chapter, some browsers will generate a security exception if they don't like the server you want to access with the XMLHttpRequest object (more on security in Chapter 3).

A better version of process() looks like that:

```
// performs a server request and assigns a callback function
function process()
{
  // continue only if xmlHttp isn't void
  if (xmlHttp)
```

```
{
  // try to connect to the server
  try
  {
    // initiate server request
    xmlHttp.open("GET", "ServerScript.aspx", true);
    xmlHttp.onreadystatechange = handleRequestStateChange;
    xmlHttp.send(null);
  }
  // display an error in case of failure
  catch (e)
  {
    alert("Can't connect to server:\n" + e.toString());
  }
}
}
```

If xmlHttp is null (or false) we don't display yet another error message, because we assume such a message was already displayed by the createXmlHttpRequestObject function. We make sure to signal any other connection problems though.

Handling the Server Response

When making an asynchronous request (such as in the code snippets presented earlier), the execution of xmlHttp.send() doesn't freeze until the server response is received; instead, the execution continues normally. In the process() function shown earlier, the handleRequestStateChange() function is defined as the callback method that should handle request state changes.

Usually, handleRequestStateChange() is called four times, for each time the request enters a new stage. The readyState property can have one the following values representing the possible stages of the request:

```
0 = uninitialized
1 = loading
2 = loaded
3 = interactive
4 = complete
```

Except state 3, all the other states have pretty self-explaining names. The *interactive* state is an intermediate state when the response has been partially received. In our AJAX applications we will only use the *complete* state, which marks that a response has been fully received from the server.

The typical implementation of `handleRequestStateChange()` is shown in the following code snippet, which highlights the portion where you actually get to read the response from the server:

```
// function executed when the state of the request changes
function handleRequestStateChange()
{
  // continue if the process is completed
  if (xmlHttp.readyState == 4)
  {
    // continue only if HTTP status is "OK"
    if (xmlHttp.status == 200)
    {
      // retrieve the response
      response = xmlHttp.responseText;
      // do something with the response
      // ...
      // ...
    }
  }
}
```

Before attempting to read the received data, we also verify that the response status code is 200. Sending such a code indicating the status of the request is part of the HTTP protocol, and 200 is the status code that specifies that the request completed successfully. Other popular HTTP status codes are 404, which indicates that the requested resource couldn't be found, and 500, which indicates a server error.

Once again we can use `try/catch` blocks to handle errors that could happen while initiating a connection to the server, or while reading the response from the server. A safer version of the `handleRequestStateChange()` function looks like this:

```
// function executed when the state of the request changes
function handleRequestStateChange()
{
  // continue if the process is completed
  if (xmlHttp.readyState == 4)
  {
    // continue only if HTTP status is "OK"
    if (xmlHttp.status == 200)
    {
      try
      {
        // retrieve the response
        response = xmlHttp.responseText;
        // do something with the response
        // ...
```

```
      // ...
   }
   catch(e)
   {
      // display error message
      alert("Error reading the response: " + e.toString());
   }
 }
 else
 {
   // display status message
   alert("There was a problem retrieving the data:\n" +
        xmlHttp.statusText);
 }
  }
 }
}
```

OK, let's see how these functions work in action.

Time for Action—Making Asynchronous Calls with XMLHttpRequest

1. In your Atlas website, create a **Text File** called `async.txt`, and add the following text to it:

    ```
    Hello, client!
    ```

2. Create an **HTML Page** file called `Async.html`, and modify the template like this:

    ```
    <!DOCTYPE html PUBLIC "-//W3C//DTD XHTML 1.0 Transitional//EN"
    "http://www.w3.org/TR/xhtml1/DTD/xhtml1-transitional.dtd">
    <html xmlns="http://www.w3.org/1999/xhtml" >
      <head>
        <title>AJAX Tutorial: XMLHttpRequest</title>
        <script type="text/javascript" src="async.js"></script>
      </head>
      <body onload="process()">
        <p>Hello, server!</p>
        <div id="myDivElement" />
      </body>
    </html>
    ```

3. Create a JScript file called `Async.js` with the following contents:

    ```
    // holds an instance of XMLHttpRequest
    var xmlHttp = createXmlHttpRequestObject();

    // creates an XMLHttpRequest instance
    function createXmlHttpRequestObject()
    ```

```
{
  // xmlHttp will store the reference to the XMLHttpRequest object
  var xmlHttp;
  // try to instantiate the native XMLHttpRequest object
  try
  {
    // create an XMLHttpRequest object
    xmlHttp = new XMLHttpRequest();
  }
  catch(e)
  {
    // assume IE6 or older
    try
    {
      xmlHttp = new ActiveXObject("Microsoft.XMLHttp");
    }
    catch(e) { }
  }
  // return the created object or display an error message
  if (!xmlHttp)
    alert("Error creating the XMLHttpRequest object.");
  else
    return xmlHttp;
}

// performs a server request and assigns a callback function
function process()
{
  // continue only if xmlHttp isn't void
  if (xmlHttp)
  {
    // try to connect to the server
    try
    {
      // initiate reading the async.txt file from the server
      xmlHttp.open("GET", "async.txt", true);
      xmlHttp.onreadystatechange = handleRequestStateChange;
      xmlHttp.send(null);
    }
    // display an error in case of failure
    catch (e)
    {
      alert("Can't connect to server:\n" + e.toString());
    }
  }
}

// function that handles the HTTP response
```

```
function handleRequestStateChange()
{
  // obtain a reference to the <div> element on the page
  myDiv = document.getElementById("myDivElement");

  // display the status of the request
  if (xmlHttp.readyState == 1)
  {
    myDiv.innerHTML += "<p>Request status: 1 (loading)</p>";
  }
  else if (xmlHttp.readyState == 2)
  {
    myDiv.innerHTML += "<p>Request status: 2 (loaded)</p>";
  }
  else if (xmlHttp.readyState == 3)
  {
    myDiv.innerHTML += "<p>Request status: 3 (interactive)</p>";
  }
  // when readyState is 4, we also read the server response
  else if (xmlHttp.readyState == 4)
  {
    // continue only if HTTP status is "OK"
    if (xmlHttp.status == 200)
    {
      try
      {
        // read the message from the server
        response = xmlHttp.responseText;
        // display the message
        myDiv.innerHTML +=
        "<p>Request status: 4 (complete). Server said:</p>";
        myDiv.innerHTML += response;
      }
      catch(e)
      {
        // display error message
        alert("Error reading the response: " + e.toString());
      }
    }
    else
    {
      // display status message
      alert("There was a problem retrieving the data:\n" +
            xmlHttp.statusText);
    }
  }
}
```

4. Load the `Async.html` file through the HTTP server by loading `http://localhost/Atlas/Async.html` in your browser (you *must* load it through HTTP; local access won't work this time). The script can also be tested online at `http://www.cristiandarie.ro/asp-ajax/Async.html`. Expect to see results similar to those shown in Figure 2-8.

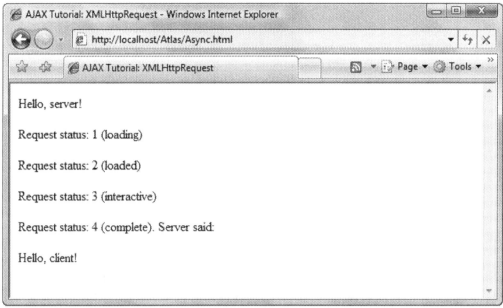

Figure 2-8. The Four HTTP Request Status Codes

 Don't worry if your browser doesn't display all the messages. Some `XMLHttpRequest` implementations simply ignore some status codes. Opera, for example, will only fire the event for status codes 3 and 4. Internet Explorer 6 will report status codes 2, 3, and 4 when using a more recent `XMLHttp` version.

What Just Happened?

To understand the exact flow of execution, let's start from where the processing begins—the `Async.html` file:

```html
<html>
  <head>
    <title>AJAX Tutorial: XMLHttpRequest</title>
    <script type="text/javascript" src="async.js"></script>
  </head>
  <body onload="process()">
```

This bit of code hides some interesting functionality. First, it references the async. js file, at which moment that file is parsed. The code residing in JavaScript functions does not execute automatically, but the rest of the code does. All the code in our JavaScript file is packaged as functions, except one line:

```
// holds an instance of XMLHttpRequest
var xmlHttp = createXmlHttpRequestObject();
```

This way we ensure that the xmlHttp variable contains an XMLHttpRequest instance right from the start. The XMLHttpRequest instance is created by calling the createXmlHttpRequestObject() function that you encountered a bit earlier.

The process() method is executed when the onload event fires. The process() method can rely on the xmlHttp object being already initialized, so it only focuses on initializing a server request. The proper error-handling sequence is used to guard against potential problems. The code that initiates the server request is:

```
// initiate reading the async.txt file from the server
xmlHttp.open("GET", "async.txt", true);
xmlHttp.onreadystatechange = handleRequestStateChange;
xmlHttp.send(null);
```

 Note that you cannot load the script locally, directly from the disk using a file:// resource. Instead, you need to load it through HTTP. To load it locally, you would need to specify the complete access path to the .txt file, but you may still meet a security problem that we will deal with later.

Supposing that the HTTP request was successfully initialized and executed asynchronously, the handleRequestStateChange() method will get called every time the state of the request changes. In real applications we will ignore all states except 4 (which signals the request has completed), but in this exercise we print a message with each state so you can see the callback method actually gets executed as advertised.

The code in handleRequestStateChange() is not that exciting by itself, but the fact that it's being called for you is very nice indeed. Instead of waiting for the server to reply with a synchronous HTTP call, making the request asynchronously allows your script to continue doing other tasks until a response is received.

The handleRequestStateChange() function starts by obtaining a reference to the HTML element called myDivElement, which is used to display the various states the HTTP request is going through:

```
// function that handles the HTTP response
function handleRequestStateChange()
{
  // obtain a reference to the <div> element on the page
  myDiv = document.getElementById("myDivElement");
```

```
// display the status o the request
if (xmlHttp.readyState == 1)
{
  myDiv.innerHTML += "<p>Request status: 1 (loading)</p>";
}
else if (xmlHttp.readyState == 2)
...
...
```

When the status hits the value of 4, we have the typical code that deals with reading the server response, hidden inside xmlHttp.responseText:

```
// when readyState is 4, we also read the server response
else if (xmlHttp.readyState == 4)
{
  // continue only if HTTP status is "OK"
  if (xmlHttp.status == 200)
  {
    try
    {
      // read the message from the server
      response = xmlHttp.responseText;
      myDiv.innerHTML +=
        "<p>Request status: 4 (complete). Server said:</p>";
      myDiv.innerHTML += response;
    }
    catch(e)
    {
      // display error message
      alert("Error reading the response: " + e.toString());
    }
  }
  else
  {
    // display status message
    alert("There was a problem retrieving the data:\n" +
          xmlHttp.statusText);
  }
}
```

Apart from the error-handling bits, it's good to notice the xmlHttp.responseText property that contains the response from the server. This property has a bigger brother called xmlHttp.responseXml, which can be used when the response from the server is in XML format.

Summary

This chapter walked you through many fields — HTML, JavaScript, CSS, the DOM, and, XMLHttpRequest — which are all important to understand before you can implement AJAX applications. In the chapter that follows we'll investigate one more important topic that you need to master before starting to work with the Microsoft AJAX Library: object-oriented programming with JavaScript.

3
Object-Oriented JavaScript

In this chapter, you'll learn about OOP (Object-Oriented Programming) and how it relates to JavaScript. As an ASP.NET developer, you probably have some experience working with objects, and you may even be familiar with concepts such as *inheritance*. However, unless you're already an experienced JavaScript programmer, you probably aren't familiar with the way JavaScript objects and functions *really* work. This knowledge is necessary in order to understand how the Microsoft AJAX Library works, and this chapter will teach you the necessary foundations. More specifically, you will learn:

- What encapsulation, inheritance, and polymorphism mean
- How JavaScript functions work
- How to use anonymous functions and closures
- How to read a class diagram, and implement it using JavaScript code
- How to work with JavaScript prototypes
- How the execution context and scope affect the output of JavaScript functions
- How to implement inheritance using closures and prototypes
- What JSON is, and what a JSON structure looks like

In the next chapters you'll use this theory to work effectively with the Microsoft AJAX Library.

Concepts of Object-Oriented Programming

Most ASP.NET developers are familiar with the fundamental OOP principles because this knowledge is important when developing for the .NET development. Similarly, to develop client-side code using the Microsoft AJAX Library, you need to be familiar with JavaScript's OOP features. Although not particularly difficult, understanding these features can be a bit challenging at first, because JavaScript's OOP model is different than that of languages such as C#, VB.NET, C++, or Java.

JavaScript is an *object-based* language. Just as in C#, you can create objects, call their methods, pass them as parameters, and so on. You could see this clearly when working with the DOM, where you manipulated the HTML document through the methods and properties of the implicit document object. However, JavaScript isn't generally considered a fully object-oriented language because it lacks support for some features that you'd find in "real" OOP languages, or simply implements them differently.

Your most important goal for this chapter is to understand how to work with JavaScript objects. As an ASP.NET developer, we assume that you already know how OOP works with .NET languages, although advanced knowledge isn't necessary. A tutorial written by Cristian Darie on OOP development with C# can be downloaded in PDF format at http://www.cristiandarie.ro/downloads/.

To ensure we start off from the same square, in the following couple of pages we'll review the essential OOP concepts as they apply in C# and other languages—objects, classes, encapsulation, inheritance, and polymorphism. Then we'll continue by "porting" this knowledge into the JavaScript realm.

Objects and Classes

What does "object-oriented programming" mean anyway? Basically, as the name suggests, OOP puts objects at the centre of the programming model. The **object** is probably the most important concept in the world of OOP—a self-contained entity that has *state* and *behavior*, just like a real-world object. Each object is an instance of a **class** (also called **type**), which defines the behavior that is shared by all its objects.

We often use objects and classes in our programs to represent real-world objects, and types (classes) of objects. For example, we can have classes like Car, Customer, Document, or Person, and objects such as myCar, johnsCar, or davesCar.

The concept is intuitive: the class represents the blueprint, or model, and objects are particular *instances* of that model. For example, all objects of type Car will have the same **behavior**—for example, the ability to change gear. However, each individual Car object may be in a different gear at any particular time—each object has its particular **state**. In programming, an object's state is described by its *fields* and *properties*, and its behavior is defined by its *methods* and *events*.

You've already worked with objects in the previous chapter. First, you've worked with the built-in document object. This is a default DOM object that represents the current page, and it allows you to alter the state of the page. However, you also learned how to create your own objects, when you created the xmlHttp object. In that case, xmlHttp is an object of the XMLHttpRequest class. You could create more XMLHttpRequest objects, and all of them would have the same abilities (behavior), such as the ability to contact remote servers as you learned earlier, but each would have a different state. For example, each of them may be contacting a different server.

In OOP's world everything revolves around objects and classes, and OOP languages usually offer three specific features for manipulating them—**encapsulation**, **inheritance**, and **polymorphism**.

Encapsulation

Encapsulation is a concept that allows the use of an object without having to know its internal implementation in detail. The interaction with an object is done only via its public interface, which contains public members and methods. We can say that encapsulation allows an object to be treated as a "black box", separating the implementation from its interface. Think of the objects you've worked with so far: `document`, a DOM object, and `xmlHttp`, an `XMLHttpRequest` object. You certainly don't know how these objects do their work internally! All you have to know is the features you can use.

The "features you can use" of a class form the *public interface* of a class, which is the sum of all its public members. The public members are those members that are visible and can be used by external classes. For example, the `innerHTML` property of a DOM object (such as the default `document` object), or the `open()` and `send()` methods of `XMLHttpRequest`, are all public, because you were able to use them. Each class can also contain `private` members, which are meant for internal usage only and aren't visible from outside.

Inheritance

Inheritance allows creating classes that are specialized versions of an existing class. For example assume that you have the `Car` class, which exposes a default interface for objects such as `myCar`, `johnsCar`, or `davesCar`. Now, assume that you want to introduce in your project the concept of a **supercar**, which would have similar functionality to the car, but some extra features as well, such as the capability to fly!

If you're an OOP programmer, the obvious move would be to create a new class named `SuperCar`, and use this class to create the necessary objects such as `mySuperCar`, or `davesSuperCar`. In such scenarios, inheritance allows you to create the `SuperCar` class based on the `Car` class, so you don't need to code all the common features once again. Instead, you can create `SuperCar` as a specialized version of `Car`, in which case `SuperCar` *inherits* all the functionality of `Car`. You would only need to code the additional features you want for your `SuperCar`, such as a method named `Fly`. In this scenario, `Car` is the *base class* (also referred to as *superclass*), and `SuperCar` is the *derived* class (also referred to as *subclass*).

Inheritance is great because it encourages code reuse. The potential negative side effect is that inheritance, by its nature, creates an effect that is known as *tight coupling* between the base class and the derived classes. Tight coupling refers to the fact that any changes that are made to a base class are automatically propagated to all the derived classes. For example, if you make a performance improvement in the code of the original Car class, that improvement will propagate to SuperCar as well. While this usually can be used to your advantage, if the inheritance hierarchy isn't wisely designed such coupling can impose future restrictions on how you can expand or modify your base classes without breaking the functionality of the derived classes.

Polymorphism

Polymorphism is a more advanced OOP feature that allows using objects of different classes when you only know a common base class from which they both derive. Polymorphism permits using a base class reference to access objects of that class, or objects of derived classes. Using polymorphism, you can have, for example, a method that receives as parameter an object of type Car, and when calling that method you supply as parameter an object of type SuperCar. Because SuperCar is a specialized version of Car, all the public functionality of Car would also be supported by SuperCar, although the SuperCar implementations could differ from those of Car. This kind of flexibility gives much power to an experienced programmer who knows how to take advantage of it.

Object-Oriented JavaScript

Objects and classes are implemented differently in JavaScript than in languages such as C#, VB.NET, Java, or C++. However, when it comes to *using* them, you'll feel on familiar ground. You create objects using the new operator, and you call their methods, or access their fields using the syntax you already know from C#. Here are a few examples of creating objects in JavaScript:

```
// create a generic object
var obj = new Object();

// create a Date object
var oToday = new Date();

// create an Array object with 3 elements
var oMyList = new Array(3);

// create an empty String object
var oMyString = new String();
```

Object creation is, however, the only significant similarity between JavaScript objects and those of "typical" OOP languages. The upcoming JavaScript 2.0 will reduce the differences by introducing the concept of *classes*, private members, and so on, but until then we have to learn how to live without them.

Objects in JavaScript have the following particularities. In the following pages we'll discuss each of them in detail:

- JavaScript code is not compiled, but parsed. This allows for flexibility when it comes to creating or altering objects. As you'll see, it's possible to add new members or functions to an object or even several objects by altering their *prototype*, on the fly.

- JavaScript doesn't support the notion of *classes* as typical OOP languages do. In JavaScript, you create *functions* that can behave — in many cases — just like classes. For example, you can call a function supplying the necessary parameters, or you can create an instance of that function supplying those parameters. The former case can be associated with a C# method call, and the later can be associated with instantiating a class supplying values to its constructor.

- JavaScript functions are first-class objects. In English, this means that the *function* is regarded, and can be manipulated, just as like other data types. For example, you can pass functions as parameters to other functions, or even return functions. This concept may be difficult to grasp since it's very different from the way C# developers normally think of functions or methods, but you'll see that this kind of flexibility is actually cool.

- JavaScript supports *closures*.

- JavaScript supports *prototypes*.

Ray Djajadinata's JavaScript article at `http://msdn.microsoft.com/msdnmag/issues/07/05/JavaScript/` covers the OOP features in JavaScript very well, and you can refer to it if you need another approach at learning these concepts.

JavaScript Functions

A simple fact that was highlighted in the previous chapter, but that is often overlooked, is key to understanding how objects in JavaScript work: code that doesn't belong to a function is executed when it's read by the JavaScript interpreter, while code that belongs to a function is only executed when that function is called.

Take the following JavaScript code that you created in the first exercise of Chapter 2:

```
// declaring new variables
var date = new Date();
var hour = date.getHours();

// simple conditional content output
if (hour >= 22 || hour <= 5)
  document.write("Goodnight, world!");
else
  document.write("Hello, world!");
```

This code resides in a file named `JavaScriptDom.js`, which is referenced from an HTML file (`JavaScriptDom.html` in the exercise), but it could have been included directly in a `<script>` tag of the HTML file. How it's stored is irrelevant; what does matter is that all that code is executed when it's read by the interpreter. If it was included in a function it would only execute if the function is called explicitly, as is this example:

```
// call function to display greeting message
ShowHelloWorld();

// "Hello, World" function
function ShowHelloWorld()
{
  // declaring new variables
  var date = new Date();
  var hour = date.getHours();

  // simple conditional content output
  if (hour >= 22 || hour <= 5)
    document.write("Goodnight, world!");
  else
    document.write("Hello, world!");
}
```

This code has the same output as the previous version of the code, but it is only because the `ShowHelloWorld()` function is called that will display "**Goodnight, world!**" or "**Hello, world!**" depending on the hour of the day. Without that function call, the JavaScript interpreter would take note of the existence of a function named `ShowHelloWorld()`, but would not execute it.

Functions as Variables

In JavaScript, functions are first-class objects. This means that a function is regarded as a data type whose values can be saved in local variables, passed as parameters, and so on. For example, when defining a function, you can assign it to a variable, and then call the function through this variable. Take this example:

```
// displays greeting
var display = function DisplayGreeting(hour)
{
  if (hour >= 22 || hour <= 5)
    document.write("Goodnight, world!");
  else
    document.write("Hello, world!");
}

// call DisplayGreeting supplying an hour as parameter
display(10);
```

When storing a piece of code as a variable, as in this example, it can make sense to create it as an anonymous function—which is, a function without a name. You do this by simply omitting to specify a function name when creating it:

```
// displays greeting
var display = function(hour)
{
  ...
}
```

Anonymous functions will come in handy in many circumstances when you need to pass an executable piece of code that you don't intend to reuse anywhere else, as parameter to a function.

Let's see how we can send functions as parameters. Instead of sending a numeric hour to DisplayGreeting(), we can send a function that in turn returns the current hour. To demonstrate this, we create a function named GetCurrentHour(), and send it as parameter to DisplayGreeting(). DisplayGreeting() needs to be modified to reflect that its new parameter is a function—it should be referenced by appending parentheses to its name. Here's how:

```
// returns the current hour
function GetCurrentHour()
{
  // obtaining the current hour
  var date = new Date();
  var hour = date.getHours();

  // return the hour
  return hour;
}

// display greeting
function DisplayGreeting(hourFunc)
{
```

```
  // retrieve the hour using the function received as parameter
  hour = hourFunc();

  // display greeting
  if (hour >= 22 || hour <= 5)
    document.write("Goodnight, world!");
  else
    document.write("Hello, world!");
}

// call DisplayGreeting
DisplayGreeting(GetCurrentHour);
```

This code can be tested online at `http://www.cristiandarie.ro/asp-ajax/Delegate.html`. The output should resemble Figure 3-1.

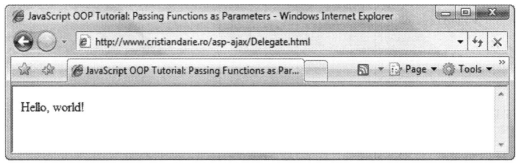

Figure 3-1. Simple demonstration of how a function can be sent as parameter to another function

 .NET languages such as C# and VB.NET support similar functionality through the concept of **delegates**. A delegate is a data type that represents a reference to a function. An instance of a delegate represents a function instance, and it can be passed as a parameter to methods that need to execute that function. Delegates are the technical means used by .NET to implement event-handling. C# 2.0 added support for anonymous methods, which behave similarly to JavaScript anonymous functions.

Anonymous Functions

Anonymous functions can be created adhoc and used instead of a named function. Although this can hinder readability when the function is more complex, you can do this if you don't intend to reuse a function's code. In the following example we pass such an anonymous function to `DisplayGreeting()`, instead of passing `GetCurrentHour()`:

```
// call DisplayGreeting
DisplayGreeting(
  function()
  {
    return (new Date()).getHours();
  }
);
```

This syntax is sure to look strange if this is the first time you have worked with anonymous functions. You can compact it on a single line if it helps understanding it better:

```
DisplayGreeting( function() { return (new Date()).getHours(); } );
```

This code can be tested online at `http://www.cristiandarie.ro/asp-ajax/AnonymousFunction.html`.

Inner Functions and JavaScript Closures

JavaScript functions implement the concept of **closures**, which are functions that are defined inside other functions, and use contextual data from the parent functions to execute. You can find a complete and technically accurate definition of closures at `http://en.wikipedia.org/wiki/Closure_(computer_science)`.

In JavaScript a function can be regarded as a named block of code that you can execute, but it can also be used as a data member inside another function, in which case it is referred to as an *inner functions*. In other words, a JavaScript function can contain other functions.

Say that we want to upgrade the initial `ShowHelloWorld()` function by separating the code that displays the greeting message into a separate function inside `ShowHelloWorld()`. This is a possible implementation, and the output continues to be the same as before:

```
// call function to display greeting message
ShowHelloWorld();

// "Hello, World" function
function ShowHelloWorld()
{
  // declaring new variables
  var date = new Date();
  var hour = date.getHours();

  // call DisplayGreeting supplying the current hour as parameter
  DisplayGreeting(hour);
```

```
  // display greeting
  function DisplayGreeting(hour)
  {
    if (hour >= 22 || hour <= 5)
      document.write("Goodnight, world!");
    else
      document.write("Hello, world!");
  }
}
```

Here, we created a function named `DisplayGreeting()` inside `ShowHelloWorld()`, which displays a greeting message depending on the `hour` parameter it receives. The execution rules apply here as well. This new function needs to be called explicitly from its parent function in order to execute.

This code can be tested online at `http://www.cristiandarie.ro/asp-ajax/JavaScriptClosure.html`.

JavaScript Classes

Not only can JavaScript functions contain other functions, but they can also be instantiated. This makes JavaScript functions a good candidate for implementing the concept of a class from traditional object-oriented programming. This is very helpful feature indeed, because JavaScript doesn't support the notion of a class in the classic sense of the word. Functions can be instantiated using the `new` operator, such as in this example:

```
var myHelloWorld = new ShowHelloWorld();
```

This line of code effectively creates an object named `myHelloWorld`, which represents an instance of the `ShowHelloWorld()` function. When the object is instantiated, the function code is executed, so creating the object has the same effect as calling `ShowHelloWorld()` as in the previous examples.

Here are a few facts that will help you port your C# OOP knowledge into the JavaScript world:

- When a function is used as a class, its body code is considered to be the *constructor*. In classic OOP, the constructor is a special method that doesn't return anything, and that is called automatically when the object is created. The same effect happens in JavaScript when creating an instance of the function: its code executes. A C# constructor is equivalent to the code in the JavaScript function—without including any inner functions (whose code doesn't execute automatically).

- In C# constructors can receive parameters, and also in JavaScript. If the code in a function represents the "class constructor", the parameters received by that function play the role of constructor parameters.

- Class fields in JavaScript are created and referenced with the `this` keyword. In a JavaScript function, `this.myValue` is a public member of the function (class), while `myValue` is a local variable that can't be accessed through function instances. Also, the local variable is destroyed after the function executes, while class fields persist their value for the entire object lifetime.

- Class methods that need to be accessible from outside the class need to be referred to using `this` as well. Otherwise the inner function will be regarded as a local function variable, rather than a "class" member.

We'll demonstrate these concepts by transforming the `ShowHelloWorld()` function that you saw earlier into a "real" class. We will:

- Change the name of the function from `ShowHelloWorld()` to `HelloWorld()`.

- Add a parameter named `hour` to the function's "constructor" so that we tell the class the hour for which we need a greeting message, when instantiating it. If this parameter is passed when creating objects of the class, we store it for future use as a class field. If this parameter is not specified, the current hour of the day should be stored instead.

- The method `DisplayGreeting()` of the class should not support the `hour` parameter any longer. Instead, it should display the greeting message depending on the hour field that was initialized by the constructor.

 Why are we changing the name of the function? Remember, OOP is a style of coding, not a list of technical requirements that a language must support. JavaScript is considered an OOP-capable language because it supports an object-based programming style. In the OOP paradigm, a class should represent an entity, and not an action. Since we intend now to use `ShowHelloWorld()` as a class, we are changing its name to one that reflects this purpose.

Once your new class is created, you use it just as you'd use a C# class. For example, this is how you'd create a new class instance, and call its `DisplayGreeting()` method:

```
// create class instance
var myHello = new HelloWorld();

// call method
myHello.DisplayGreeting();
```

A possible implementation of the `HelloWorld` class is the following:

```
// "Hello, World" class
function HelloWorld(hour)
{
  // class "constructor" initializes this.hour field
  if (hour)
  {
    // if the hour parameter has a value, store it as a class field
    this.hour = hour;
  }
  else
  {
    // if the hour parameter doesn't exist, save the current hour
    var date = new Date();
    this.hour = date.getHours();
  }

  // display greeting
  this.DisplayGreeting = function()
  {
    if (this.hour >= 22 || this.hour <= 5)
      document.write("Goodnight, world!");
    else
      document.write("Hello, world!");
  }
}
```

This code can be tested online at `http://www.cristiandarie.ro/asp-ajax/` `JavaScriptClass.html`. The `HelloWorld` class is formed of the constructor code that initializes the `hour` field (`this.hour`), and of the `DisplayGreeting()` method — `this.DisplayGreeting()`. Fans of the ternary operator can rewrite the constructor using this shorter form, which also makes use of the object detection feature that was discussed in Chapter 2:

```
// define and initialize this.hour
this.hour = (hour) ? hour : (new Date()).getHours();
```

The ternary operator is supported both by C# and JavaScript. It has the form (`condition ? valueA : valueB`). If the condition is `true`, the expression returns `valueA`, otherwise it returns `valueB`. In the shown example, object detection is used to test if a value was supplied for the `hour` parameter. If it was not, the current hour is used instead.

Class Diagrams

JavaScript classes, just like C# or VB.NET classes, can be described visually using class diagrams. There are standards such as UML (**Unified Modeling Language**), that can be used to model classes and the relationships between them. In this book we'll show quite a few class diagrams using the notation used by Visual Studio 2005. Using this notation, the HelloWorld class shown earlier would be described as shown in Figure 3-2.

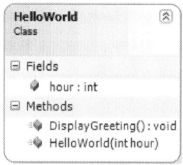

Figure 3-2. HelloWorld class diagram

The diagrams to this book follow typical conventions for C# classes, which don't translate to JavaScript exactly. For example, the diagram in Figure 3-2 says that the HelloWorld class has an integer field named hour. However, JavaScript doesn't support specifying data types for variables or class fields. The data type of the field makes the diagram helpful in specifying the intended purpose and type of the field, but that type isn't used in the actual implementation of the class.

The diagram also mentions the HelloWorld() constructor, which receives an integer parameter. As you know, JavaScript doesn't support "real" constructors. However, by reading the diagram you can tell that the HelloWorld() function receives a parameter named hour, which is supposed to be an integer value.

Appendix A contains more details about the conventions used in class diagrams throughout this book.

C# and JavaScript Classes

For the purpose of demonstrating a few more OOP-related concepts, we'll use another class. Our new class is named Table, and it has two public fields (rows, columns), and one method, getCellCount(). The getCellCount() method should return the number of rows multiplied by the number of columns. The class constructor should receive two parameters, used to initialize the rows and columns fields. This class could be represented by the class diagram in Figure 3-3.

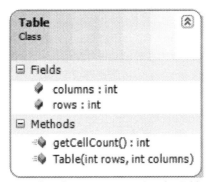

Figure 3-3. Class diagram representing the Table class

The C# version of this class would look like this:

```
public class Table
{
  // public members
  public int rows = 0;
  public int columns = 0;

  // constructor
  public Table(int rows, int columns)
  {
    this.rows = rows;
    this.columns = columns;
  }

  // method returns the number of cells
  public int getCellCount()
  {
    return rows * columns;
  }
}
```

You'd instantiate and use the class like this:

```
Table t = new Table(3,5);
int cellCount = t.getCellCount();
```

 In a production-quality C# implementation you may want to implement `rows` and `columns` as properties with `get` and `set` assessors, rather than public fields. That implementation, however, would make its JavaScript version more complicated than necessary for the purposes of our examples.

The `Table` class can be easily implemented in JavaScript as shown in the following code snippet, and it would resemble very much its C# version:

```
function Table (rows, columns)
{
  // "constructor"
  this.rows = rows;
  this.columns = columns;

  // getCellCount "method"
  this.getCellCount = function()
  {
    return this.rows * this.columns;
  };
}
```

After having declared the object, we can instantiate it by using the `new` operator and use its properties and methods:

```
var t = new Table(3,5);
var cellCount = t.getCellCount();
```

There are a few subtle points you need to notice regarding the JavaScript implementation of `Table`:

- You don't declare public members explicitly. You simply need to reference them using `this`, and assign some value to them; from that point on, they're both declared and defined.

- JavaScript allows you to implement most of the design specifications defined in class diagrams, but the implementation can't reflect the specification as accurately as a C# implementation can. For example, the line **Table (int rows, int columns)** in the diagram in Figure 3-3 refers to the constructor of the class. In JavaScript, as you know, classes as implemented using functions neither have real constructors, nor support specifying data types for their parameters.

- When objects are created, each object has its own set of data — to maintain its own state. However, C# and JavaScript are different in that in JavaScript functions are first-class objects. In C#, the "state" is made of the object's fields. The object functionality, as defined by its methods, is the same for all objects of the same type. For example, if you create many objects of the type `Table` in C#, each object will have its own set of `rows` and `columns`, but internally they all use the same copy of the `getCellCount()` method. In JavaScript, however, functions are treated like any other variable. In other words, creating a new `Table` object in JavaScript will result not only in creating a new set of `rows` and `columns` values, but also in a new copy of the `getCellCount()` method. Usually, you don't need (or want) this behavior.

The last mentioned problem is commonly referred to as a "memory leak", although technically it's just inefficient JavaScript object design. When we design our JavaScript "classes" as we do in typical OOP languages, we don't need each class to create its own set of methods. It's only state (fields) that need to be individual, and not methods' code. The good news is that JavaScript has a neat trick that we can use to avoid replicating the inner function code for each object we create: referencing external functions.

Referencing External Functions

Instead of defining member functions ("methods") inside the main function ("class") as shown earlier, you can make references to functions defined outside your main function, like this:

```
function Table (rows, columns)
{
  // "constructor"
  this.rows = rows;
  this.columns = columns;

  // getCellCount "method"
  this.getCellCount = getCellCount;
}

// returns the number of rows multiplied by the number of columns
function getCellCount()
{
  return this.rows * this.columns;
}
```

Now, all your `Table` objects will share the same instance of `getCellCount()`, which is what you will usually want.

Thinking of Objects as Associative Arrays

A key element in understanding JavaScript objects is understanding the notion of **associative arrays**, which are nothing more than collections of (**key**, **value**) pairs. As a .NET developer you have worked with associative arrays represented by classes such as `NameValueCollection`, `Hashtable`, dictionaries, and others. Unlike with normal arrays, where the key is numeric (as in `bookNames[5]`), the key of an associative array is usually a string, or even other kinds of objects that can represent themselves as strings. For example, take a look at the following code snippet, where we retrieve the name of the book by specifying a unique string value that identifies that book:

```
// retrieve the name of the book
bookName = bookNames["ASP_AJAX"];
```

The concept is simple indeed. In this case, the key and the value of the `bookNames` associative array are both strings. This associative array could then be represented by a table like this:

Key	Value
ASP_AJAX	Microsoft AJAX Library Essentials
AJAX_PHP	AJAX and PHP: Building Responsive Web Applications
SEO_ASP	Professional Search Engine Optimization with ASP.NET

The table above can be represented in JavaScript, as an associative array, like this:

```
// define a simple associative array
var bookNames =
{ "ASP_AJAX" : "Microsoft AJAX Library Essentials",
  "AJAX_PHP" : "AJAX and PHP: Building Responsive Web Applications",
  "SEO_ASP" : "Professional Search Engine Optimization with ASP.NET"
};
```

The key of an element doesn't have to be literal; it can even be specified through a variable:

```
// store the book ID in a variable
var bookId = "ASP_AJAX";

// display the name of the book
document.write("The name of " + bookId +
               " is " + bookNames[bookId] + "<br />");
```

In JavaScript, however, the implementation of the associative array is more powerful, in that it makes no restriction on the type of the value of the (key, value) pair. The value can be a number, a string, a date, or even a function! This flexibility allows us to represent JavaScript objects as associative arrays. For example, an instance of the `Table` class that we discussed earlier can be represented like this:

```
// create Table object
var t =
  { rows : 3,
    columns : 5,
    getCellCount : function () { return this.rows * this.columns; }
  };

// display object field values
document.writeln("Your table has " + t.rows + " rows" +
                 " and " + t.columns + " columns<br />");

// call object function
document.writeln("The table has " + t.getCellCount() +
                 " cells<br />");
```

This example, and the one presented earlier with book names, can be tested online at `http://www.cristiandarie.ro/asp-ajax/Associative.html`, and the result is presented in Figure 3-4.

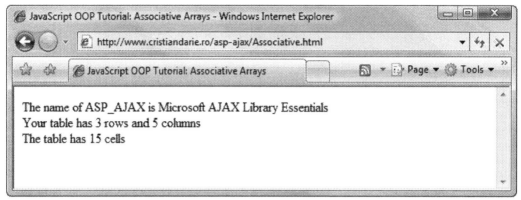

Figure 3-4. Testing JavaScript associative arrays

> The literal notation of creating JavaScript objects has one weakness—it can only be used to describe objects. In other words, using the literal notation you can only define (key, value) pairs, but you can't create classes, class constructors, or other reusable components of code.

Creating Object Members on the Fly

One major difference between OOP in C# and ASP.NET, and OOP in JavaScript, is that JavaScript allows creating object members "on the fly". This is true for objects and classes that you create yourself and also for JavaScript's own objects and types as well. Here's an example where we add a field named `ImADate` to a JavaScript `Date` object:

```
// create a Date object
var myDate = new Date();

// create a new member named ImADate in the oDate object
myDate.ImADate = "I'm a Date!";

// display the value of oDate.ImADate
document.write(myDate.ImADate);
A typical OOP language such as C#, VB.NET, or Java, doesn't allow you
to create members on the fly, like JavaScript does. Instead, each
member must be defined formally in the definition of the class.
```

Private Members

JavaScript doesn't support the notion of private members as C# does, but you can simulate the functionality by using variables inside the function. Variables are declared with the `var` keyword or are received as function parameters.
They aren't accessed using `this`, and they aren't accessible through function instances, thus acting like private members. Variables can, however, be accessed by closure functions.

If you want to test this, modify the `Table` function as shown below.

```
function Table (rows, columns)
{
  // save parameter values to local variables
  var _rows = rows;
  var _columns = columns;

  // return the number of table cells
  this.getCellCount = function()
  {
    return _rows * _columns;
  };
}
```

This time we persist the values received as parameters as local variables named `_rows` and `_columns`. Note they aren't referred to using `this` any more. Local variables names don't need to start with an underscore, but this is a useful naming convention that specifies they are meant to be used as private members. You can make a short test that the "private" members can't be accessed from outside the function, and that `getCellCount()` still works, using code such as the following. The results are shown in Figure 3-5.

```
// create a Table object
var t = new Table(3,5);

// display object field values
document.write("Your table has " + t._rows + " rows" +
               " and " + t._columns + " columns<br />");

// call object function
document.write("The table has " + t.getCellCount() + " cells<br />");
```

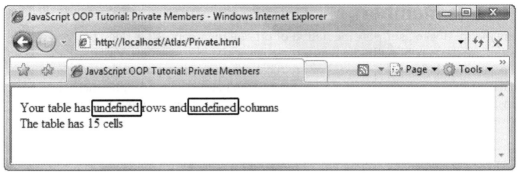

Figure 3-5. JavaScript example demonstrating "private" members

This exercise reveals that _rows and _columns aren't accessible from outside the function's scope. Their values read **undefined** because there are no fields named _rows and _columns in the Table function. The getCellCount() function, on the other hand, can read _rows and _columns as variables because they are in the same closure. As you can see, although the implementation and behavior are somewhat different than in C#, you still have a way of defining internal (private) members inside a function.

Prototypes

You learned earlier that in JavaScript you should define "class methods" outside the body of the "class", in order to prevent their multiplication for each instantiated object. Prototyping is a JavaScript language feature that allows attaching functions and properties to the "blueprint" of a function. When functions are added to a class (function) prototype, they are not replicated for each object of the class (function). This reflects quite well the behavior of classes in C#, although the core mechanism and the specific implementation details differ greatly. A few facts that you should keep in mind about prototypes are:

- Every JavaScript function has a property named prototype. Adding members to the function's prototype is implemented by adding them to the prototype property of the function.

- Private variables of a function aren't accessible through functions added to its prototype.

- You can add members to a function's prototype at any time, but this won't affect objects that were already created. It will affect only any new ones.

- You can add members to a function's prototype only after the function itself has been defined.

The `Table` "class" from the previous example contains a "method" named `getCellCount()`. The following code creates the same class, but this time adding `getCellCount()` to its prototype:

```
// Table class
function Table (rows, columns)
{
   // save parameter values to class properties
   this.rows = rows;
   this.columns = columns;
}

// Table.getCellCount returns the number of table cells
Table.prototype.getCellCount = function()
{
   return this.rows * this.columns;
};
```

The JavaScript Execution Context

In this section we'll take a peek under the hood of the JavaScript closures and the mechanisms that allow us to create classes, objects, and object members in JavaScript. For most cases, understanding these mechanisms isn't absolutely necessary for writing JavaScript code—so you can skip it if it sounds too advanced. If, on the contrary, you should be interested in learning more about the JavaScript parser's inner workings, see the more advanced article at `http://www.jibbering.com/faq/faq_notes/closures.html`.

The JavaScript **execution context** is a concept that explains much of the behavior of JavaScript functions, and of the code samples presented earlier. The execution context represents the environment in which a piece of JavaScript code executes. JavaScript knows of three execution contexts:

- The **global execution context** is the implicit environment (context) in which the JavaScript code that is not part of any function executes.

- The **function execution context** is the context in which the code of a function executes. A function context is created automatically when a function is executed, and removed from the contexts stack afterwards.

- The **eval() execution context** is the context in which JavaScript code executed using the `eval()` function runs.

Each execution context has an associated *scope*, which specifies the objects that are accessible to the code executing within that context.

The scope of the global execution context contains the locally defined variables and functions, and the browser's `window` object. In that context, `this` is equivalent to `window`, so you can access, for example, the `location` property of that object using either `this.location` or `window.location`.

The scope of a function execution context contains the function's parameters, the locally defined variables and functions, and the variables and functions in the scope of the calling code. This explains why the `getCellCount()` function has access to the `_rows` and `_columns` variables that are defined in the outer function (`Table`):

```
// Table class
function Table (rows, columns)
{
  // save parameter values to local variables
  var _rows = rows;
  var _columns = columns;

  // return the number of table cells
  this.getCellCount = function ()
  {
    return _rows * _columns;
  };
}
```

The scope of the `eval()` execution context is identical to the scope of the calling code context. The `getCellCount()` function from the above code snippet could be written like this, without losing its functionality:

```
// return the number of table cells
this.getCellCount = function ()
{
  return eval(_rows * _columns);
};
```

var x, this.x, and x

An execution context contains a collection of (key, value) associations representing the local variables and functions, a prototype whose members can be accessed through the `this` keyword, a collection of function parameters (if the context was created for a function call), and information about the context of the calling code.

Members accessed through `this`, and those declared using `var`, are stored in separate places, except in the case of the global execution context where variables and properties are the same thing. In objects, variables declared through `var` are not accessible through function instances, which makes them perfect for implementing `private` "class" members, as you could see in an earlier exercise. On the other hand, members accessed through `this` are accessible through function instances, so we can use them to implement public members.

When a member is read using its literal name, its value is first searched for in the list of local variables. If it's not found there, it'll be searched for in the prototype. To understand the implications, see the following function, which defines a local variable x, and a property named x. If you execute the function, you'll see that the value of x is read from the local variable, even though you also have a property with the same name:

```
function BigTest()
{
  var x = 1;
  this.x = 2;

  document.write(x); // displays "1"
  document.write(this.x); // displays "2"
}
```

Calling this function, either directly or by creating an instance of it, will display 1 and 2—demonstrating that variables and properties are stored separately. Should you execute the same code in the global context (without a function), for which variables and properties are the same, you'd get the same value displayed twice.

When reading a member using its name literally (without this), if there's no local variable with that name, the value from the prototype (property) will be read instead, as this example demonstrates:

```
function BigTest()
{
  this.x = 2;
  document.write(x); // displays "2"
}
```

Using the Right Context

When working with JavaScript functions and objects, you need to make sure the code executes in the context it was intended for, otherwise you may get unpredictable results. You saw earlier that the same code can have different output when executing inside a function or in the global context.

Things get a little more complicated when using the this keyword. As you know, each function call creates a new context in which the code executes. When the context is created, the value of this is also decided:

- When an object is created from a function, this refers to that object.
- In the case of a simple function call, no matter if the function is defined directly in the global context or in another function or object, this refers to the global context.

The second point is particularly important. Using this in a function that is meant to be called directly, rather than instantiated as an object, is a bad programming practice, because you end up altering the global object. Take this example that demonstrates how you can overwrite a global variable from within a function:

```
x = 0;
function BigTest()
{
    this.x = 1; // modify a variable of the global context
}
BigTest();
document.write(x); // displays "1"
```

Modifying the global object can be used to implement various coding architectures or features, but abusing of this technique can be dangerous. On the other hand, if BigTest is instantiated using the new keyword, the this keyword will refer to the new object, rather than the global object. Modifying the previous example as highlighted below, we can see the x variable of the global context remains untouched:

```
x = 0;
function BigTest()
{
    this.x = 1; // create an internal object property
}
var obj = new BigTest();
document.write(x); // displays "0"
```

When creating your own code framework, you can enforce that a function's code is executed through a function instance. The little trick involves creating a new object on the spot if the function was called directly, and using that object for further processing. This allows you to ensure that a function call will not modify any members of the global context. It works like this:

```
x = 0;
function BigTest()
{
    if (!(this instanceof BigTest)) return new BigTest();
    this.x = 1;
}
BigTest();
document.write(x); // displays "0"
```

The highlighted line simply checks if the this keyword refers to an instance of BigTest (the instanceof keyword is used for this). If it's not, a new BigTest instance is returned, and execution stops. The BigTest instance, however, is executed, and this time this will be a BigTest instance, so the function will continue executing in the context of that object.

This ends our little incursion into JavaScript's internals. The complete theory is more complicated than that, and it's comprehensively covered by David Flangan's *JavaScript: The Definitive Guide, Fifth Edition* (O'Reilly, 2006). The FAQ at http://www.jibbering.com/faq/ will also be helpful if you need to learn about the more subtle aspects of JavaScript.

Inheritance using Closures and Prototypes

There are two significant techniques for implementing the OOP concept of inheritance with JavaScript code. The first technique uses closures, and the other technique makes use of a feature of the language named prototyping.

Early implementations of the Microsoft AJAX library made use of closures-based inheritance, and in the final stage the code was rewritten to use prototypes. In the following few pages we'll quickly discuss both techniques.

Inheritance Using Closures

In classic OOP languages such as C#, C++, or Java, you can extend classes through inheritance. Closure-based inheritance is implemented by creating a member in the derived class that references the base class, and calling that member. This causes the derived class to inherit all the base class members, effectively implementing the concept of inheritance.

To demonstrate this technique, we'll implement two classes: Car and SuperCar. The Car class constructor receives a car name as parameter, and it has a method named Drive(). The class SuperCar inherits the functionality of Car, and adds a new method named Fly(), reflecting the additional functionality it has in addition to what Car has to offer. The diagram in Figure 3-6 describes these two classes.

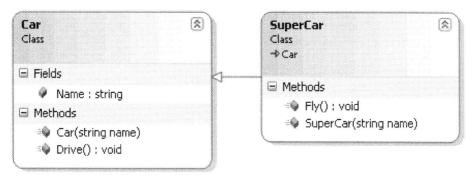

Figure 3-6. Car and SuperCar class diagram

Rember that in JavaScript the implementation of a class diagram can be achieved in multiple ways. The code reflects the concept of the diagram, but not also the implementation details, as the C# code would. Here's a possible implementation of Car and SuperCar:

```
<script type="text/javascript">
  // to be used as the Drive method of Car
  function Drive()
  {
    document.write("My name is " + this.Name +
                   " and I'm driving. <br />");
  }

  // class Car
  function Car(name)
  {
    // create the Name property
    this.Name = name;

    // Car knows how to drive
    this.Drive = Drive;
  }

  // to be used as the Fly method of SuperCar
  this.Fly = function()
  {
    document.write("My name is " + this.Name + " and I'm flying! <br
/>");
  }

  // class SuperCar
  function SuperCar(name)
  {
    // implement closure inheritance
    this.inheritsFrom = Car;
    this.inheritsFrom(name);

    // SuperCar knows how to fly
    this.Fly = Fly;
  }

  // create a new Car and then Drive
  var myCar = new Car("Car");
  myCar.Drive();

  // create SuperCar object
  var mySuperCar = new SuperCar("SuperCar");
```

```
    // SuperCar knows how to drive
    mySuperCar.Drive();

    // SuperCar knows how to fly
    mySuperCar.Fly();
</script>
```

Loading this script in a browser would generate the results shown in Figure 3-7. It can be tested online at `http://www.cristiandarie.ro/asp-ajax/JavaScriptClosureInheritance.html`.

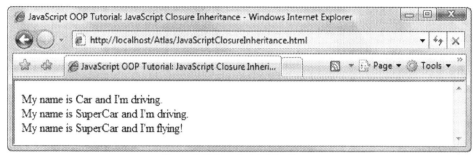

Figure 3-7. JavaScript Inheritance

The exercise demonstrates that inheritance really works. `SuperCar` only defines the capability to `Fly()`, yet it can `Drive()` as well. The capability to `Drive()` and the `Name` property are inherited from `Car`.

At the first sight the code can look a bit complicated, especially if you're a C# veteran. The `Drive()` and `Fly()` functions aren't defined inside `Car` and `SuperCar`, as you'd do in a C# class. Instead, we stored these methods/functions in the global context, and referenced them in `Car` and `SuperCar`, to avoid the memory leaks that were discussed earlier in this chapter. You can, however, define `Drive()` inside `Car`, and `Fly()` inside `SuperCar`, without losing any functionality.

If you comment the execution of `this.inheritsFrom(name)` from `SuperCar`, it won't inherit the capabilities of `Car` any more. If you make this test in FireFox, you'll see the following eloquent error message in the **Error Console** window of Firefox:

Figure 3-8. Signs of failed inheritance

The problem with the presented inheritance solution is that it's not very elegant. Writing all functions and classes in the global context can quickly degenerate into chaos; and things get even more complicated if you want to have classes that have functions with the same name. Needless to say, this isn't something you need to be dealing with when writing your code. Luckily, JavaScript has a very neat feature that allows us implement inheritance in a much cleaner way: **prototyping**.

Inheritance Using Prototyping

Once again, prototyping can help us implement an OOP feature in a more elegant way than when using closures. Prototype-based inheritance makes use of the behavior of JavaScript prototypes. When accessing a member of a function, that member will be looked for in the function itself. If it's not found there, the member is looked for in the function's prototype. If it's still not found, the member is looked for in the prototype's prototype, and so on until the prototype of the implicit Object object.

In closure-based inheritance, the derived class inherits the base class methods and properties by "loading" them into itself. Here's the code again for your reference:

```
// class SuperCar
function SuperCar(name)
{
  // implement closure inheritance
  this.inheritsFrom = Car;
  this.inheritsFrom(name);

  // SuperCar knows how to fly
  this.Fly = Fly;
}
```

When implementing inheritance through prototyping, we can "load" the base class properties and methods by adding them to the derived class prototype. That way, an object of the derived class will have access to the class methods and properties, but also to the base class methods and properties since they exist in the derived class prototype. To successfully implement prototype-based inheritance with JavaScript, you need to:

- Add a base class instance to the derived class prototype property, as in SuperCar.prototype = new Car(). This creates Car as SuperCar's prototype.
- The prototype property has a constructor property that needs to point back to the function itself. Since now the SuperCar's prototype is a Car, its constructor property points back to the constructor of Car. To fix this, we need to set the constructor property of the prototype property of the derived class to the class itself, as in SuperCar.prototype.constructor = SuperCar.

- Create the derived class constructor, and call the base class constructor from there, eventually passing any necessary parameters. In other words, when a new SuperCar is instantiated, its base class constructor should also execute, to ensure correct base class functionality.

- Add any additional derived class members or functions to its prototype.

This is so very complicated! In practice you'll find that the code doesn't look that scary, although the complete theory is a little more complex than this. A nice article describing a few additional theoretical aspects can be found at http://mckoss.com/jscript/object.htm.

The new implementation of Car and SuperCar, this time using prototypes, is the following, with the inheritance mechanism highlighted. The Drive() and Fly() methods have also been created through prototyping, although the old version using closures would work as well. The code can be checked online at http://www.cristiandarie.ro/seo-asp/JavaScriptPrototypeInheritance.html.

```
<script type="text/javascript">
  // class Car
  function Car(name)
  {
    // create the Name property
    this.Name = name;
  }

  // Car.Drive() method
  Car.prototype.Drive = function()
  {
    document.write("My name is " + this.Name +
                   " and I'm driving. <br />");
  }

  // SuperCar inherits from Car
  SuperCar.prototype = new Car();
  SuperCar.prototype.constructor = SuperCar;

  // class SuperCar
  function SuperCar(name)
  {
    // call base class constructor
    Car.call(this, name);
  }

  // SuperCar.Fly() method
  SuperCar.prototype.Fly = function()
  {
```

```
        document.write("My name is " + this.Name +
                    " and I'm flying! <br />");
    }

    // create a new Car and then Drive
    var myCar = new Car("Car");
    myCar.Drive();

    // create SuperCar object
    var mySuperCar = new SuperCar("SuperCar");

    // SuperCar knows how to drive
    mySuperCar.Drive();

    // SuperCar knows how to fly
    mySuperCar.Fly();
</script>
```

Here, instead of creating a `Car` instance in `SuperCar`'s constructor, we declare `Car` as `SuperCar`'s prototype.

Introducing JSON

In AJAX applications, client-server communication is usually packed in XML documents, or in the **JSON** (JavaScript Object Notation) format. Interestingly enough, JSON's popularity increased together with the AJAX phenomenon, although the AJAX acronym includes XML. JSON is the format used by the Microsoft AJAX Library and the ASP.NET AJAX Framework to exchange data between the AJAX client and the server, which is why it deserves a quick look here. As you'll learn, the Microsoft AJAX Library handles JSON data packaging through `Sys.Serialization.JavaScriptSerializer`, which is described in the Appendix—but more on this later.

Perhaps the best short description of JSON is the one proposed by its official website, `http://www.json.org`: "JSON (JavaScript Object Notation) is a lightweight data-interchange format. It is easy for humans to read and write. It is easy for machines to parse and generate."

If you're new to JSON, a fair question you could ask would be: why another data exchange format? JSON, just like XML, is a text-based format that it is easy to write and to understand for both humans and computers. The key word in the definition above is "lightweight". JSON data structures occupy less bandwidth than their XML versions.

To get an idea of how JSON compares to XML, let's take the same data structure and see how we would represent it using both standards:

```xml
<?xml version="1.0" encoding="UTF-8" standalone="yes"?>
<response>
  <clear>false</clear>
  <messages>
    <message>
      <id>1</id>
      <color>#000000</color>
      <time>2006-01-17 09:07:31</time>
      <name>Guest550</name>
      <text>Hello there! What's up?</text>
    </message>
    <message>
      <id>2</id>
      <color>#000000</color>
      <time>2006-01-17 09:21:34</time>
      <name>Guest499</name>
      <text>This is a test message</text>
    </message>
  </messages>
</response>
```

The same message, written in JSON this time, looks like this:

```json
[
  {"clear":"false"},
  "messages":
    [
      {"message":
        {"id":"1",
         "color":"#000000",
         "time":"2006-01-17 09:07:31",
         "name":"Guest550",
         "text":"Hello there! What's up?"}
      },
      {"message":
        {"id":"2",
         "color":"#000000",
         "time":"2006-01-17 09:21:34",
         "name":"Guest499",
         "text":"This is a test message"}
```

```
        }
    ]
  }
]
```

As you can see, they aren't *very* different. If we disregard the extra formatting spaces that we added for better readability, the XML message occupies 396 bytes while the JSON message has only 274 bytes.

JSON is said to be a *subset* of JavaScript because it's based on the associative array-nature of JavaScript objects. JSON is based on two basic structures:

- **Object**: This is defined as a collection of name/value pairs. Each object begins with a left curly brace ({) and ends with a right curly brace (}). The pairs of names/values are separated by a comma. A pair of name/value has the following form: *string:value.*

- **Array**: This is defined as a list of values separated by a coma (,).

We've mentioned `strings` and `values`. A `value` can be a `string`, a `number`, an `object`, an `array`, `true` or `false`, or `null`. A `string` is a collection of Unicode characters surrounded by double quotes. For escaping, we use the backslash (\).

It's obvious that if you plan to use JSON, you need to be able to parse and generate JSON structures in both JavaScript and ASP.NET, at least if the communication is bidirectional. JSON libraries are available for most of today's programming languages: ActionScript, C, C++, C#, VB.NET, Delphi, E, Erlang, Java, JavaScript, Lisp,Lua, ML and Ruby, Objective CAML, OpenLazslo, Perl, PHP, Python, Rebol, Ruby, and Squeak. When we said almost every programming language we were right, weren't we!

If you plan to work with JSON data outside of the Microsoft AJAX Library, you can use the library listed at `http://www.json.org/js.html`.

Summary

This chapter walked you through many fields. Working with OOP in JavaScript is certainly no easy task, especially if you haven't been exposed to the implied concepts before. Where you don't feel confident enough, have a look at the additional resources we've referenced. When you feel ready, proceed to Chapter 4, where you will have an overview of the architecture and features of the Microsoft AJAX Library.

4
Introducing the Microsoft AJAX Library

In the previous chapters you've learned the basics of AJAX and object-oriented JavaScript, and in Chapter 1 you even created a very simple AJAX-enabled form validation page using ASP.NET code for the server.

On small projects it's acceptable to implement the features you need from scratch, occasionally reinventing the wheel. However, when developing more complex ASP. NET projects, the decision of "whether to use ASP.NET AJAX or not" becomes "how much of ASP.NET AJAX to use ". In this chapter we'll quickly investigate the features offered by the Microsoft AJAX Library, and at the end we'll even use it to update the Quickstart example that was presented in Chapter 1.

In this chapter, you will:

- Learn about the components of the ASP.NET AJAX Framework and the Microsoft AJAX Library
- Understand the asynchronous communication model of the Microsoft AJAX Library
- Go through a quickstart exercise

Let's get started!

Microsoft AJAX Library Components

You learned in Chapter 1 that the ASP.NET AJAX Framework is made of three componenets: the *Microsoft AJAX Library*, the *ASP.NET AJAX Extensions*, and the *ASP.NET AJAX Control Toolkit*. The first two are available for download at http://www.asp.net/, while the control toolkit is a project under development at CodePlex (http://www.codeplex.com/AtlasControlToolkit).

These components are shown in Figure 4-1.

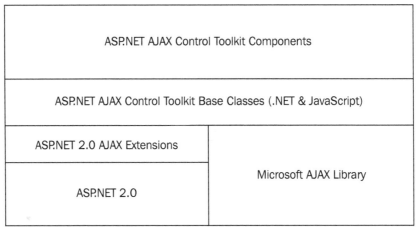

Figure 4-1. The World of ASP.NET AJAX

The Microsoft AJAX Library, the subject of this book, is the client-side component of the ASP.NET AJAX Framework. It comes in the form of a JavaScript file named `MicrosoftAjax.js`, which has about 80 kilobytes, and (obviously) needs to travel to the client when a visitor loads a website that uses the library. This potential drawback, together with the complexity of the library, which may require a long learning curve, needs to be taken into account when deciding whether to use this library. If the AJAX features you need to implement are very simple, you can write the AJAX code yourself, such as in the simple example from Chapter 1.

For larger projects, the Microsoft AJAX Library gives a helping hand offering the following features:

- **Cross-browser compatibility**: We don't need to worry about having our applications running on multiple browsers.
- **Server-side agnostic**: The Microsoft AJAX Library is a JavaScript library that can integrate with any server-side technology.
- **Object orientation**: The Microsoft AJAX Library builds on the basic OOP capabilities you learned in Chapter 3, to create a framework that permits coding in a way that resembles very much the way you code for the .NET Framework.

These features will help you:

- Avoid the problems related to working with the different DOM implementations in today's web browsers.
- Implement asynchronous postbacks easily, using an improved API.

- Benefit from the power of a framework that exposes features that aren't typically available to JavaScript programmers, such as namespaces, common types, type reflection, and more.

The features of the Microsoft AJAX Library are implemented in a layered architecture that is described in Figure 4-2.

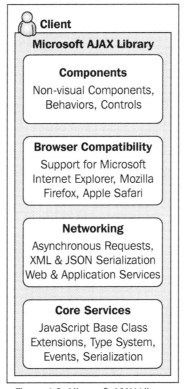

Figure 4-2. Microsoft AJAX Library

- **Core Services :** This layer was inspired from the .NET BCL (Base Class Library), and extends JavaScript by adding features you'd expect to meet in a .NET environment: namespaces, classes, interfaces, inheritance, enumerations, delegates, data types, serialization, event handling, extended error handling with debugging and tracing, string builders, etc.
- **Networking:** This layer handles all the communication with the web services and application services as well as calls using web requests.
- **Browser Compatibility:** This layer provides the abstraction needed in order to avoid compatibility problems across browsers.
- **Components:** This layer contains non-visual components, controls, and behaviors that enable the AJAX experience.

Asynchronous Communication

In Chapter 2, you learned about the XMLHttpRequest object that represents the core of any AJAX-enabled application. Asynchronous client-server communication is also a pillar of the Microsoft AJAX Library. Although this library does a great job at abstracting the low-level details from the developer, XMLHttpRequest is still used to handle the background client-server communication.

The Microsoft AJAX Library client can call server-side web service methods. Its networking layer binds together the client presentation layer and the business layer of the server side. This approach has the advantage of loosely coupling the JavaScript client to the ASP.NET server, providing an interface for them to communicate.

The networking layer in Microsoft AJAX Library works as described in Figure 4-3.

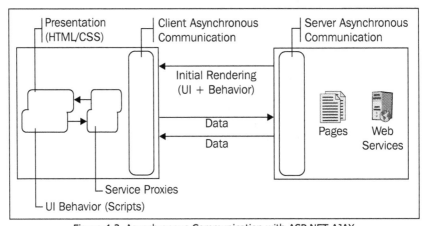

Figure 4-3. Asynchronous Communication with ASP.NET AJAX

The Microsoft AJAX Library client can use the networking layer to do one of the following:

- Make calls to server pages
- Make calls to the server services (authentication, profile) automatically exposed as web services by using their corresponding JavaScript proxies
- Make calls to page methods as if they were web services
- Make calls to web services
- Carry out serialization/deserialization using JSON

Client Asynchronous Communication

Figure 4-4 describes the components of the Microsoft AJAX Library networking layer.

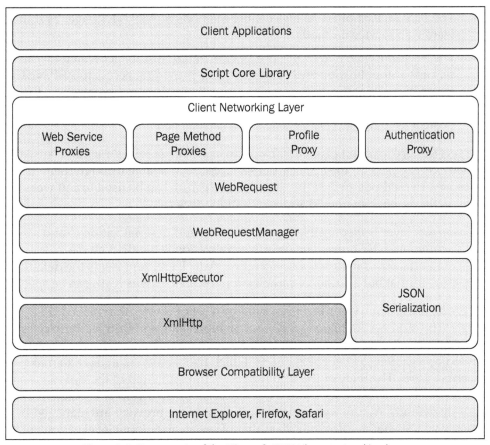

Figure 4-4. Components of the Microsoft AJAX Library networking layer

At a higher level, the client asynchronous communication (networking layer) can be divided into three parts:

- Core communication layer
- Conversion layer
- Proxies layer

The *Proxies* layer consists of all the proxies that access functionality from the server side:

- The *Web Service* proxy enables us to call web service methods directly from the client script.

- The *Page Method* proxy allows calling methods of ASP.NET pages as if they were web service methods.

- The *Authentication* and *Profile* proxies are automatically generated by the server's authentication and profile services providing access to ASP.NET's authentication and profile services respectively. Using these proxies, the user can be authenticated and his or her profile retrieved without additional postbacks to the server.

These services are invoked in a similar way to how web services' methods are called. The methods exposed by the application services are available through their client proxies as web methods so that the same infrastructure can be used to call web service methods, page methods, and application services.

The *Conversion* layer is responsible for serialization and deserialization to and from the common .NET types. The default serialization is handled by the `Sys.Serialization.JavaScriptSerializer` class. JSON represents the default serialization format but additional serialization formats such as XML can be specified.

The *Core communication* layer is represented by a set of classes that make HTTP requests. The `Sys.Net.WebRequestExecutor` represents an "abstract" base class by convention, offering a generic interface for making web requests. The class is extended by `Sys.Net.XmlHttpExecutor`, which uses `XMLHttpRequest` to make the web requests. The logic of the web request is implemented in the `Sys.Net.WebRequest` class, which uses a `WebRequestExecutor` object (`XmlHttpExecutor` is used by default). All the web requests initiated by the browser are managed by the `Sys.Net.WebRequestManager` class that offers an additional level of control by exposing new properties, events, and methods.

See Appendix A for reference regarding these classes. We'll use them in practice in the upcoming exercise.

Server Asynchronous Communication

This book is dedicated to the client-side of the ASP.NET AJAX Framework — in other words, the Microsoft AJAX Library. You should be aware, however, that the ASP.NET AJAX Framework includes server-side capability as well, including an asynchronous communication layer. This layer is made of the components described in Figure 4-5.

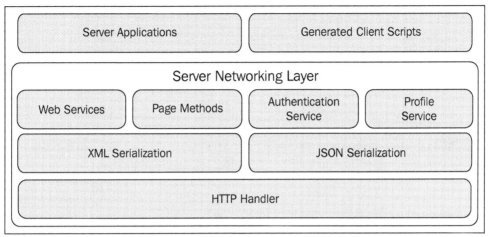

Figure 4-5. Server Asynchronous Communication

This architecture can also be split into three layers, just like its client-side counterpart:

- Core communication layer
- Conversion layer
- Application services layer

The *Core communication* layer consists of the web services that are the entry point for each request initiated from the client side. Remember that we said that page methods and application services are exposed as web service methods.

The *Conversion* layer consists of JSON serialization/deserialization by default, and allows custom serialization and deserialization of common .NET types.

The *Application services* layer consists of a set of services that generate client proxies in order to enable invocation from the client side. Once configured, they provide the client with the necessary proxies.

Working with WebRequest

For the rest of this chapter, we'll go through two simple exercises to implement the QuickStart example from Chapter 1, but this time using the Microsoft AJAX Library. This exercise will demonstrate how the `WebRequest` class can be used to perform AJAX requests. Look ahead at Figures 4-6 and 4-7 to see where we're heading, and start typing.

Time for Action—WebRequest

1. Open the `http://localhost/Atlas` web application in Visual Web Developer 2005.

2. Create a folder named `Scripts` in your project. We'll use this folder to store the files of the Microsoft AJAX Library, and other JavaScript files we'll create.

3. Copy all the files in `\Program Files\Microsoft ASP.NET\ASP.NET 2.0 AJAX Extensions\version\MicrosoftAjaxLibrary\ System.Web.Extensions\version\` to your `Scripts` folder. After this operation, your `Scripts` folder should contain `MicrosoftAjax.js`, `MicrosoftAjaxTimer.js`, `MicrosoftAjaxWebForms.js`, their debug versions, and other JavaScript source files. The files we're interested in are `MicrosoftAjax.js` and `MicrosoftAjax.debug.js`.

4. Create a new **HTML Page** in your project named `AtlasQuickstart.html` and modify it as highlighted below:

```
<!DOCTYPE html PUBLIC "-//W3C//DTD XHTML 1.1//EN"
    "http://www.w3.org/TR/xhtml11/DTD/xhtml11.dtd">
<html>
<head>
  <title>Microsoft AJAX Library: Quickstart</title>
</head>
<body>
  <form>
    <!-- load debug version of Microsoft AJAX Library -->
    <script type="text/javascript" src="Scripts/MicrosoftAjax.
debug.js"></script>

    <div>
      <h1>Microsoft AJAX Library: Quickstart</h1>

      Server wants to know your name:
      <input type="text" id="myName" />

      <h2>OnWebRequestCompleted</h2>
      <div id="response"></div>
    </div>
  </form>

  <script type="text/javascript">
    // get references to the response div element
    responseDiv = $get("response");

    // initialize application
    function pageLoad()
```

```
{
  // make web request
  makeWebRequest();
}

// performs asynchronous server request
function makeWebRequest()
{
  // set request parameters
  var param = "?name=" +
        encodeURIComponent($get("myName").value);
  var url = "AtlasQuickstartServer.ashx" + param;
  var timeout = 10000;
  var httpVerb = "GET";

  // create new WebRequest object and set its properties
  req = new Sys.Net.WebRequest();
  req.set_timeout(timeout);
  req.set_httpVerb(httpVerb);
  req.add_completed(OnWebRequestCompleted);
  req.set_url(url);

  // perform asynchronous server call
  req.invoke();
}

// executed when the message is received from the server
function OnWebRequestCompleted(executor, eventArgs)
{
  // if the request timed out...
  if(executor.get_timedOut())
  {
    responseDiv.innerHTML = "The request timed out!";
  }
  // if the request was aborted...
  else if(executor.get_aborted())
  {
    responseDiv.innerHTML = "The request aborted!";
  }
  // if the request completed successfully
  else if(executor.get_responseAvailable())
  {
    // use get_object() to deserialize response JSON data
    result = executor.get_object();

    // display the response
    responseDiv.innerHTML = result.response;
  }
```

```
        // restart sequence after one second
        setTimeout("makeWebRequest();", 1000);
    }
  </script>
</body>
</html>
```

5. Add a new **Generic Handler** file in your project, named
    `AtlasQuickstartServer.ashx`.

6. The code in `AtlasQuickstartServer.ashx` is similar to `Quickstart.aspx`
    that you created in Chapter 1, except that now we have a Generic Handler
    instead of a Web Form, and we encode the server response in JSON format.
    Here is the code of `AtlasQuickstartServer.ashx`:

```csharp
<%@ WebHandler Language="C#" Class="AtlasQuickstartServer" %>

using System;
using System.Web;

public class AtlasQuickstartServer : IHttpHandler
{
  public void ProcessRequest(HttpContext context)
  {
    // declare the names that are recognized by the server
    string[] names = new string[] { "CRISTIAN", "BOGDAN",
                                     "YODA" };

    // retrieve the current name sent by the client
    string currentUser = context.Request.QueryString["name"] + "";

    // set the response content type
    context.Response.ContentType = "application/json";

    // declare the response string format, and the response text
    string response = "{{response:\"{0}\"}}";
    string responseText = "";

    // if the name is empty...
    if (currentUser.Length == 0)
    {
      responseText = "Stranger, please tell me your name!";
    }
```

```csharp
      // if the typed name is in the names array
      else if (Array.IndexOf(names, currentUser.ToUpper().Trim())
                                                          >= 0)
      {
        responseText = "Hello, master " + currentUser + "!";
      }
      // if the name is neither empty nor recognized
      else
      {
        responseText = currentUser + ", I don't know you!";
      }

      // fill in the response
      response = string.Format(response, responseText);

      // output the response
      context.Response.Write(response);

      // flush the response stream
      context.Response.Flush();
    }

    public bool IsReusable
    {
      get
      {
        return false;
      }
    }
  }
```

7. Select `AtlasQuickstart.html` and execute it, or right-click on it, and choose **View in Browser**.

8. If you don't type anything in the text box, the message from the server will read **Stranger, please tell me your name!**, as shown in Figure 4.6:

Figure 4-6. Sample output from AtlasQuickstart.html

9. Type John Doe in the box, and note the updated message received from the server — see Figure 4-7:

Figure 4-7. Server doesn't know John Doe

What Just Happened?

The example shows how to make simple web requests using the Microsoft AJAX Library. As advertised, we'll go into the nitty gritty details of working with this library starting with Chapter 5. You can test the example online at `http://www.cristiandarie.ro/asp-ajax/AtlasQuickstart.html`.

The purpose of this exercise was to get you a first exposure to the Microsoft AJAX Library. As you could see, the major difference between this example and the Quickstart example presented in Chapter 1 is the client-side code.

Before looking at the code itself, here are a few conclusions we can draw straight away:

- The Microsoft AJAX Library offers a powerful, event-based, and completely object-oriented interface to the AJAX web development paradign. You implemented the required functionality by handling a few events. You didn't execute the `XMLHttpRequest` calls manually.

- If all you need is to implement trivial AJAX functionality, you may be better off without the Microsoft AJAX Library, which requires an additional learning curve, plus 80 kilobytes for your visitors to load. Chapter 2 taught you most of what you needed to know to do just that.

Let's analyze our project in detail now. The client requests are handled at the server side by a Generic Handler named `AtlasQuickstartServer.ashx`. A Generic Handler is an ASP.NET-supported file type, which can be used to write scripts that don't need the typical functionality of `.aspx` Web Forms. In our case we only needed a simple script that is able to output simple content depending on the parameter received as the query string.

ASP.NET Web Forms (files with the `.aspx` extension) are essentially classes that derive from `System.Web.UI.Page`. This is a powerful class that contains the functionality needed to render web pages, and includes support for features such as master pages, controls, code-behind files, and so on.

ASP.NET Generic Handlers (files with the `.ashx` extension), on the other hand, don't derive from `System.Web.UI.Page`. This makes them useful for creating web-accessible functionality without the overhead implied by inheriting from `Page`.

Generic Handlers must implement the `System.Web.IHttpHandler` interface. This interface contains two members: `IsReusable`—a `Boolean` property that specifies whether the handler instance can be reused for more requests, and `ProcessRequest()`—the method that executes when the handler is loaded. When creating a new Generic Handler in Visual Web Developer, you get a very simple handler template, which simply outputs "Hello World".

You're already familiar with most of this script from the Quickstart exercise in Chapter 1. Just as a short reminder, this script reads the name parameter sent through the query string. For example, you could load this URL:

```
http://localhost/Atlas/AtlasQuickstartServer.ashx?name=Yoda
```

The script replies by packaging the response—this time in JSON format, such as:

```
{response:"Hello, master Yoda!"}
```

This output is created using the String.Format() method, and the following formatting string (the curly bracket is doubled to lose its special meaning):

```
string response = "{{response:\"{0}\"}}";
```

Let's see what happens at the client side now. Your visitor loads AtlasQuickstart. html, whose body is pretty simple. Apart from the input text box and the <div> element where we write the response, we also have reference to the debug version of the Microsoft AJAX Library script—MicrosoftAjax.debug.js.

```
<form>
  <!-- load debug version of Microsoft AJAX Library -->
  <script type="text/javascript" src="Scripts/MicrosoftAjax.debug.
js"></script>

  <div>
    <h1>Microsoft AJAX Library: Quickstart</h1>

    Server wants to know your name:
    <input type="text" id="myName" />
    <h2>OnWebRequestCompleted</h2>
    <div id="response"></div>
  </div>
</form>
```

Later in AtlasQuickstart.html, we can find the JavaScript code that uses the Microsoft AJAX Library to call AtlasQuickstartServer.ashx asynchronously. The first thing we do is to obtain a reference to the <response> element from our document, which we'll populate with the response received from the server:

```
<script type="text/javascript">
  // get references to the response div element
  responseDiv = $get("response");
```

$get() is just a shortcut to the Sys.UI.DomElement.getElementById() function of the Microsoft AJAX Library, which is basically a wrapper for the getElementById() JavaScript function. In other words, $get() obtains a reference to the object with the specified ID.

Remember that Appendix A contains the Microsoft AJAX Library API reference. Use it when you need more details about classes or methods in the Microsoft AJAX Library.

Next there is the `pageLoad()` function. Although it's not referenced anywhere else, this is called automatically when the Microsoft AJAX Library loads. Here we call `makeWebRequest()`, which starts calling the server.

```
// initialize application
function pageLoad()
{
  // make web request
  makeWebRequest();
}
```

The code in `makeWebRequest()` starts looking familiar and making some sense, at last. This function makes the asynchronous request to `AtlasQuickstartServer.ashx`, and sends the text typed by the visitor as a parameter. It starts by setting a number of parameters that will be used for making the request: the timeout value in milliseconds, the URL to access, and the HTTP method. We use `$get()` to read the text typed by the visitor, and we use `encodeURIComponent()` to encode it for transferring it safely to the server as a query string parameter:

```
// set request parameters
var param = "?name=" + encodeURIComponent($get("myName").value);
var url = "AtlasQuickstartServer.ashx" + param;
var timeout = 10000;
var httpVerb = "GET";
```

Once these variables are set, we create the `WebRequest` object. This is the Microsoft AJAX Library object that encapsulates all the functionality required to perform asynchronous web requests. Although it is more complex than that, it's easy to see that `WebRequest` is a wrapper for the `XMLHttpRequest` object. Instead of creating `XMLHttpRequest` objects and performing the requests ourselves, now we create a `WebRequest` object.

After creating the `WebRequest` object, you need to set the parameters that you've just defined as variables: the URL to call, the timeout, and the HTTP method, which in our case is GET because we're passing the parameters through the query string. Additionally you set the event handler for the `Completed` event. This is similar to setting the `onreadystatechange()` method of the `XMLHttpRequest` object. In our case we set `OnWebRequestCompleted()` as the method to be called when the response from the server is received:

```
// create new WebRequest object and set its properties
req = new Sys.Net.WebRequest();
req.set_timeout(timeout);
req.set_httpVerb(httpVerb);
req.add_completed(OnWebRequestCompleted);
req.set_url(url);
```

Finally, we call the `invoke()` method of `WebRequest`, which initiates the asynchronous server call:

```
// perform asynchronous server call
req.invoke();
}
```

The code in `OnWebRequestCompleted()` will also look familiar, as it's very similar to the `handleServerResponse()` function you wrote in Chapter 2 to handle the server response. This event handler is the one responsible for retrieving the response data. However, here we no longer manually verify the state and status code of the request as we did before. Instead, we check properties of the `executor` parameter to find the status of the request:

```
// executed when the message is received from the server
function OnWebRequestCompleted(executor, eventArgs)
{
    // if the request timed out...
    if(executor.get_timedOut())
    {
        responseDiv.innerHTML = "The request timed out!";
    }
    // if the request was aborted...
    else if(executor.get_aborted())
    {
        responseDiv.innerHTML = "The request aborted!";
    }
    // if the request completed successfully
    else if(executor.get_responseAvailable())
    {
        ...
    }
}
```

If `executor.get_responseAvailable()` is `true`, then we know the response has arrived successfully from the server. In this case we read the server's response using the `get_object()` method of `executor`:

```
// if the request completed successfully
else if(executor.get_responseAvailable())
{
```

```
    // use get_object() to deserialize response JSON data
    result = executor.get_object();
    // display the response
    responseDiv.innerHTML = result.response;
}
```

In order to make your code totally bulletproof, you can also check for the response code using `get_responseCode()`. The result of this method call should be 200, indicating that the server successfully replied to the request. Note that the `get_object()` method of `WebRequestExecutor` internally executes `JavaScriptSerializer.deserialize()`, which is used to deserialize incoming JSON data, so the highlighted line of code is equivalent to:

```
result = Sys.Serialization.JavaScriptSerializer.deserialize(executor.
get_responseData());
```

At the end of our `OnWebRequestCompleted()` function, we restart the sequence by using `setTimeout()` to execute `makeWebRequest()` after one second:

```
    // restart sequence after one second
    setTimeout("makeWebRequest();", 1000);
```

More WebRequests

After going through the previous example, you could think that using `WebRequest` isn't that different from working with `XMLHttpRequest` directly—but, that is because we only scratched the functionality of the Microsoft AJAX Library.

In the exercise we handled the completed event of `WebRequest` to read the server response. In the last little experiment for this chapter we will handle two events of the `WebRequestManager` class: `invokingRequest` and `completedRequest`.

Time for Action—More WebRequest

1. While still in the `Atlas` project, modify the `pageLoad()` function in `AtlasQuickstart.html` like this:

```
// initialize WebRequestManager on page load
function pageLoad()
{
    // create WebRequestManager and assign event handlers
    var wrm = Sys.Net.WebRequestManager;
    wrm.add_invokingRequest(OnWebRequestManagerInvoking);
    wrm.add_completedRequest(OnWebRequestManagerCompleted);
    // make web request
    makeWebRequest();
}
```

2. Add the highlighted elements to the form:

```
<div>
  <h1>Microsoft AJAX Library: Quickstart</h1>

  Server wants to know your name:
  <input type="text" id="myName" />
  <h2>OnWebRequestCompleted</h2>
  <div id="response"></div>

  <h2>OnWebRequestManagerInvoking</h2>
  <div id="responseWRMI"></div>

  <h2>OnWebRequestManagerCompleted</h2>
  <div id="responseWRMC"></div>
</div>
```

3. Obtain references to the new `<div>` elements by writing this code:

```
<script type="text/javascript">
  // get references to the response div element
  responseDiv = $get("response");
  responseWRMIDiv = $get("responseWRMI");
  responseWRMCDiv = $get("responseWRMC");
```

4. Add the following two event handlers, before the closing `</script>` tag:

```
function OnWebRequestManagerInvoking(sender, eventArgs)
{
  var req = eventArgs.get_webRequest();
  responseWRMIDiv.innerHTML =
      "Date: " + new Date().toString() + "<br />" +
      "URL : " + req.getResolvedUrl() + "<br />" +
      "Timeout : " + req.get_timeout() + "<br />" +
      "Method : " + req.get_httpVerb() + "<br />";
}

function OnWebRequestManagerCompleted(executor, eventArgs)
{
  responseWRMCDiv.innerHTML =
      "Date: " + new Date().toString() + "<br />" +
      "Timed out: " + executor.get_timedOut()   + "<br />" +
      "Aborted: " + executor.get_aborted() + "<br />";

  if (executor.get_responseAvailable())
  {
    responseWRMCDiv.innerHTML +=
        "Status code: " + executor.get_statusCode() + "<br />" +
```

```
                "Status text: " + executor.get_statusText() + "<br />" +
                "Headers: " + executor.getAllResponseHeaders()+ "<br />";
    }
}
```

5. Load the application again, type **Yoda**, and expect to see the results shown in Figure 4-8.

Figure 4-8: Reading more data about the request

What Just Happened?

We used the page's `load` event to register the event handlers for
`WebRequestManager`'s `invokingRequest` and `completedRequest` events.

```
// create WebRequestManager and assign event handlers
var wrm = Sys.Net.WebRequestManager;
wrm.add_invokingRequest(OnWebRequestManagerInvoking);
wrm.add_completedRequest(OnWebRequestManagerCompleted);
```

The event handler for the `invokingRequest` event simply logs all the details for
the web request: URL, timeout, and the HTTP method. Our event handler displays
this data:

```
function OnWebRequestManagerInvoking(sender, eventArgs)
{
  var req = eventArgs.get_webRequest();

  responseWRMIDiv.innerHTML =
      "Date: " + new Date().toString() + "<br />" +
      "URL : " + req.getResolvedUrl() + "<br />" +
      "Timeout : " + req.get_timeout() + "<br />" +
      "Method : " + req.get_httpVerb() + "<br />";
}
```

The handler for the `completedRequest` event logs data about the response: whether
it is timed out or not, whether it is aborted or not, the response code, the response
text, and all the response headers:

```
function OnWebRequestManagerCompleted(executor, eventArgs)
{
  responseWRMCDiv.innerHTML =
      "Date: " + new Date().toString() + "<br />" +
      "Timed out: " + executor.get_timedOut()  + "<br />" +
      "Aborted: " + executor.get_aborted() + "<br />";

  if (executor.get_responseAvailable())
  {
    responseWRMCDiv.innerHTML +=
        "Status code: " + executor.get_statusCode() + "<br />" +
        "Status text: " + executor.get_statusText() + "<br />" +
        "Headers: " + executor.getAllResponseHeaders()+ "<br />";
  }
}
```

During the life cycle of a request these two methods will provide information about
the request's general information.

Summary

Wasn't this chapter short! You've learned about the main architectural principles built into the Microsoft AJAX Library, and you now know about its main components. We also touched a bit on the asynchronous communication features in the library. In Chapter 5, you'll continue your journey by investigating the inner details of this library.

5

OOP with the Microsoft AJAX Library

Microsoft AJAX Library is a large set of functions that can be used for developing powerful client-side functionality. This chapter will help you understand the environment created by those functions, and how to adapt to it when writing your own code. You will learn the architectural fundamentals that make the Microsoft AJAX Library work, and you'll test its features in a few small projects.

The developers of the Microsoft AJAX Library have invested a lot of effort to create, with JavaScript, an environment that is similar — to the extent that is possible — to the .NET framework. You will find support for the major features you'd expect to find in a professional development environment: namespaces, interfaces, class and interface inheritance, properties and events, and more.

Please remember to use Appendix A for detailed reference for the classes discussed. The official reference at `http://ajax.asp.net/docs/` will also be helpful for the areas that we couldn't afford to cover with enough depth. At the end of this chapter, you will have a good understanding of the following aspects of the Microsoft AJAX Library:

- The JavaScript base classes extensions
- The Type system
- Namespaces
- Inheritance and interfaces
- Properties and events
- Enumerations

Let's get started!

The New Features

We hope the list of features you'll learn in this chapter didn't look very intimidating! To get you accustomed to the world of the Microsoft AJAX Library, let's have a high-level look at these features, before discussing at length the details:

- *Classes* in JavaScript are reference types derived from `Object`.
- *Reflection* is supported through `Type`, which is a special class that defines an extended area of features available implicitly to all classes written within the Microsoft AJAX Library ecosystem.
- *JavaScript Base Classes Extensions* (`Array`, `Boolean`, `Date`, `Error`, `Number`, `Object`, `String`) are classes that represent the basic data types exposed by the Microsoft AJAX Library and that extend those in JavaScript.
- *Namespaces*, just like in .NET, offer the means for grouping classes in a hierachical fashion, for improved project management and type collision avoidance.
- *Inheritance*, *interfaces*, and *enumerations* are also supported or enhanced by the Microsoft AJAX Library.
- *Properties* and *events* are supported through special conventions for naming and using them.

The fact that Microsoft AJAX Library introduces classes, namespaces, inheritance, interfaces, properties, events, enumerations, and reflection, might not seem much. However, in comparison to what JavaScript offers by default, there's quite a great deal of new functionality at your disposal.

JavaScript Base Classes Extensions

The Microsoft AJAX Library base classes are: `Array`, `Boolean`, `Date`, `Error`, `Number`, `Object`, and `String`. For detailed reference, apart from Appendix A, we recommend that you check the cheat sheets published at `http://aspnetresources.com/`. The complete links are too long to type, but you can easily find them googling for "microsoft ajax cheat sheet".

You create objects of a base class the same way you create other kinds of objects. For example, here's how you create an array of three string elements:

```
var myArray = new Array("one", "two", "three");
```

JavaScript's loose typing, although admittedly feeling a bit unnatural to many .NET programmers, has its advantages when it comes to coding flexibility. For example, you can create arrays containing objects of any type. Moreover, each array element can be of any type. The flip side is that you need to be careful when the data type is not clear. For example, take this array:

```
var myArray = new Array("12/23/1980");
```

Although it may look like a date, this is an array that contains one string. Trying to use `myArray[0]` as a `Date` will have unexpected results because `Date`-specific methods aren't recognized by strings, and those that are have different functionality. To store the date as a `Date`, you would need to do something like this:

```
var myDate = Date.parseInvariant("1980/12/23", "yyyy/MM/dd");
var myArray = new Array(myDate);
```

This time, the array contains a `Date` object, thus inheriting all functionality provided by the `Date` type.

To demonstrate some typical coding involving base classes extensions, we'll go through a simple example where we use the Bubble Sort algorithm to sort an array of dates, in ascending order of the date.

 Bubble Sort is one of the simplest sorting algorithms to implement. It involves parsing the list of elements multiple times, comparing each element with the one that comes after it, and swapping their values if needed. The process is repeated until no swaps happen when parsing the entire list.

Note that Bubble Sort isn't one of the most efficient sorting algorithms, but we're using it in this exercise for its simplicity. If you're not familiar with this algorithm, we recommend that you read its description at `http://en.wikipedia.org/wiki/Bubble_sort`.

Time for Action: Bubble Sort and Base Classes Extensions

1. Open the `http://Atlas/` website in Visual Web Developer.

2. Make sure you have the Microsoft AJAX Library files in your `Scripts` folder, as instructed in the first exercise of Chapter 4.

3. Create a new **HTML Page** file in your project named `BubbleSort.html`.

4. Modify the generated template for `BubbleSort.html` like this:

```
<!DOCTYPE html PUBLIC "-//W3C//DTD XHTML 1.0 Transitional//EN"
"http://www.w3.org/TR/xhtml1/DTD/xhtml1-transitional.dtd">
<html xmlns="http://www.w3.org/1999/xhtml">
<head runat="server">
  <title>Microsoft AJAX Framework: Base Classes Extensions
    and Bubble Sort</title>
  <script src="Scripts/MicrosoftAjax.js" type="text/javascript">
  </script>
  <script src="Scripts/BubbleSort.js" type="text/javascript">
  </script>
</head>
```

```
<body>
  <h1>Base Classes Extensions and Bubble Sort
    with the Microsoft AJAX Library</h1>

  <p>Here are the original dates:</p>
  <div id="originalDates"></div>

  <p>Here are the sorted dates:</p>
  <div id="sortedDates"></div>

  <script language="JavaScript">
    // executed by MS AJAX Library on page load
    function pageLoad()
    {
       bubbleSort();
    }
  </script>
</body>
</html>
```

5. Create a new **JScript File** in the Scripts folder, named BubbleSort.js, and type this code in:

```
// sorts dates using bubble sort algorithm
function bubbleSort()
{
  // get reference to the div elements
  originalDiv = $get("originalDates");
  sortedDiv = $get("sortedDates");

  // define an array of strings containing dates
  var dateArr = new Array(
    Date.parseInvariant("08/13/1981", "MM/dd/yyyy"),
    Date.parseInvariant("12/23/1984", "MM/dd/yyyy"),
    Date.parseInvariant("04/22/1977", "MM/dd/yyyy"),
    Date.parseInvariant("09/22/1979", "MM/dd/yyyy"));

  // display the original dates
  for (i=0; i<dateArr.length; i++)
    originalDiv.innerHTML +=
      dateArr[i].format("dddd, dd MMMM yyyy <br />");

  // bubble sort the dates
  do
  {
    // initialize swapped to false
    swapped = false;
```

```
    // bubble sort
    for (i=0; i<dateArr.length - 1; i++)
    {
      // if condition is met, swap dates and set the swapped flag
      if (dateArr[i] > dateArr[i+1])
      {
        tempDate = dateArr[i];
        dateArr[i] = dateArr[i+1];
        dateArr[i+1] = tempDate;
        swapped = true;
      }
    }
  }
  while (swapped);

  // display the sorted dates
  for (i=0; i<dateArr.length; i++)
    sortedDiv.innerHTML +=
      dateArr[i].format("dddd, dd MMMM yyyy <br />");
}
```

6. Load `http://localhost/Atlas/BubbleSort.html`. You should get the results shown in Figure 5-1.

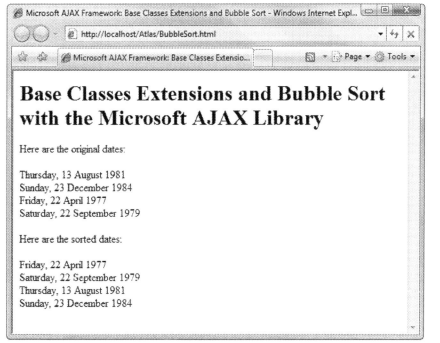

Figure 5-1. Testing the base classes extensions in the Microsoft AJAX Library

What Just Happened?

This little exercise demonstrated a few relevant ways of working with Microsoft AJAX Framework's base classes extensions. You can test it online at http://www.cristiandarie.ro/asp-ajax/BubbleSort.html.

The HTML page, BubbleSort.html, contains these essential elements:

- Two <div> elements that we use to display the original and sorted dates
- A reference to BubbleSort.js, which contains our bubble sort code
- A reference to MicrosoftAjax.js, which contains the Microsoft AJAX Library
- A function named pageLoad() that the Microsoft AJAX Library calls on page load

The BubbleSort.js file contains just one function, named bubbleSort(), which is executed from pageLoad() of BubbleSort.html:

```
<script language="JavaScript">
  // executed by MS AJAX Library on page load
  function pageLoad()
  {
      bubbleSort();
  }
</script>
</body>
</html>
```

The bubbleSort() function starts by using $get to obtain references to the two <div> elements, originalDates and sortedDates. These are used to display the original dates and the sorted dates. (Remember that $get() is a shortcut to the Sys.UI.DomElement.getElementById() function of the Microsoft AJAX Library, which is basically a wrapper for the getElementById() JavaScript function.)

```
function bubbleSort()
{
  // get reference to the div elements
  originalDiv = $get("originalDates");
  sortedDiv = $get("sortedDates");
```

Next, we created an array of Date objects. As you can read from the reference in Appendix A, Date contains quite a few useful methods. This time we've used parseInvariant(), which takes as parameter a string in the specified format, and transforms it into a Date.

```
// define an array of strings containing dates
var dateArr = new Array(
  Date.parseInvariant("08/13/1981", "MM/dd/yyyy"),
  Date.parseInvariant("12/23/1984", "MM/dd/yyyy"),
  Date.parseInvariant("04/22/1977", "MM/dd/yyyy"),
  Date.parseInvariant("09/22/1979", "MM/dd/yyyy"));
```

Once the `Array` is created, we display its elements. You can see how we parse the array, and how we call the `format()` function on each `Date` element of the array, to display the date as a string.

```
// display the original dates
for (i=0; i<dateArr.length; i++)
  originalDiv.innerHTML +=
    dateArr[i].format("dddd, dd MMMM yyyy <br />");
```

Next, the Bubble Sort algorithm is implemented to sort the array in ascending order of the dates. The detail to notice here is the direct comparison we're making between two array elements. Because the array elements are `Date` objects, the comparison isn't a string comparison, but a date comparison!

```
// if condition is met, swap dates and set the swapped flag
if (dateArr[i] > dateArr[i+1])
{
  tempDate = dateArr[i];
  dateArr[i] = dateArr[i+1];
  dateArr[i+1] = tempDate;
  swapped = true;
}
```

At the end, we display the sorted list, this time in the `<sortedDates>` div element.

We used the release version of the Microsoft AJAX Library (`MicrosoftAjax.js`). Feel free to use the debug version instead (`MicrosoftAjax.debug.js`). The differences between these versions of the library are:

- The debug version contains de-obfuscated, readable code. The release version is stripped of all spaces and comments to be smaller for download.

- The debug version contains XML descriptions for some functions, to be used by the IntelliSense features of Visual Studio "Orcas" edition.

- The debug version verifies function parameters using `Function._validateParams()`.

We hope you enjoyed this little example. You'll meet more examples of working with the base classes in the following pages.

Classes in Microsoft AJAX Library

You've learned about JavaScript classes and objects in Chapter 3. Here we're providing a quick refresher, with additional details as they relate to the features of Microsoft AJAX Library.

In JavaScript, classes are reference types that derive from JavaScript's `Object`. Classes can have four types of members: *fields*, *properties*, *methods*, and *events*.

Fields and properties have the same meaning as in C#. Public fields hold the state of an object of the class. Properties are mechanisms that offer getter and setter functions for retrieving and modifying field values, which is useful when additional code needs to run when setting or reading a field value. When a property is created to expose a field, the field's value should only be accessed through that property. This restriction is *by convention only*; field values can be accessed directly, but the convention requires using the getter and setter methods.

Because we use conventions, the implementation will differ from what you see in a class diagram. The class field that stores the property value is named with a leading underscore (_), suggesting that it's not meant to be accessed directly. The getter and setter methods are prefixed with `get_` and `set_` followed by the property name. For example, a property called `name` could be implemented like this:

```
this._name = myvalue;
...
get_name: function(){
   return this._name;
},
set_name: function(value){
   this._name = value;
}
```

Methods are functions inside a class. The term comes from the OOP world, but in the case of JavaScript, methods are implemented as functions.

Events represent notifications that an action has occurred. The implementation for events in JavaScript is very similar to the one chosen in the .NET case. If you aren't familiar with the .NET implementation, please refer to the OOP tutorial you can download at `http://www.cristiandarie.ro/downloads/`. Having in mind the approach chosen in .NET, the implementation for an event named `change` in JavaScript looks like this:

```
this._events = new Sys.EventHandlerList();
...
add_change: function(handler) {
  this.get_events().addHandler("change", handler);
```

```
},
// unregister a change event handler
remove_change: function(handler) {
  this.get_events().removeHandler("change", handler);
}
```

When an event is raised, one or more functions, called *event handlers*, can be invoked in response. Handlers can be registered and deregistered from an event. Each event handler would typically have a signature like the following:

```
function MyHandler(source, eventArgs)
```

Here, `source` represents the object that raised the event, and `eventArgs` contains an object derived from `Sys.EventArgs` as the parameters for our event. As can be easily seen, this closely matches the .NET implementation of event handlers.

Events are implemented by using the `Sys.EventHandlerList` class in a similar fashion to the classic .NET approach. This class is mapped as a property having only a getter accessor, so we cannot modify (by convention) the default reference to `Sys.EventHandlerList`. The exercises that follow will demonstrate these concepts in practice.

The Type, Namespaces, and Events

The Microsoft AJAX Library contains a special class named `Type` (which is an alias for JavaScript's Function constructor), which defines a set of properties and methods that provide typing and type-reflection capability, and other common features required when building ASP.NET AJAX applications. `Type` provides these features:

- Typing system and type-reflection
- Namespace registration
- Registration of classes, interfaces, and enumerations

As in typical .NET development, *namespaces* offer the means for avoiding type collision, and are used as containers for classes. They provide a simple yet efficient way to group common functionality implemented in classes in tree-like structures. It takes less effort to narrow our search when finding a class when guided by the namespaces at each step. Searching inside the current namespace is certainly easier than having to search in the global namespace that might contain hundreds of classes. In order to create a new namespace and to register it, we use the `registerNamespace()` static method of `Type`:

```
Type.registerNamespace("Samples");
```

Namespaces are registered as property objects of the JavaScript's `window` object. This means they become available to all the running scripts. Root namespaces like the one defined on the previous page are also registered in the `__rootNamespaces` property of the `window` object. This property is an array of all the registered root namespaces allowing us to declare nested namespaces that are registered as properties of their parent namespaces (rather than as properties of the `window` object). For example, we can declare the following nested namespace:

```
Type.registerNamespace ("Samples.Chapter5");
```

In this case, the `Chapter5` namespace will be added as an `Object` property to the `Samples` entry in the `__rootNamespaces` array.

In the exercise that follows, we will build a class (`Person`) that exposes a single property (`name`) and a single event (`change`). The `name` property can be read or modified through the `get_name()` and `set_name()` accessor methods. As you know, it is possible to register several event handlers for the same event. To demonstrate this, we will register programmatically two event handlers for the `change` event. These functions will execute when the `change` event is fired, and we will see how our event handlers are notified. Use Figure 5-2 as reference, and proceed to the exercise.

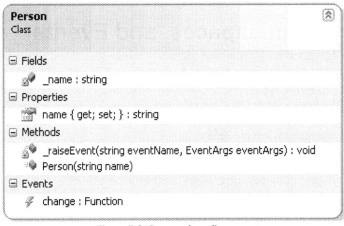

Figure 5-2. Person class diagram

Time for Action—Creating and Using the Person Class

1. Open your Atlas project in Visual Web Developer and add a **HTML Page** named `Person.html`.

2. Update the generated code in `Person.html` as shown in the following code snippet:

```
<!DOCTYPE html PUBLIC "-//W3C//DTD XHTML 1.0 Transitional//EN"
"http://www.w3.org/TR/xhtml1/DTD/xhtml1-transitional.dtd">
<html xmlns="http://www.w3.org/1999/xhtml" >
<head>
  <title>Microsoft AJAX Library: Classes and Namespaces</title>
  <script type="text/javascript" src="Scripts/MicrosoftAjax.js">
  </script>
</head>
<body>
  <script type="text/javascript" src="Scripts/Person.js">
  </script>
  <script type="text/javascript" src="Scripts/PersonTest.js">
  </script>

  <textarea id="TraceConsole" cols="70" rows="10"></textarea>

  <script type="text/javascript">
    function pageLoad()
    {
      loadPersonTest();
    }
  </script>
</body>
</html>
```

3. Add a **JScript File** named Person.js to the Scripts folder, and type the following code in. This file contains the Person class, and it registers this class under a namespace named AjaxTutorial. We'll add all the classes we create in this chapter to the AjaxTutorial namespace, to keep our code structure tidy.

```
// register a new namespace
Type.registerNamespace("AjaxTutorial");

// create the Person class and constructor
AjaxTutorial.Person = function(name)
{
  // initialize person name
  this._name = name;

  // notify person creation
  Sys.Debug.trace("Person created: " + name);
}

// define the instance members of the person class
AjaxTutorial.Person.prototype =
{
```

```
// getter function for the name property
get_name: function() {
  return this._name;
},

// setter function for the name property
set_name: function(value) {
  if(value != this._name) {
    // set the new name and raise the change event
    this._name = value;
    this._raiseEvent("change");
  }
},

// returns the events of the class
get_events: function() {
  if (!this._events) {
    this._events = new Sys.EventHandlerList();
  }
  return this._events;
},

// raises an event
_raiseEvent: function(eventName, eventArgs) {
  // obtain the event handler for the specified event name
  var handler = this.get_events().getHandler(eventName);

  // continue only if there is at least one registered handler
  if (handler) {
    // if no event args have been supplied, create empty
    //EventArgs
    if (!eventArgs) eventArgs = Sys.EventArgs.Empty;
    // call the event handlers
    handler(this, eventArgs);
  }
},

// register a change event handler
add_change: function(handler) {
  this.get_events().addHandler("change", handler);
},

// unregister a change event handler
remove_change: function(handler) {
  this.get_events().removeHandler("change", handler);
}
}
// register the Person class
AjaxTutorial.Person.registerClass("AjaxTutorial.Person");
```

4. Add a new JScript file to the project named `PersonTest.js`, and type the following code:

```
// tests the functionality of the Person class
function loadPersonTest()
{
  // create a Person named Mike
  var Mike = new AjaxTutorial.Person("Mike");

  // register two handlers for the change event
  Mike.add_change(OnChangeHandler);
  Mike.add_change(OnChange2Handler);

  // change the name, causing the change event to fire
  Mike.set_name("Michael");

  // remove one event handler
  Mike.remove_change(OnChange2Handler);

  // change the name again
  Mike.set_name("Mike");
}


// handler for Person's change event
function OnChangeHandler(sender, args)
{
  Sys.Debug.trace("OnChangeHandler: The name has changed to: " +
                  sender.get_name());
}


// another handler for Person's change event
function OnChange2Handler(sender, args)
{
  Sys.Debug.trace("OnChange2Handler: The name has changed to: " +
                  sender.get_name());
}
```

5. Execute your application or choose *View in Browser* from the context menu of Person.html. You should get the output shown in Figure 5-3.

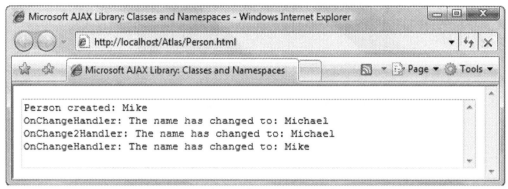

Figure 5-3. Working with Namespaces and Events

What Just Happened?

You can test the page online at http://www.cristiandarie.ro/asp-ajax/ Person.html. Let's see what the messages displayed by the application represent. The application is made of one HTML file—Person.html, and three external JavaScript files: Person.js, PersonTest.js, and (unsurprisingly) MicrosoftAjax.js.

The pageLoad() function in Person.html is automatically executed by the Microsoft AJAX Library, and it calls in turn the loadPersonTest() function in order to test our Person class:

```
<script language="javascript">
  function pageLoad()
  {
    loadPersonTest();
  }
</script>
```

Person.js contains the definition of a class named Person, located in a namespace named AjaxTutorial. PersonTest.js is a script file that we use to test the functionality of the Person class. Let's analyze these files one at a time.

Person.js starts by registering the AjaxTutorial namespace. This is not strictly related to the Person class, but since Person is part of the AjaxTutorial namespace, we think it's easier to define AjaxTutorial here instead of creating a separate JavaScript file for it. If you create more classes, in separate files, but in the same namespace, it's safe to register that namespace multiple times, in each of those files—the Microsoft AJAX Library will only register the namespace once.

```
// register a new namespace
Type.registerNamespace("AjaxTutorial");
```

After registering the namespace, we created the `Person` class, according to the diagram you saw earlier in Figure 5-2. The class has a private field called _name, which stores the person's name, and which is accessible through a property called name. Because there's no support for properties in JavaScript as there is in C#, the name property is implemented in practice through getter/setter functions, which are called `get_name()` and `set_name()`.

The class diagram also shows a private method called `_raiseEvent()`, which is used to raise events, and the `change` event. In practice we implement the support for the `change` event through getter/setter functions named `add_change()` and `remove_change()`, and the getter method named `get_events()`, which returns an object representing the class's list of events.

> We try to use the coding conventions used by the developers of the Microsoft AJAX Library. We name private members of a class starting with an underscore, such as _name or _raiseEvent(). Note that these fields are only *private by convention*, because in practice they are public members. Getter and setter functions for properties are named like get_*propertyName* and set_*propertyName*. For events, they are named add_*eventName*, remove_*eventName*, and get_events(). The rest of the functions and fields are named using camel casing, where the first letter of each word is in upper case except the first—as in _raiseEvent(). Class names use Pascal casing, where the first letter of each word is in upper case, as in Person.

Let's get back to the implementation now. After creating the `AjaxTutorial` namespace, we created the body of the `Person` function, which implements the `Person` class and also serves as its constructor. (Please review the OOP theory in Chapter 3 if this sounds awkward to you.)

```
// create the Person class and constructor
AjaxTutorial.Person = function(name)
```

The class receives as parameter the person's name, and is meant to be instantiated like this:

```
// create a Person named Mike
var Mike = new AjaxTutorial.Person("Mike");
```

> Note that unlike in .NET languages such as C# and VB.NET, you can't import a namespace, and refer to its classes without appending the namespace name. With Microsoft AJAX Library, you must always use the fully qualified name of a class, which includes its entire namespace hierarchy. In our particular case, the Person class needs to be referred to as AjaxTutorial.Person.

To understand how the class instantiation works, let's further analyze the definition of AjaxTutorial.Person. As you know, in JavaScript the function definition also functions as its constructor. The parameter name is a parameter that the class receives when it's instantiated. We save its value to a private field, so that a Person instance will retain its name:

```
// create the Person class and constructor
AjaxTutorial.Person = function(name)
{
   // initialize person name
   this._name = name;

   // notify person creation
   Sys.Debug.trace("Person created: " + name);
}
```

Apart from saving the name, the constructor also displays a message on the <TraceConsole> element using Sys.Debug.trace() to acknowledge execution (for debugging purposes).

> What's Sys.Debug.trace()? This is one of the static functions of the Debug class, which displays debugging data to a <textarea> element of the page that must be called TraceConsole. As you can see, we have such an element in Person.html. Review Chapter 7 for more information on the debugging features of Microsoft AJAX Library; for now, suffice to say that we have an easy way to output testing data.

Next, we extend Person using its prototype object, to add property, event, and function definitions to the class. The first definitions we add are those for the get_name() and set_name() functions. These are the getter and setter functions for our person's name property, which is stored internally into a "private" field called _name. This way, when get_name() is called, it returns the value of _name, and when set_name() is called, its argument is saved as _name, but only if it's different than the already existing name. Also, when setting a new name the change event is fired:

```
// define the instance members of the person class
AjaxTutorial.Person.prototype =
{
   // getter function for the name property
   get_name: function() {
     return this._name;
   },

   // setter function for the name property
   set_name: function(value) {
      if(value != this._name) {
```

```
      // set the new name and raise the change event
      this._name = value;
      this._raiseEvent("change");
    }
  },
```

Then we have two methods that support class event handling (get_events(),
_raiseEvent()), and two methods that deal particularly with the change event
(add_change() and remove_change()).

> When events are involved, there are always two parties involved: the
> class that generates (fires) the events, and the class that is listening to
> those events. In our scenario, Person is the class that generates (fires)
> events, and the event handlers are functions in the classes that use
> Person, and listen to its events. We've tested the Person class, and
> listened to its events, in the PersonTest.js file. The class or program
> that listens to events (PersonTest.js), informs the class that throws
> the events (Person) of one or more event handlers, which are methods
> to be executed when the event happens. In other words, to fire events, the
> Person class simply executes one or more methods in PersonTest.js.
> For each event, one or more event handlers can be registered.

When adding an event to a JavaScript class, you need to take care of five things:

- Declare an add_*eventName* method in order to enable adding handlers to
  the event
- Declare a remove_*eventName* method in order to enable removing handlers
  from the event
- Create a helper function named get_events() that creates and returns an
  event handler list (Sys.EventHandlerList) for the class.
- Declare the _raiseEvent() function that raises events
- Use the _raiseEvent() function to raise the event whenever necessary

Let's see get_events() first. While it's not necessary to create a special function for
creating a new Sys.EventHandlerList, we choose to do so to keep the code clean.
This function is by convention the getter function of a read-only property named
events. We'll find ourselves calling get_events() whenever we need to manipulate
the events of our class.

```
  // returns the events of the class
  get_events: function() {
    if (!this._events) {
      this._events = new Sys.EventHandlerList();
    }
    return this._events;
  },
```

The code is quite straightforward: we check if we already have a `Sys.EventHandlerList` object in the `_events` field. If not we declare it and hold it in a private field named `_events`. The object is then returned to the caller.

> The `Sys.EventHandlerList` class manages a dictionary containing events as keys, and their corresponding handlers as an array of values. It contains three methods: `addHandler()` adds a new handler for the id event, `removeHandler()` removes a handler from the list of handler for the id event, and `getHandler()` returns a function that can be invoked to call all the handlers for the id event. This class is extensively used when dealing with custom Microsoft AJAX Library components, but in our case we will use it only to keep track of the events and their handlers for our simple person example.

The `_raiseEvent()` function fires an event. When this happens, the handlers for the event need to be executed. It receives two parameters: a string containing the name of the event, and a class derived from the `EventArgs` object containing the details (arguments) of the event. The function retrieves a method that calls all the handlers of the event, and invokes it. The function is obtained using `getHandler()`:

```
// raises an event
_raiseEvent: function(eventName, eventArgs) {
    // obtain the event handler for the specified event name
    var handler = this.get_events().getHandler(eventName);
```

Next, if there is at least one handler for the event, it's executed by supplying the class instance—which is the object firing the event, mentioned using the `this` keyword—and the list of arguments in the form of an `EventArgs` object. If no additional arguments are needed for the event handler, we supply an empty list of arguments in the form of `Sys.EventArgs.Empty`. This is the standard way of firing events from a class using the Microsoft AJAX Library:

```
    // continue only if there is at least one registered handler
    if (handler) {
        // if no event args have been supplied, create empty EventArgs
        if (!eventArgs) eventArgs = Sys.EventArgs.Empty;

        // call the event handlers
        handler(this, eventArgs);
    }
},
```

Once `get_events()` and `_raiseEvent()` are in place, the getter/setter methods for the `change` event—namely `add_change()` and `remove_change()`, are easy to implement. They are simple wrappers for `EventHandlerList`'s `addHandler()` and removeHandler() methods. The EventHandlerList object for our object is returned by get_events(). These methods receive the name of the event, and the event handler to register or unregister for that event.

```
// register a change event handler
add_change: function(handler) {
  this.get_events().addHandler("change", handler);
},

// unregister a change event handler
remove_change: function(handler) {
  this.get_events().removeHandler("change", handler);
}
```

Remember that an event can have multiple event handlers registered. Typically there will be methods of various classes or programs using our class, but in our case we'll use a single program—the code in PersonTest.js—to register and use two event handlers for the change event of Person.

After creating the Person class, we register it using the registerClass() method, which is provided by Type. Class registration is somewhat similar to namespace registration. Each class name is put inside the __registeredTypes and __classes fields of the window object offering the means to avoid registering two classes or types with the same name.

```
// register the Person class
AjaxTutorial.Person.registerClass("AjaxTutorial.Person");
```

This gets us to PersonTest.js, which, at least compared to the Person class, contains fairly easy code. Once the foundations have been programmed, it's easy to use them. PersonTest.js contains three functions: loadPersonTest() is the function that we call from Person.html at load time; OnChangeHandler() and OnChange2Handler() are the two event handlers that we register for Person's change event.

loadPersonTest() starts by creating an instance of the AjaxTutorial.Person class, named Mike. Note that unlike with C#, if a class has been created in a namespace, it has to be **always** instantiated (and referred to) using the fully qualified name. This is due to the fact that in Microsoft AJAX Library there is no keyword like using that we find in C#. Then loadPersonTest() registers two event handlers for the change event. By convention, this is done using add_*eventName* functions:

```
// tests the functionality of the Person class
function loadPersonTest()
{
  // create a Person named Mike
```

```
    var Mike = new AjaxTutorial.Person("Mike");

    // register two handlers for the change event
    Mike.add_change(OnChangeHandler);
    Mike.add_change(OnChange2Handler);
```

After adding the event handlers, we change the person's name:

```
    // change the name, causing the change event to fire
    Mike.set_name("Michael");

    // remove one event handler
    Mike.remove_change(OnChange2Handler);

    // change the name again
    Mike.set_name("Mike");
}
```

At this moment, both the `change` event fires, and the two event handlers that listen to this event are executed. `OnChangeHandler()` and `OnChange2Handler()` have minimal implementations—all they do is to display a message on the `<messages>` element, so that we can test they were indeed executed as planned, as we could see in Figure 5-3.

At the end in `loadPersonTest()`, also for testing purposes, we called `Mike.remove_ change()` to remove one event handler, and changed the person's name again, to test that the second time only the first event handler is executed.

Inheritance

You're already familiar with the concept of inheritance. As an ASP.NET developer you know how inheritance works with C#, and you've learned about inheritance with JavaScript in Chapter 3.

The Microsoft AJAX Library implements a more involved mechanism for achieving inheritance. The `Type` class contains five `register` methods (`registerBaseMethod()`, `registerClass()`, `registerInterface()`, `registerNamespace()`, `registerEnum()`), which are used to initialize several fields such as the type name, the list of interfaces it implements, and the list of base classes.

When registering a class we can specify a base class and also an array of interfaces it implements. This additional information is stored inside the registered class's `__baseType` and `__interfaces` fields, and is used to implement the inheritance mechanism and to check for the correct use of base classes and interfaces.

The `initializeBase()` method is responsible for creating the impression of inheritance. You usually call this method in the first line of the constructor of your class, and it executes the constructor of the base class and loads all the members of the base class. This mechanism, as implemented by the Microsoft AJAX Library, provides some improvements on the default JavaScript approach for inheritance.

The `isInstanceOfType()` and `inheritsFrom()` methods that your classes inherit from `Type` can be used to test if an object is of a specified type, or if a class derives from another (this is where the `__baseType` and `__interfaces` fields are used). For example, `Person.isInstanceOfType(myObject)` will return `true` if `myObject` is a Person `object`.

In the following exercise we'll create a new class named `SmartPerson` that inherits from `Person`, and adds a property named `iq`, which stores the person's IQ. The relationship between `Person` and `SmartPerson` is described in the class diagram in Figure 5-4.

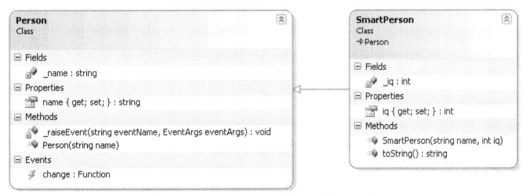

Figure 5-4. Diagram representing SmartPerson inheriting from Person

We will also use inheritance to create a class named `PersonPropertyChangedEventArgs`, which derives from `Sys.PropertyChangedEventArgs`, and contains the old and new values of a `change` event. This class is created before calling `_raiseEvent()` in `Person` and will be passed as the second parameter when firing the `change` event. The class exposes three read-only properties:

- `propertyName`: will contain the name of the property that changed (inherited from `Sys.PropertyChangedEventArgs`)
- `oldValue`: will contain the property value before the change
- `newValue`: will contain the property value after the change

This new class is presented below in Figure 5-5.

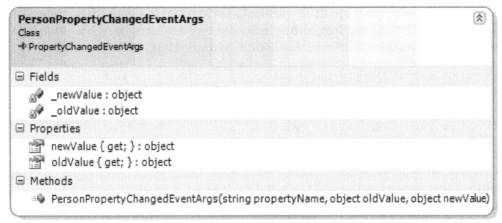

Figure 5-5. Diagram representing AjaxTutorial.PersonPropertyChangedEventArgs inheriting from
Sys.PropertyChangedEventArgs

Let's implement and use the `PersonPropertyChangedEventArgs` and `SmartPerson`
classes in a *Time for Action* exercise, and we'll discuss the details afterwards.

Time for Action—Implementing Inheritance using Microsoft AJAX Library

1. Create a JScript file in your `Scripts` folder named `Utils.js`, and type the
   following code in.

```
// register namespace
Type.registerNamespace("AjaxTutorial");

// create PersonPropertyChangedEventArgs class and constructor
AjaxTutorial.PersonPropertyChangedEventArgs = function(
  propertyName, oldValue, newValue)
{
  // initialize the base class
  AjaxTutorial.PersonPropertyChangedEventArgs.initializeBase(
    this, [propertyName]);

  // initialize oldValue and newValue property values
  this._oldValue = oldValue;
  this._newValue = newValue;
}

// create the members of PersonPropertyChangedEventArgs
AjaxTutorial.PersonPropertyChangedEventArgs.prototype =
```

```
{
  // get accessor for oldValue property
  get_oldValue: function(){
    return this._oldValue;
  },

  // get accessor for newValue property
  get_newValue: function(){
    return this._newValue;
  }
}

// register the class mentioning the base class
AjaxTutorial.PersonPropertyChangedEventArgs.registerClass(
  "AjaxTutorial.PersonPropertyChangedEventArgs",
  Sys.PropertyChangedEventArgs);
```

2. Create a new file in your `Scripts` folder named `SmartPerson.js`, and type the following code in.

```
// create the SmartPerson class and its constructor
AjaxTutorial.SmartPerson = function(name, iq)
{
  // call the Person base class constructor
  AjaxTutorial.SmartPerson.initializeBase(this, [name]);
  this._iq = iq;

  // notify SmartPerson creation
  Sys.Debug.trace(
    String.format("{0} was created with an IQ of {1}",
                  this.get_name(), this.get_iq()));
}

// register the SmartPerson class
AjaxTutorial.SmartPerson.registerClass("AjaxTutorial.SmartPerson",
  AjaxTutorial.Person);

// define the instance members of the SmartPerson class
AjaxTutorial.SmartPerson.prototype =
{
  // getter function for the iq property
  get_iq: function() {
    return this._iq;
  },

  // setter function for the iq property
  set_iq: function(value) {
    if(value != this._iq) {
```

```
     // create eventArgs that contains the old and new values
     var eventArgs =
       new AjaxTutorial.PersonPropertyChangedEventArgs("IQ",
         this._iq, value);

     // set the new iq and raise the change event
     this._iq = value;
     this._raiseEvent("change", eventArgs);
   }
 },

 // returns string description of object
 toString: function() {
   return String.format('{{name:"{0}", IQ:{1}\}}',
                         this._name, this._iq);

 }
}
```

3. In the Scripts folder, create a copy of Person.js named Person2.js, and modify its code as highlighted:

```
// setter function for the name property
set_name: function(value) {
  if(value != this._name) {
    // create eventArgs that contains the old and new values
    var eventArgs =
              new AjaxTutorial.PersonPropertyChangedEventArgs(
              "name", this._name, value);

    // set the new name and raise the change event
    this._name = value;
    this._raiseEvent("change", eventArgs);
  }
},
```

4. In the Scripts folder make a copy of PersonTest.js named PersonTest2.js, and modify the loadPersonTest() function to make use of the new SmartPerson class. The new code is highlighted opposite. We've removed some of the old code, including the references to OnChange2Handler(), to keep the focus on the matter at hand.

```
// executed on page load
function loadPersonTest()
{
  // get the messages <div> element
  messagesDiv = $get("messages");

  // create a Person named Mike
```

```
    var Mike = new AjaxTutorial.Person("Mike");

    // register a handler for the change event
    Mike.add_change(OnChangeHandler);

    // change the name, causing the change event to fire
    Mike.set_name("Michael");

    // create a SmartPerson named John with the IQ of 200
    var John = new AjaxTutorial.SmartPerson("John", 200);

    // register an event handler for SmartPerson's change event
    John.add_change(OnChangeHandler);

    // change John's IQ
    John.set_iq(100);

    // change John's name
    John.set_name("Johnny");
}
```

5. Also in `PersonTest2.js`, modify `OnChangeHandler()` to display different messages for events raised by `Person` and by `SmartPerson`, and to use the new `PropertyChangedEventArgs` class received as parameter. You can delete the other event handler (`OnChange2Handler()`) because we aren't using it any more in this exercise.

```
// handler for change event of Person and SmartPerson
function OnChangeHandler(sender, args)
{
  // display info for events fired by Person
  if (AjaxTutorial.Person.isInstanceOfType(sender))
  {
    Sys.Debug.trace(
      String.format("Person changed its {0} from {1} to {2}",
        args.get_propertyName(), args.get_oldValue(),
        args.get_newValue()));
  }

  // display info for events fired by SmartPerson
  else if (AjaxTutorial.SmartPerson.isInstanceOfType(sender))
  {
    Sys.Debug.trace(
      String.format(
        "SmartPerson {0} changed its {1} from {2} to {3}",
        sender, args.get_propertyName(),
        args.get_oldValue(), args.get_newValue()));
  }
}
```

6. Make a copy of `Person.html` in your project named `Person2.html`, and modify it as highlighted:

```html
<!DOCTYPE html PUBLIC "-//W3C//DTD XHTML 1.0 Transitional//EN"
"http://www.w3.org/TR/xhtml1/DTD/xhtml1-transitional.dtd">
<html xmlns="http://www.w3.org/1999/xhtml" >
<head>
  <title>Microsoft AJAX Library: Inheritance</title>
  <script type="text/javascript" src="Scripts/MicrosoftAjax.js">
  </script>
</head>
<body>
  <script type="text/javascript" src="Scripts/Utils.js">
  </script>
  <script type="text/javascript" src="Scripts/Person2.js">
  </script>
  <script type="text/javascript" src="Scripts/SmartPerson.js">
  </script>
  <script type="text/javascript" src="Scripts/PersonTest2.js">
  </script>

  <textarea id="TraceConsole" cols="70" rows="10"></textarea>

  <script type="text/javascript">
    function pageLoad()
    {
      loadPersonTest();
    }
  </script>
</body>
</html>
```

7. Load `Person2.html`. The results should resemble Figure 5-6. You can also check the example online at `http://www.cristiandarie.ro/asp-ajax/Person2.html`.

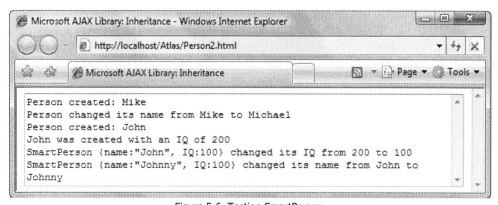

Figure 5-6. Testing SmartPerson

What Just Happened?

In this exercise we've created a new class named `SmartPerson`, which inherits from `Person`, and a class named `PersonPropertyChangedEventArgs` that inherits from `Sys.PropertyChangedEventArgs`.

The inheritance mechanism is implemented using `initializeBase()`, inherited from `Type`, in the first line of the derived class's constructor. This imports all the members of the base class into the derived class simulating in this way the "real" inheritance you're accustomed to from the world of .NET, Java, or C++.

```
// create the SmartPerson class and its constructor
AjaxTutorial.SmartPerson = function(name,iq)
{
    // call the Person base class constructor
    AjaxTutorial.SmartPerson.initializeBase(this, [name]);
    this._iq = iq;
```

As you can see, we call `initializeBase()` by supplying as parameters the current class instance, and an array with the parameters for the base class contructor. This is similar to the `base(..)` syntax of C#. To test that inheritance actually works, the constructor in `SmartPerson` displays a message that includes both the person's name, and the person's IQ. The person's name is referenced through `this.get_name()`, which, as you know, is defined in `Person`.

```
// notify SmartPerson creation
Sys.Debug.trace(
    String.format("{0} was created with an IQ of {1}",
                this.get_name(), this.get_iq()));
```

Apart from inheriting the properties, methods, and events of `Person`, `SmartPerson` added the `iq` property, implementing it using `get_iq()` and `set_iq()`. We have also overridden the `toString()` method that is provided by default by JavaScript's `Object`. You can see these in Figure 5-4, and we're displaying them again in Figure 5-7 for your convenience.

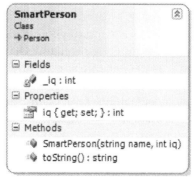

Figure 5-7. Class diagram for SmartPerson class

Next we called `registerClass()` to register the new class, this time also specifying the base class:

```
// register the SmartPerson class
AjaxTutorial.SmartPerson.registerClass("AjaxTutorial.SmartPerson",
    AjaxTutorial.Person);
```

When using the `SmartPerson` class in `PersonTest2.js` we've made a few tests to ensure the inheritance works fine. For starters, we created a new `SmartPerson` named John, with an IQ of 200:

```
// create a SmartPerson named John with the IQ of 200
var John = new AjaxTutorial.SmartPerson("John", 200);
```

If you look at the debugging messages in Figure 5-6, you'll see that the constructor of `Person` is called first, as a result of executing `initializeBase()` in `SmartPerson`, and then the rest of `SmartPerson`'s constructor is executed. This behavior is similar to the natural inheritance mechanism that you find in server-side .NET programming with C#.

Then we registered an event handler for the `change` event of `SmartPerson`. This is another demonstration that inheritance works, because the `change` event is defined in `Person`, and inherited by `SmartPerson`.

```
// register an event handler for SmartPerson's change event
John.add_change(OnChangeHandler);
```

Then we changed John's name and IQ, to ensure that `OnChangeHandler()` fires correctly when both the name and the IQ are changed:

```
// change John's IQ
John.set_iq(100);

// change John's name
John.set_name("Johnny");
}
```

The last function in `PersonTest2.js` is `OnChangeHandler()`, which is the event handler that handles the `change` event of `Person` and `SmartPerson`. One of the design goals for this function was to continue supporting the functionality that we had for the `Person` class, and display the old value and the new value of a property that is being changed. However, in order to support this feature for `SmartPerson` we needed to extend our architecture a little bit by creating a class named `PersonPropertyChangedEventArgs`.

This class is designed to hold the name of the property that is being changed (such as "name" or "iq"), the old value of the property, and the new value of that property.

Whenever SmartPerson fires a change event, it creates a
PersonPropertyChangedEventArgs object that contains this data, and supplies this
object to the event handler. The event handler uses this data to display information
about the change event of SmartPerson:

```
// handler for change event of Person and SmartPerson
function OnChangeHandler(sender, args)
{
  // display info for events fired by Person
  if (AjaxTutorial.Person.isInstanceOfType(sender))
  {
    Sys.Debug.trace(
      String.format("Person changed its {0} from {1} to {2}",
        args.get_propertyName(), args.get_oldValue(),
        args.get_newValue()));
  }

  // display info for events fired by Person
  else if (AjaxTutorial.SmartPerson.isInstanceOfType(sender))
  {
    Sys.Debug.trace(
      String.format(
        "SmartPerson {0} changed its {1} from {2} to {3}",
        sender, args.get_propertyName(),
        args.get_oldValue(), args.get_newValue()));
  }
}
```

If you're curious to see how the args parameter is created as a
PersonPropertyChangedEventArgs object, see the set_iq() function in
SmartPerson. There you'll see how the event data is created, and how the event
is created (a similar approach was implemented in the Person class in the
set_name() function):

```
// setter function for the iq property
set_iq: function(value) {
  if(value != this._iq) {
    // create eventArgs that contains the old and new values
    var eventArgs =
      new AjaxTutorial.PersonPropertyChangedEventArgs("IQ",
        this._iq, value);

    // set the new iq and raise the change event
    this._iq = value;
    this._raiseEvent("change", eventArgs);
  }
},
```

PersonPropertyChangedEventArgs is a class that derives from Sys.
PropertyChangedEventArgs, which in its turn derives from Sys.EventArgs. The
names of these classes reveal their purpose, and as always you can read more about
them in Appendix A. The inheritance mechanism is the standard one, as you can see
in the class definition in Utils.js. First we called initializeBase() to initialize
the base class, and afterwards we created the additional properties that we needed to
implement in PersonPropertyChangedEventArgs:

```
// create PersonPropertyChangedEventArgs class and constructor
AjaxTutorial.PersonPropertyChangedEventArgs = function(
  propertyName, oldValue, newValue)
{
  // initialize the base class
  AjaxTutorial.PersonPropertyChangedEventArgs.initializeBase(
    this, [propertyName]);

  // initialize oldValue and newValue property values
  this._oldValue = oldValue;
  this._newValue = newValue;
}
```

So the class differs from Sys.PropertyChangedEventArgs in that it adds two
properties next to the propertyName property (which is provided by the base class):
the "before" and "after" values of the property. These are implemented as read-only
properties "by convention" by creating only the getter accessors:

```
// create the members of PersonPropertyChangedEventArgs
AjaxTutorial.PersonPropertyChangedEventArgs.prototype =
{
  // get accessor for oldValue property
  get_oldValue: function(){
    return this._oldValue;
  },

  // get accessor for newValue property
  get_newValue: function(){
    return this._newValue;
  }
}
```

After creating the PersonPropertyChangedEventArgs class, we registered it inside
the new namespace:

```
// register the class mentioning the base class
AjaxTutorial.PersonPropertyChangedEventArgs.registerClass(
  "AjaxTutorial.PersonPropertyChangedEventArgs",
  Sys.PropertyChangedEventArgs);
```

Before moving on to the next topic, it's worth noticing the way `SmartPerson` overrode JavaScript's default implementation for `toString()`. When `SmartPerson` needs to display itself as a string, it will do so in a form like `{name: "John", IQ: 150}`. This string obviously resembles the JSON format, but it doesn't need to. We just needed a string representation of the smart person, so that we could identify the object when displaying the `change` event data in the event handler.

Enumerations

Enumerations represent a set of finite identifiers for integers. It is much easier to work with labels instead of brute values. Typically, only one enumeration identifier can be assigned to a variable. In order to declare enumerations we need to use the `registerEnum()` method like this:

```
// create an enum named Days
AjaxTutorial.Days = function() {};
AjaxTutorial.Days.prototype = {
        Su : 1,
        Mo : 2,
        Tu : 3,
        We : 4,
        Th : 5,
        Fr : 6,
        Sa : 7
}

// register the Days enum
AjaxTutorial.Days.registerEnum("AjaxTutorial.Days");

// example of reading an enum value
alert(AjaxTutorial.Days.Sa);
```

When declaring flags the values can be combined using bitwise operators. In this case we must supply `true` for the second parameter of `registerEnum`. Here's an example:

```
// create a flag enumeration named ConnectionStatus
AjaxTutorial.ConnectionStatus = function() {};
AjaxTutorial.ConnectionStatus.prototype = {
        UNINITIALIZED : 0x0,
        LOADING : 0x2,
        LOADED : 0x4,
        INTERACTIVE : 0x8,
        COMPLETE : 0x10
}

// register the flags enumeration
AjaxTutorial.ConnectionStatus.registerEnum(
  "AjaxTutorial.ConnectionStatus", true);
```

```
// example of combining flag values
alert(AjaxTutorial.ConnectionStatus.UNINITIALIZED |
    AjaxTutorial.ConnectionStatus.COMPLETE);
```

Interfaces

An *interface* is a contract that specifies a list of methods that need to be implemented by the classes that adhere to it. However, this contract is not checked when an object is registered (as it is in C#, for example), and not even when the object is created, so we must be extra careful when using interfaces with JavaScript and the Microsoft AJAX Library. For example, an interface method could contain code that is inherited if the method is not overridden in the class that implements the interface. This is obviously not a desirable case, as it breaks the rules of interface-based programming.

Interface registration is very similar to class registration, except that it's done using the `registerInterface()` method of `Type`. The interface name is saved internally inside the `__registeredTypes` field of the `window` object offering the means to avoid registering two interface or types with the same name, or implementing from a base type that is not an interface.

The `isImplementedBy()` and `implementsInterface()` methods (both provided by `Type`) can be used to test if an interface has a relation with a class.

To demonstrate the implementation of interfaces and more features in Microsoft AJAX Library's OOP architecture, we'll implement the class design presented in Figure 5-8.

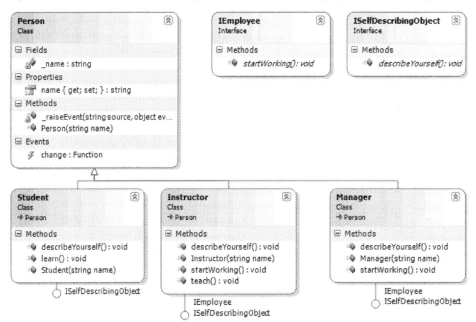

Figure 5-8. Class diagram that uses inheritance and interfaces

The diagram describes a simple class structure formed of four classes: Person, and three classes that inherit from it: Student, Instructor, and Manager. We also have two interfaces: IEmployee, and ISelfDescribingObject. Classes that implement IEmployee must implement a method named startWorking(), which is defined by that interface. The ISelfDescribingObject interface contains a method named describeYourself(), which must be implemented by classes that implement the interface.

As the diagram shows, Student implements ISelfDescribingObject, so it contains a method named describeYourself(). It also has a method named learn().

Instructor implements both IEmployee and ISelfDescribingObject, so it contains the required methods describeYourself() and startWorking(). It also contains a method named teach().

Manager also implements both IEmployee and ISelfDescribingObject, but unlike Instructor it doesn't add any more features on top of those required by the interfaces.

Follow the exercise to implement this structure of classes using JavaScript and the Microsoft AJAX Library.

Time for action—Inheritance and Interfaces

1. Create a **JScript File** in your Scripts folder named ISelfDescribingObject.js, and type the following code:

```
// register the AjaxTutorial namespace
Type.registerNamespace("AjaxTutorial");

// define the ISelfDescribingObject interface
AjaxTutorial.ISelfDescribingObject = function() { }

AjaxTutorial.ISelfDescribingObject.prototype = {
  describeYourself : function() {}
}

// register the ISelfDescribingObject interface
AjaxTutorial.ISelfDescribingObject.registerInterface(
  "AjaxTutorial.ISelfDescribingObject");
```

2. Create a new **JScript File** in your Scripts folder named IEmployee.js, and type the following code:

```
// register the AjaxTutorial namespace
Type.registerNamespace("AjaxTutorial");

// define the IEmployee interface
AjaxTutorial.IEmployee = function() { }
```

```
AjaxTutorial.IEmployee.prototype = {
  startWorking : function() {}
}

// register the IEmployee interface
AjaxTutorial.IEmployee.registerInterface("AjaxTutorial.IEmployee");
```

3. Create a **JScript File** in your `Scripts` folder named `Student.js`, and type the following code:

```
// register the AjaxTutorial namespace
Type.registerNamespace("AjaxTutorial");

// define the Student class
AjaxTutorial.Student = function(name)
{
  // initialize base class
  AjaxTutorial.Student.initializeBase(this, [name]);

  // notify student creation
  Sys.Debug.trace("Student created: " + name);
}

// create Student instance members
AjaxTutorial.Student.prototype =
{
  // Student must implement this method of ISelfDescribingObject
  describeYourself: function()
  {
    Sys.Debug.trace(
      String.format("Hello man, I'm {0}. I'm a cool student!",
      this._name));
  },

  // Student has the function to learn
  learn: function()
  {
    Sys.Debug.trace("Student wakes up, yawns, " +
      "stratches head, and tries to look interested.");
  }
}

// register the Student class
AjaxTutorial.Student.registerClass("AjaxTutorial.Student",
  AjaxTutorial.Person, AjaxTutorial.ISelfDescribingObject);
```

4. Create a **JScript File** in your `Scripts` folder named `Instructor.js`, and type the following code:

```
// register the AjaxTutorial namespace
Type.registerNamespace("AjaxTutorial");

// define the Instructor class
AjaxTutorial.Instructor = function(name)
{
  // initialize base class
  AjaxTutorial.Instructor.initializeBase(this, [name]);

  // notify instructor creation
  Sys.Debug.trace("Instructor created: " + name);
}

// define Instructor instance members
AjaxTutorial.Instructor.prototype =
{
  // method of ISelfDescribingObject interface
  describeYourself: function()
  {
    Sys.Debug.trace("Good morning class. My name is " +
      this._name + " and I'm your instructor.");
  },

  // method of IEmployeeInterface
  startWorking : function()
  {
    Sys.Debug.trace("Going to my dear students.");
  },

  // method specific to Instructor
  teach: function()
  {
    Sys.Debug.trace("Instructor bubbles incomprehensibly");
  }
}

// register the Instructor class
AjaxTutorial.Instructor.registerClass("AjaxTutorial.Instructor",
  AjaxTutorial.Person, AjaxTutorial.ISelfDescribingObject,
  AjaxTutorial.IEmployee);
```

5. Create a **JScript File** in your `Scripts` folder named `Manager.js`, and type the following code:

```
// register the AjaxTutorial namespace
Type.registerNamespace("AjaxTutorial");

// define the Manager class
AjaxTutorial.Manager = function(name)
{
  // initialize base class
  AjaxTutorial.Manager.initializeBase(this, [name]);

  // notify manager creation
  Sys.Debug.trace("Manager created: " + name);
}

// define Manager instance members
AjaxTutorial.Manager.prototype =
{
  // method of ISelfDescribingObject interface
  describeYourself : function()
  {
    Sys.Debug.trace(String.format(
      "I'm {0}. I'm the boss around here.", this._name));
  },

  // method of IEmployee interface
  startWorking: function()
  {
    Sys.Debug.trace("No, it's my golf day!");
  }
}

// register the Manager class
AjaxTutorial.Manager.registerClass("AjaxTutorial.Manager",
  AjaxTutorial.Person, AjaxTutorial.ISelfDescribingObject,
  AjaxTutorial.IEmployee);
```

6. Make a copy of `PersonTest2.js` created in the previous exercise, name it `PersonTest3.js`, and modify the `loadPersonTest()` function like this:

```
// executed on page load
function loadPersonTest()
{
  // testing Student
  Sys.Debug.trace("Working with Student Joe");
  var student = new AjaxTutorial.Student("Joe");
```

```
student.add_change(OnChangeHandler);
student.set_name("Joe v2");
student.describeYourself();

Sys.Debug.trace("---");

// testing Instructor
Sys.Debug.trace("Working with Instructor Pamela");
var instructor = new AjaxTutorial.Instructor("Pamela");
instructor.startWorking();

Sys.Debug.trace("---");

// testing Manager
Sys.Debug.trace("Working with Manager Mr. Barneson");
var manager = new AjaxTutorial.Manager("Mr. Barneson");
manager.add_change(OnChangeHandler);
manager.startWorking();
manager.describeYourself();
manager.set_name("Mr. Listentomecarefully");
}
```

7. Make a copy of `Person2.html`, name that copy `Person3.html`, and update it as highlighted:

```
<!DOCTYPE html PUBLIC "-//W3C//DTD XHTML 1.0 Transitional//EN"
"http://www.w3.org/TR/xhtml1/DTD/xhtml1-transitional.dtd">
<html xmlns="http://www.w3.org/1999/xhtml" >
<head>
    <title>Microsoft AJAX Library: Inheritance and Interfaces
    </title>
    <script type="text/javascript" src="Scripts/MicrosoftAjax.js">
    </script>
</head>
<body>
    <script type="text/javascript" src="Scripts/Utils.js">
    </script>
    <script type="text/javascript" src="Scripts/Person2.js">
    </script>
    <script type="text/javascript"
            src="Scripts/ISelfDescribingObject.js">
    </script>
    <script type="text/javascript" src="Scripts/IEmployee.js">
    </script>
    <script type="text/javascript" src="Scripts/Student.js">
    </script>
```

```
<script type="text/javascript" src="Scripts/Instructor.js">
</script>
<script type="text/javascript" src="Scripts/Manager.js">
</script>
<script type="text/javascript" src="Scripts/PersonTest3.js">
</script>

<textarea id="TraceConsole" cols="70" rows="20"></textarea>

<script type="text/javascript">
  function pageLoad()
  {
    loadPersonTest();
  }
</script>
</body>
</html>
```

8. Load `Person3.html`. The results should resemble Figure 5-9. You can also
   find it online at `http://www.cristiandarie.ro/asp-ajax/Person3.html`.

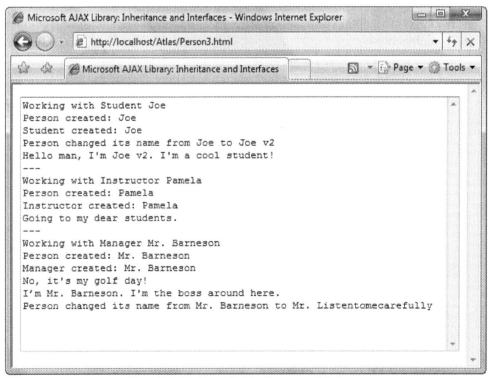

Figure 5-9. Working with inheritance and interfaces

What Just Happened?

The goal of this exercise was to demonstrate how interfaces, class inheritance, and interface inheritance can be used in client-side programming.

You used two interfaces (ISelfDescribingObject and IEmployee), a base class (Person), and three derived classes (Student, Instructor, and Manager) that extend the base class and implement the interfaces. The base class Person is the same as the one used in the previous exercise.

Each of the two interfaces exposes one method and uses the registerInterface() method to register itself. Here's the example from IEmployee.js:

```
// register the AjaxTutorial namespace
Type.registerNamespace("AjaxTutorial");

// define the IEmployee interface
AjaxTutorial.IEmployee = function() { }

AjaxTutorial.IEmployee.prototype = {
  startWorking : function() {}
}

// register the IEmployee interface
AjaxTutorial.IEmployee.registerInterface("AjaxTutorial.IEmployee");
```

Declaring the two interfaces (IEmployee and ISelfDescribingObject) is very simple as they have empty constructors and each method is also empty.

Each of the newly defined classes (Student, Instructor, and Manager) extends the Person base class and implements one or two interfaces.

Each of the new classes receives as parameter for its contructor the name of the person. The constructors of the newly derived classes first call the constructor of the Person base class, passing in turn the person's name, and then display a short debugging message to signal object creation:

```
// define the Manager class
AjaxTutorial.Manager = function(name)
{
  // initialize base class
  AjaxTutorial.Manager.initializeBase(this, [name]);

  // notify manager creation
  Sys.Debug.trace("Manager created: " + name);
}
```

`Student` implements the `ISelfDescribingObject` interface by implementing the `describeYourself()` method, and adds a new method named `learn()`. The interface is implemented by defining the method exposed by the interface:

```
// create Student instance members
AjaxTutorial.Student.prototype =
{
  // Student must implement this method of ISelfDescribingObject
  describeYourself: function()
  {
    Sys.Debug.trace(
      String.format("Hello man, I'm {0}. I'm a cool student!",
      this._name));
  },

  // Student has the function to learn
  learn: function()
  {
    Sys.Debug.trace("Student wakes up, yawns, " +
      "stratches head, and tries to look interested.");
  }
}
```

`Student` inherits from `Person`, and implements the `ISelfDescribingObject` interface. This information is specified at registration time, when the base class is specified as the second parameter of `registerClass()`, and the interfaces it implements are specified using the third parameter:

```
// register the Student class
AjaxTutorial.Student.registerClass("AjaxTutorial.Student",
  AjaxTutorial.Person, AjaxTutorial.ISelfDescribingObject);
```

Things are similar for the `Instructor` class, except that it implements two interfaces and it adds a new teach method. When the `Instructor` class is registered we add the two interfaces it implements as the last parameters of the `registerClass()` method:

```
// register the Instructor class
AjaxTutorial.Instructor.registerClass("AjaxTutorial.Instructor",
  AjaxTutorial.Person, AjaxTutorial.ISelfDescribingObject,
  AjaxTutorial.IEmployee);
```

The `Manager` class is very similar to the `Instructor` class as it implements both interfaces but it doesn't expose any new methods.

With this example we covered the most important details of the OOP model you can implement using the Microsoft AJAX Library.

OOP Recommendations

Before putting aside the rather theoretical area of OOP programming, here are a few guidelines for you to follow when writing your object-oriented JavaScript code with the Microsoft AJAX Library.

- Declare all fields, properties and events in the class constructor.
- Prefix the "private by convention" field names with an underscore (_).
- Declare the variables as instance fields using the `this` keyword.
- In the prototype, declare all the methods, accessor methods for properties, and events.
- Call `initializeBase()` in the first line of your constructor if deriving from a base class.

Summary

This chapter introduced you to the core of Microsoft AJAX Library and the client-side programming. It is very important to have a good understanding of what was presented here as it will represent the foundation to build upon in the next chapters.

This chapter was not intended to be an exhaustive presentation of Microsoft AJAX Library but merely a solid introduction to the client-side platform offered by Microsoft. In the next chapter you'll use this knowledge to create client-side components using this library.

6
Creating Client Components

In this chapter you learn how to create client-side components using the Microsoft AJAX Library. This implies working with elements of the page, registering events, creating controls and behaviors, and more. At the end of this chapter, you will have the thoeritical foundation of:

- Working with DOM elements and events
- Application object and page life cycle
- Components, controls, and behaviors

As usual, Appendix A will serve as your reference for the classes and methods discussed. You won't find much code in this chapter. Instead, Chapter 7 will put the concepts into practice through a detailed case study.

DOM Elements and Events

One of the problems developers face when writing client-side JavaScript code regards writing code that is compatible with all existing browsers. Internet Explorer in particular has historically raised the most problems because of its non-compliance with the W3C standards.

For example, to attach or detach an event handler for a particular event of an object in Internet Explorer, you need to use `attachEvent()` or `detachEvent()`. You can easily find examples of working with these functions by googling for "attachevent javascript example". On the other hand, standards-compliant browsers use `addEventListener()` and `removeEventListener()`. There are examples with these functions at `http://www.quirksmode.org/js/events_advanced.html`.

The differences don't stop here! The events themselves sometimes have different names. For example, the event that is raised when a button is clicked is named `onclick` in Internet Explorer, and is named `click` in other browsers. The differences continue with the parameters the event handlers receive.

Internet Explorer (including IE 7) takes these parameters from the window.event object whereas in other browsers the event object is passed as a parameter to the event handler itself. The list of issues can continue with mouse button's values and so on. The point is made. There are so many differences between the web browsers! To overcome these browser incompatibilities when it comes to working with DOM elements and events, the Microsoft AJAX library provides a set of *static* helper functions and properties grouped in two classes: Sys.UI.DomElement and Sys.UI.DomEvent. These classes offer a unified API that correctly performs the functionality you need implemented for any web browser.

> You've already worked with these classes in this book. For example, you've used the $get() function, which is a shortcut for the Sys.UI.DomElement.getElementById() function.

You can sneak peek how the Microsoft AJAX Library implements the browser compatibility layer by looking, for example, at the definition of $addHandler() in MicrosoftAjax.debug.js. Here it is a stripped portion of this function, which highlights the code that verifies if the user's browser supports addEventListener() or attachEvent():

```
var $addHandler = Sys.UI.DomEvent.addHandler = function Sys$UI$DomEven
t$addHandler(element, eventName, handler)
{
...
...
...
  if (element.addEventListener) {
    browserHandler = function(e) {
      return handler.call(element, new Sys.UI.DomEvent(e));
    }
    element.addEventListener(eventName, browserHandler, false);
  }
  else if (element.attachEvent) {
    browserHandler = function() {
      return handler.call(element,
                          new Sys.UI.DomEvent(window.event));
    }
    element.attachEvent("on" + eventName, browserHandler);
  }
  eventCache[eventCache.length] =
    {handler: handler, browserHandler: browserHandler};
}
```

The Microsoft AJAX Library offers an API that hides the various differences between browsers, while offering a model that is close to the standard API. This API is part of the **browser compatibility layer** of the library (see Figures 4-2 and 4-4 from Chapter 4). This layer is made of the `Sys.UI.DomElement` and `Sys.UI.DomEvent` classes, along with some other classes and enumerations inside the `Sys.UI` namespace (`Sys.UI.Bounds`, `Sys.UI.Key`, `Sys.UI.MouseButton`, `Sys.UI.Point`, and `Sys.UI.VisibilityMode`). They provide the user a seamless way of working across different browsers. The following browsers are supported:

- Internet Explorer 6.0 or higher
- Firefox 1.5 or higher
- Opera 9.0 or higher
- Safari 2.0 or higher

`Sys.UI.DomElement` contains a set of static methods that manipulate DOM elements. These include the very useful `getElementById()` function, methods for working with CSS classes (`addCssClass()`, `containsCssClass()`, `removeCssClass()`, `toggleCssClass()`), and with the element's position (`getLocation()`, `setLocation()`) and coordinates (`getBounds()`). These methods are very handy when working with the DOM elements and can save us a lot of time when we need to write non-trivial cross-browser code.

`Sys.UI.DomEvent` exposes a set of static methods that help us registering/deregistering event handlers for different events: `addHandler()`, `addHandlers()`, `removeHandler()`, and `clearHandlers()`. All these methods have corresponding shortcut methods: `$addHandler()`, `$addHandlers()`, `$removeHandler()`, `$clearHandlers()`.

Each event handler added using these methods should have the following signature:

```
function MyEventHandler(domEvent)
{...}
```

where the `domEvent` parameter is a `Sys.UI.DomEvent` object.

While in Chapter 5 you saw how you can fire an AJAX event, you might just wonder how we can do the same for events that occur in browser or DOM. DOM events can be categorized as: user interface events, HTML events, mouse events, and mutation events (events that notify changes in the structure of the document). Being able to fire DOM events (`click`, `mousedown`, `mouseup`, `change`, `focus`, `blur`, etc.) gives an enormous power for controlling what happens in the browser.

The Microsoft AJAX Library doesn't include this feature yet, but we will see that is fairly simple to do it ourselves. Here are some references:

- `http://www.w3.org/TR/DOM-Level-2-Events/events.html`
- `http://developer.mozilla.org/en/docs/DOM:document.createEvent`
- `http://www.webreference.com/js/tips/000722.html`

In our code we could implement a uniform interface for raising DOM events, in the form of a method named `_raiseDomEvent()`. It does not represent the ultimate solution to raising events, but it will come in handy. Please refer to the `www.w3.org` reference mentioned above for more details on DOM events. Here's the code for our `_raiseDomEvent()` function:

```
// raise a DOM event
_raiseDomEvent: function(eventName)
{
  // FireFox + Safari + Opera
  if (document.createEvent) {
    var onEvent = document.createEvent("HTMLEvents");
    onEvent.initEvent(eventName, true, true);

    this.get_element().dispatchEvent(onEvent);
  }
  // IE
  else if(document.createEventObject) {
    this.get_element().fireEvent("on" + eventName);
  }
}
```

In the next example we will see that we add it to our custom client control, but we could extend the `Sys.UI.DomEvent` with a static method as well. The static method would differ from the above implementation of `_raiseDomEvent()` in that it would also receive as parameter the DOM element it applies to.

Components, Behaviors, and Controls

Components represent objects that inherit from the `Sys.Component` class. They have no user interface representation and no DOM element associated to them and their lifetime is managed by Microsoft AJAX.

The components of an application are managed by the Sys.Application class, which is also a component and has no representation in the user interface and therefore inherits from Sys.Component. Adding a component to the application means adding it to Sys.Application's bag of components. By implementing the Sys.IContainer interface, Sys.Application declares itself as a component that can contain other components. This ability translates into a series of methods exposed by Sys.Application (addComponent(), getComponents(), removeComponent(), findComponent(), or its shortcut $find().

Sys.Component is the base class for components, but there are two other important classes that derive from Sys.Component and represent base classes for specialized client components: Sys.UI.Behavior and Sys.UI.Control. Objects that derive from these classes have specific names: *behavior* and *control* respectively.

Behaviors represent components that extend the behavior of DOM elements they are attached to and typically do not modify their existing markup. If they are assigned a name they can be referenced through a custom expando attribute of the DOM element. A DOM element can have multiple behaviors. The control toolkit includes behavior examples such as Slider (for text boxes), SlideShow (for images), TextBoxWatermark (for text boxes), and RoundedCorners (works with any element; adds rounded corners around it).

Controls represent components that typically change the behavior of DOM elements in order to provide new functionality. A DOM element can have a single control attached to them. They can also be referenced by using the control expando of the DOM element.

The Sys.Component class implements the Sys.INotifyPropertyChange interface. This interface exposes the propertyChanged event, which can be used internally by the control or externally by other objects that register to this event. It is recommended that every class implementing this interface and thus every component, behavior, or control uses it to notify registered listeners about changes of different properties.

Every handler registered to the propertyChanged event typically receives a Sys.PropertyChangedEventArgs object as the event argument parameter. We can raise this event for a specific property using the Sys.Component's raisePropertyChanged() method.

Creating Components

The Sys.Component class has the create() static method, as shown in Figure 6-1. The shortcut version for it is $create().

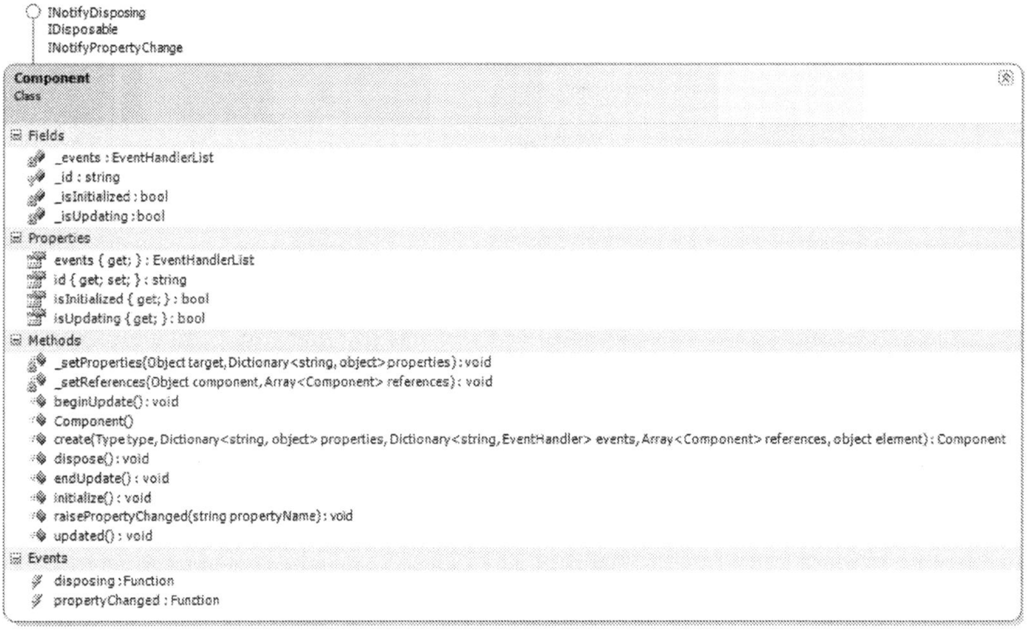

Figure 6-1. Class diagram for Sys.Component

The signature of create() is particularly interesting, because it's the key for creating new components. This method must receive at least one parameter: the type of component being created:

```
Component create (Type type,
                  Dictionary<string, object> properties,
                  Dictionary <string, Delegate> events,
                  Array<Component> references,
                  object element)
```

Quite often we might want to pass other information such as the default property values, handlers for events exposed by the component, or the references to other components. This information can be passed in as it follows:

- For property values, as the second parameter of the create() method
  { propertyName: value, propertyName2: value2 }

- For events handlers, as the third parameter of the create() method
  { eventName: handler, eventName2: handler2}

- For referenced components, as the fourth parameter of the `create()` method

  `{ component1, component2 }`

- The DOM element the component is attached to, as the fifth parameter of the `create()` method

When the `create()` method is called, there are two phases in which the component is created. In the first phase the component's constructor is called and the optional properties and events handlers specified as parameters are set.

At the beginning of this phase the component is marked as being updated, the state being reflected by the `isUpdating` property. At the end of this phase we have a new component created and added to the `Sys.Application`'s bag of components.

The second phase involves initializing the component by calling its `initialize()` method. The `isUpdating` property is set to `false` reflecting the completion of the first phase.

`Sys.Component` defines an `initialize()` method that simply marks the component as initialized through the `isInitialized` property. Another two properties that are frequently used in applications are:

- `id` is a unique identifier that represents the component. The `id` can be set only once, and it's recommended to set it using the properties parameter of the `create()` method, when creating the component. We can use the `Sys.Application.find()` method (or its shortcut `$find()`) to retrieve a component by its `id`.

- `events` is a read-only property that represents the `Sys.EventHandlerlist` object of the component.

Disposing of Components

The `Sys.Component` class also implements the `Sys.IDisposable` interface. This interface contains the `dispose()` method that is used for closing, releasing, or resetting resources held. After the method executed, an object instance is ready to be deleted. The method is very similar to the `Dispose()` method used in server-side programming for releasing unmanaged resources.

The `Sys.Component` class also implements the `Sys.INotifyDisposing` interface. This interface exposes the `disposing` event. This event allows other objects to hook to when a component is disposed in order to implement some custom logic typically involving cleanup and self disposal.

By implementing the `IDisposable` and `INotifyDisposing` interfaces we make sure that every component gets the chance to do cleanup operations before its life ends.

Sys.Application and Client Page Life-Cycle Events

In ASP.NET it is important to know the server page life cycle, and the events that are raised at every stage. The Microsoft AJAX Library ports these concepts to the client, and raises client events during the client page life cycle. These client events offer the means for controlling the user interface. Microsoft AJAX uses Sys.Application to raise application events.

In ASP.NET 2.0 we have the Page server control that raises events like init, load, and unload. The Page server control derives from the base class Control. The Microsoft AJAX Library keeps this hierarchy having the Sys.Component control similar to Control on the server, and the Sys.Application class similar to Page. The Sys.Application class inherits from Sys.Component and implements the Sys.IContainer interface.

The Sys.Application object is created by default inside the Microsoft AJAX Library so we don't have to bother about it. It provides the events and methods that fully support the development of client components. Figure 6-2 displays the public interface of this class.

Beside the addComponent(), removeComponent(), getComponents(), and findComponent() (or $find()) methods for components management, we have two methods for objects that implement the Sys.IDisposable interface to register themselves as disposable: registerDisposableObject() and unregisterDisposableObject().

Inside its constructor, the Sys.Application object registers a handler for two events that occur in every browser: load and unload of the window object. These two events represent the hooks of Microsoft AJAX Library in the browser's events.

The window's load event is raised when all the page content is loaded (including scripts and images)

Figure 6-2. Class diagram for Sys.Application

The init Event

Sys.Application is registered to the window's load event, which allows it to initialize itself. During this phase the _initializing field is set to true and its own init event is raised. Sys.Application's init event fires at the time we can create our components. We can register our own handler for this event like this:

```
<script>
  // define handler for init event
  Sys.Application.add_init(pageInit);

  // page init
  function pageInit(sender, eventArgs)
  {
    ...
  }
</script>
```

The registered handler for this event receives the Sys.Application object as its first parameter, and Sys.EventArgs.Empty as its second parameter.

Before calling the handlers registered to this event, Sys.Application sets its isCreatingComponents property to true. Anyone should check this property before tampering with the components during this early phase.

Each handler registered to the init event can create components by using the $create() method. At the end of the init event we have the page fully loaded and the components created and properly initialized.

After successfully completing the init event, Sys.Application raises another event: load.

The load Event

Similarly to what happens on the server side, the init event is followed by one of the best known and most used events: the load event. The init event is raised only when the page is initially loaded, whereas the load event is raised during the initial page load and during partial page updates.

All the handlers registered to this event should have the following signature:

```
function OnLoadHandler(sender, eventArgs)
{
}
```

The sender parameter contains the Sys.Application object and the eventArgs parameter contains a Sys.ApplicationLoadEventArgs object. The Sys.ApplicationLoadEventArgs object has two properties:

- components – returns an array containing the created components.

- isPartialLoad – returns false if Sys.Application's _initializing field is true, and true otherwise. (Remember that the _initializing field is set to true only during the initial page load when the Sys.Application object initializes itself.)

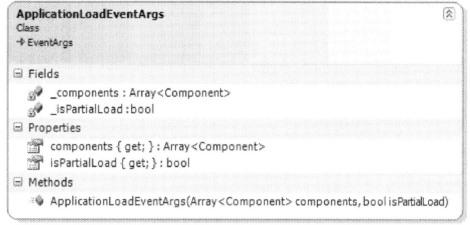

Figure 6-3. ApplicationLoadEventArgs class diagram

The pageLoad() Method

After raising the load event, the page's pageLoad() method is called, if it exists. The signature for this method should be:

```
function pageLoad(sender, eventArgs)
{
}
```

The parameters for pageLoad() are the same as for the handlers registered for the load event.

After these events are raised, the Sys.Application object is fully initialized (it's not necessary to initialize Sys.Application many times).

The pageUnload() Method

At the other end of the page life cycle we have the `window`'s `unload` event. As we have seen above, `Sys.Application` hooks to this event inside its constructor. The `Sys.Application` object calls its `dispose()` method and does the necessary cleanup.

At the end of the page life cycle events, methods, and events are called and raised in reverse order: first the `pageUnload()` method (the pair of the `pageLoad()` method) and then the `unload` event (the pair of the `load` event). The signature for this method should be:

```
function pageUnload(sender, eventArgs)
{
}
```

The `sender` parameter contains the `Sys.Application` object and the `eventArgs` parameter contains a `Sys.EventArgs.Empty` object.

The unload Event

After calling the `pageUnload()` method, the `unload` event is fired. All the handlers registered to this event should have the following signature:

```
function OnUnloadHandler(sender, eventArgs)
{
}
```

The parameters are the same as with the `pageUnload()` method.

This event represents the best place for disposing the components as it is the last event before the page is unloaded by the browser. At this moment we might want to display some sort of message or release different resources.

After this event the `dispose()` method is called on all the components registered as disposable.

Behaviors

The `Sys.UI.Behavior` class (described in Figure 6-4) represents the base class for developing behavior components. As stated before, a DOM element can have multiple behaviors, but a behavior can be attached to a single DOM element. Generally they do not modify the markup of the elements they are attached to.

Because `Behavior` inherits from `Sys.Component`, we are able to set its `id` property. We are also able to set a new property it exposes, `name`, which stores the name of the behavior.

Depending on whether the `id` and/or `name` properties are set, the overridden getter method for the `id` property returns:

- the `id` of the behavior if set

- an empty string if the DOM element's `id` is not set

- the DOM element's `id` appended with `$` and the behavior's `name`

If the `name` property is set with `$create()`, the behavior can be accessed directly through a custom expando attribute of the DOM element like this:

```
domElement[behaviorName]
```

If you set the behavior name later than at creation time, the behavior won't be accessible throught the custom expando attribute of the DOM element.

The constructor of the behavior receives as parameter the associated DOM element, which is stored inside the `element` property.

There are also three additional static methods of `Sys.UI.Behavior` that allow retrieving behaviors for a DOM element: `getBehaviorByName()`, `getBehaviors()`, and `getBehaviorsByType()`.

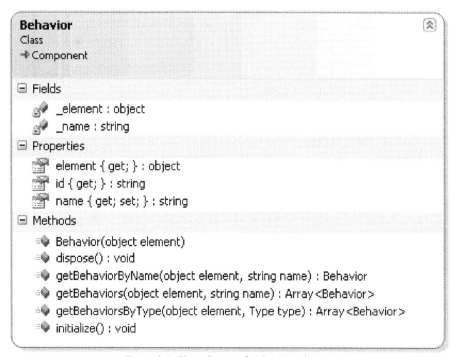

Figure 6-4. Class diagram for Sys.UI.Behavior

Controls

The `Sys.UI.Control` class (Figure 6-5) represents the base class for developing control components. Unlike behaviors they cannot be attached to more than one DOM element and they typically provide new functionality. They can be easily accessed throught the `control` expando of the DOM element they are associated to:

```
domElement.control
```

The `id` property returns the DOM element's `id`.

Beside the `element` property that (as for behaviors) exposes the DOM element, `Control` also provides the `parent` property, which represents the parent `Sys.UI.Control` component. The getter method for `parent` tries to return the first `Sys.UI.Control` associated to a DOM element up in the DOM hierarchy if the `parent` property is not set.

The control also has another two interesting properties: `visible` and `visibilityMode`.

As you might have already guessed, these two properties are related one to another: the `visibilityMode` property specifies how the control will behave when the `visible` property is set to `false`. The `visibilityMode` property can have two values defined by the `Sys.UI.VisibilityMode` enumeration: `hide` or `collapse`. Here's an example of how to set the `visibilityMode` for a control to `hide`:

```
control.set_visibilityMode(Sys.UI.VisibilityMode.hide);
```

The `visible` property is related to the `display` CSS property, where `visibilityMode` is related to the `visibility` CSS property.

`Sys.UI.Control` offers wrapper methods with the same names as the static methods of `Sys.UI.DomElement`: `addCssClass()`, `removeCssClass()`, and `toggleCssClass()`.

Another two interesting methods of `Control` are `raiseBubbleEvent()` and `onBubbleEvent()`. The `raiseBubbleEvent()` method receives as parameters a `sender` object and an `eventArgs` object, and the `onBubbleEvent()` method is called with these parameters for each parent control up in the hierarchy until one `onBubbleEvent()` returns `true` or we have reached the top of the hierarchy. This resembles very much the way a DOM event bubbles up the DOM hierarchy, except that we have the flexibility of passing custom `eventArgs` objects containing different information.

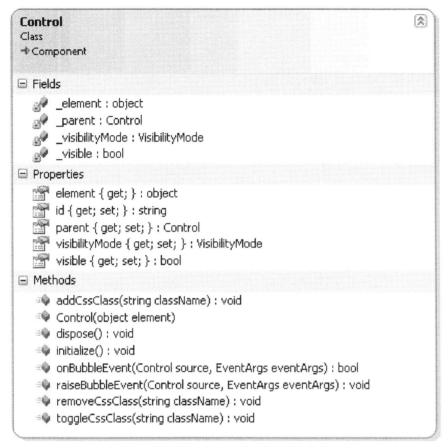

Figure 6-5. Class diagram for Sys.UI.Control

After having gone through all that's related to components and getting a grasp on client page life-cycle events, it's time to see how we can create our own components.

Quicksteps for Creating Custom Client Components

This section is intended to represent a general reference when creating our custom client components. It will represent a reference point when we analyze the custom components we create.

When developing a custom client component we have to keep in mind a few steps that can be as followed for guidance:

- Register the namespace for the component
- Declare the component's constructor
- Call the component's inherited `initializeBase()` method
- Declare the fields and properties
- Declare the component's prototype
- Declare an overridden `initialize()` method
- Call the initialize method of the base class using `callBaseMethod()`
- Initialize private fields, register event handlers
- Declare an overridden `dispose()` method
- Close and release any resources held
- Remove any handlers added during the initialize phase or during the component's life
- Call the `dispose()` method of the base class using `callBaseMethod()`
- Declare the getters and setters for the component's properties
- Declare the "private" and "public" methods
- Declare the events
- Register the new component

Summary

This short and admittedly very theoretical chapter laid the foundations for creating custom client components using the Microsoft AJAX Library. Chapter 7 will walk you through a practical example that demonstrates this theory into practice.

7
Case Study: Timer and EnhancedTextBox

In this chapter you will apply the theory you've learned so far in this book, while creating two client-side components: `Timer` and `EnhancedTextBox`. Building components represents the final challenge when working with the Microsoft AJAX Library.

The `Timer` component is one of the client components that didn't make it into ASP.NET AJAX 1.0. We will create it here, however, to help us create the component we're interested in: a behavior named `EnhancedTextBox`. This behavior extends the normal HTML input text control by implementing the word suggest/auto-complete feature based on the letters typed by the user inside the text box.

The Timer Component

The timer component is very useful because it can be used in a variety of scenarios that involve repetitive tasks. This component has a very simple logic: based on two properties named `interval` and `enabled`, the component fires a `tick` event informing the registered handlers of the elapsed period of time.

Figure 7-1 represents the class diagram for this component.

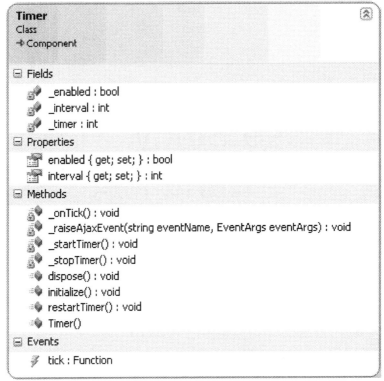

Figure 7-1. Class diagram for the Timer component

The timer component inherits from Sys.Component as it doesn't have a visual representation.

The EnhancedTextBox Behavior

The EnhancedTextBox behavior enriches the classic HTML input text with one of the most appreciated features brought by today's web applications: suggest and auto-complete. While the user is typing text inside the text box, it is auto-completed using a dictionary of known names. You can move back and forth between known names using the "up" and "down" arrow keys.

EnhancedTextBox is a behavior component thus inheriting from Sys.UI.Behavior as it is attached to a visual element but it does not modify it. You can see its list of members in the diagram in Figure 7-2.

Figure 7-2. Class diagram for EnhancedTextBox behavior

EnhancedTextBox makes use of a class named Dictionary, which stores the possible words for auto-completion, and has a method named getMatchingItems() that returns the matches that start with the prefix provided as parameter.

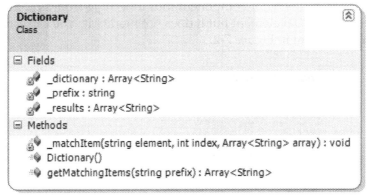

Figure 7-3. Diagram representing the Dictionary class

Creating Timer and EnhancedTextBox

We'll create and test the `Timer` and `EnhancedTextBox` in the following step-by-step exercise, and we'll discuss more details about them afterwards. We will also create a helper class named `Dictionary`, which stores the dictionary of known words used by `EnhancedTextBox` for word auto-completion, and performs keyword matching through a function named `getMatchingItems()`.

Figure 7-4 shows the demo page in action: after typing the letters "**Bo**" the text was auto-completed to the first match, "Bobby". When hitting the down arrow on the keyboard, the text was auto-completed to the next known name to start with "Bo," which according to our current dictionary is "**Bogdan**".

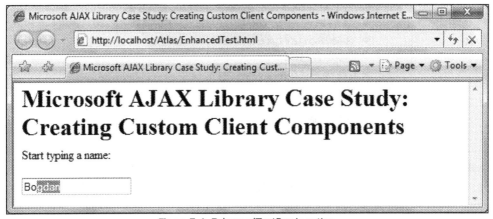

Figure 7-4. EnhancedTextBox in action

Time for Action—Creating Custom Client Components

1. Open the `http://localhost/Atlas/` project in Visual Web Developer.

2. Create a new **JScript File** in your `Scripts` folder named `Timer.js`, and type the following code in.

```
// Register the AjaxTutorial namespace
Type.registerNamespace("AjaxTutorial");

// Timer constructor
AjaxTutorial.Timer = function()
{
  // initialize base class
  AjaxTutorial.Timer.initializeBase(this);
  // set up class members
  this._interval = 1000;
  this._enabled = false;
  this._timer = null;
}

// Timer members
AjaxTutorial.Timer.prototype =
{
  // initialize the timer
  initialize: function()
  {
    // initialize base class
    AjaxTutorial.Timer.callBaseMethod(this, "initialize");

    // start the timer if it's enabled
    if(this._enabled) this._startTimer();
  },

  // dispose of the timer
  dispose: function()
  {
    // make sure the timer is stopped
    this._stopTimer();

    // be sure to call base.dispose()
    AjaxTutorial.Timer.callBaseMethod(this, "dispose");
  },

  // interval getter
  get_interval: function()
  {
    return this._interval;
```

```
  },

  // interval setter
  set_interval: function(value)
  {
    if (this._interval !== value) {
      this._interval = value;
      this.raisePropertyChanged("interval");
      // do not restart the timer during the creation phase
      if (!this.get_isUpdating() && this._timer !== null)
        this._restartTimer();
    }
  },
  // enabled getter
  get_enabled: function()
  {
    return this._enabled;
  },

  // enabled setter
  set_enabled: function(value)
  {
    if (value !== this._enabled) {
      this._enabled = value;
      this.raisePropertyChanged("enabled");
      // do not enable the timer during the creation phase
      if (!this.get_isUpdating())
        if(this._enabled)
          this._startTimer();
        else
          this._stopTimer();
    }
  },

  // tick event
  add_tick: function(handler)
  {
    this.get_events().addHandler("tick", handler);
  },

  remove_tick: function(handler)
  {
    this.get_events().removeHandler("tick", handler);
  },

  // callback function for the tick event
  _onTick: function()
```

```
  {
    this._raiseAjaxEvent("tick");
  },

  // start or restart the timer
  restartTimer: function()
  {
    this._stopTimer();
    this._startTimer();
  },

  // start the timer
  _startTimer: function()
  {
    // save timer cookie
    this._timer = window.setInterval(Function.createDelegate(this,
this._onTick), this._interval);
  },

  // stop the timer
  _stopTimer: function()
  {
    // prevent multiple calls
    if(this._timer) {
      window.clearInterval(this._timer);
      this._timer = null;
    }
  },

  // raise an AJAX event
  _raiseAjaxEvent: function(eventName, eventArgs)
  {
    // obtain the event handler for the specified event name
    var handler = this.get_events().getHandler(eventName);

    // continue only if there is at least one handler for the event
    if (handler) {
      // if no event args have been supplied, create empty EventArgs
      if (!eventArgs) eventArgs = Sys.EventArgs.Empty;
      // call the event handlers
      handler(this, eventArgs);
    }
  }
}

// register the Timer class
AjaxTutorial.Timer.registerClass("AjaxTutorial.Timer",
Sys.Component);
```

3. Create a new **JScript File** in your `Scripts` folder named `EnhancedTextBox.js`, and type the following code in.

```
// Register our namespaces
Type.registerNamespace("AjaxTutorial");

// EnhancedTextBox constructor
AjaxTutorial.EnhancedTextBox = function(element)
{
  // initialize base class
  AjaxTutorial.EnhancedTextBox.initializeBase(this, [element]);

  // set up the initial behavior state
  this._onKeyUpHandler = null;
  this._onKeyPressHandler = null;
  this._onFocusHandler = null;
  this._dictionary = null;
  this._index = 0;
  this._prefix = "";
  this._timer = null;
  this._interval = 2000;
  this._onTickHandler = null;
  this._wasKeyUpDownPressed = false;
  this._wasAnyKeyPressed = false;
}

// EnhancedTextBox members
AjaxTutorial.EnhancedTextBox.prototype =
{
  // initialize
  initialize: function()
  {
    // initialize base class
    AjaxTutorial.EnhancedTextBox.callBaseMethod(this, "initialize");

    // create the dictionary
    this._dictionary = new AjaxTutorial.Dictionary();

    // KeyUp
    this._onKeyUpHandler = Function.createDelegate(this, this._
onKeyUp);
    $addHandler(this.get_element(), "keyup", this._onKeyUpHandler);

    // KeyPress
    this._onKeyPressHandler = Function.createDelegate(this, this._
onKeyPress);
    $addHandler(this.get_element(), "keypress", this._
onKeyPressHandler);
        // Focus
```

```
       this._onFocusHandler = Function.createDelegate(this, this._
onFocus);
       $addHandler(this.get_element(), "focus", this._onFocusHandler);

       // Tick
       this._onTickHandler = Function.createDelegate (this, this._
onTick);

       this._timer = $create(AjaxTutorial.Timer, {interval:this._
interval, enabled:true}, {tick:this._onTickHandler}, null, null);

       // focus on the DOM element
       this.get_element().focus();
    },
    // dispose
    dispose: function()
    {
       // remove the event handlers
       $removeHandler(this.get_element(), "keyup", this._
onKeyUpHandler);
       $removeHandler(this.get_element(), "keypress", this._
onKeyPressHandler);
       $removeHandler(this.get_element(), "focus", this._
onFocusHandler);

       // make sure the timer is not enabled
       if(this._timer) {
          this._timer.remove_tick(this._onTickHandler);
       }

       // call dispose of the base calss
       AjaxTutorial.EnhancedTextBox.callBaseMethod(this, "dispose");
    },

    // interval getter
    get_interval: function()
    {
       return this._interval;
    },

    // interval setter
    set_interval: function(value)
    {
       if(value != this._interval) {
          this._interval = value;
          this.raisePropertyChanged("interval");
          if(this._timer)
             this._timer.set_interval(this._interval);
       }
```

```
  },

  // onFocus handler
  _onFocus: function (e)
  {
    this._index = 0;
  },

  // onTick handler
  _onTick: function()
  {
    if(this._wasAnyKeyPressed && !this._wasKeyUpDownPressed) {
      this._index = -1;
      this._prefix = this.get_element().value;
      this._getNextMatchingItem();
      this._wasAnyKeyPressed = false;
    }
  },


  // onKeyPress handler
  _onKeyPress: function(e)
  {
    this._wasAnyKeyPressed = true;
  },

  // onKeyUp handler
  _onKeyUp: function(e)
  {
    this._wasKeyUpDownPressed = false;

    if (e.keyCode == Sys.UI.Key.down) {
      this._wasKeyUpDownPressed = true;
      this._getNextMatchingItem();
      return;
    }

    if (e.keyCode == Sys.UI.Key.up) {
      this._wasKeyUpDownPressed = true;
      this._getPreviousMatchingItem();
      return;
    }

    // fix for IE where backspace and delete keypress is not raised
    if (e.keyCode == Sys.UI.Key.backspace ||
        e.keyCode == Sys.UI.Key.del)
      this._wasAnyKeyPressed = true;
  },
```

```
// Type ahead
_selectRange : function(start,length)
{
  var element = this.get_element();
  // IE
  if (element.createTextRange)
  {
    var range = element.createTextRange();
    range.moveStart("character", start);
    range.moveEnd("character", length - range.text.length);
    range.select();
  }
  // FF
  else if (element.setSelectionRange)
  {
    element.setSelectionRange(start, length);
  }

  element.focus();
},

// Select the next matching item in the textbox
_getNextMatchingItem: function()
{
  var results = this._dictionary.getMatchingItems(this._prefix);

  if(results.length > 0)
  {
    if (this._index < results.length - 1) this._index++;
    var matchingItem = results[this._index];

    this.get_element().value = matchingItem;
    this._selectRange(this._prefix.length, matchingItem.length);
  }
},

// Select the previous matching item in the textbox
_getPreviousMatchingItem: function()
{
  var results = this._dictionary.getMatchingItems(this._prefix);

  if(results.length > 0)
  {
    if(this._index > 0) this._index--;
    var matchingItem = results[this._index];
```

```
            this.get_element().value = matchingItem;
            this._selectRange(this._prefix.length, matchingItem.length);
        }
    }
}

// register the EnhancedTextBox class
AjaxTutorial.EnhancedTextBox.registerClass(
    "AjaxTutorial.EnhancedTextBox", Sys.UI.Control);
```

4. Create a new **JScript File** in your `Scripts` folder named `Dictionary.js`, and type the following code in.

```
// JScript File
Type.registerNamespace("AjaxTutorial");

// Dictionary constructor
AjaxTutorial.Dictionary = function()
{
    this._prefix = "";
    this._results = [];
    this._dictionary = [
"Aaron", "Abdullah", "Abel", "Abraham", "Abram","Adam",
"Adan","Addison","Aden","Adin","Aditya","Adolfo","Adonis",
"Adrian","Adriel","Adrien","Aedan","Agustin","Ahmad","Ahmed",
"Aidan","Aiden","Ajax","Alan","Albert","Alberto","Alden",
"Aldo","Alec","Alejandro","Alessandro","Alex","Alexander",
"Alexandro","Alexis","Alexzander","Alfonso","Alfred",
"Alfredo","Ali","Alijah","Allan","Allen","Alonso","Alonzo",
"Alvaro","Alvin","Amare","Amari","Amarion","Amir","Anderson",
"Andre","Andreas","Andres","Andrew","Andy","Angel","Angelo",
"Anthony","Antoine","Anton","Antonio","Antony","Antwan","Ari",
"Ariel","Arjun","Armando","Armani","Arnav","Aron",
"Arthur","Arturo","Aryan","Asa","Asher","Ashton","Atticus",
"August","Augustus","Austen","Austin","Avery","Axel","Aydan",
"Ayden","Aydin","Baby","Bailey","Barrett","Beau","Ben",
"Benjamin","Bennett","Bernard","Bernardo","Billy","Blaine",
"Blaise","Blake","Blaze","Bobby","Bogdan","Brad","Braden",
"Bradley","Brady","Bradyn","Braeden","Braedon","Braiden",
"Branden","Brandon","Branson","Braulio","Braxton","Brayan",
"Brayden","Braydon","Braylen","Braylon","Brendan","Brenden",
"Brendon","Brennan","Brennen","Brent","Brenton","Brett","Brian",
"Brice","Bridger","Brock","Broderick","Brodie","Brody",
"Bronson","Brooks","Bruce","Bruno","Bryan","Bryant","Bryce",
"Brycen","Bryson","Byron","Cade","Caden","Cael","Caiden",
"Cale","Caleb","Calvin","Camden","Cameron","Campbell","Camren",
```

"Camron","Camryn","Cannon","Carl","Carlo","Carlos","Carlton",
"Carmelo","Carmine","Carson","Carter","Casey","Cash","Cason",
"Cayden","Cedric","Cesar","Chad","Chaim","Chance","Chandler",
"Charles","Charlie","Chase","Chaz","Chris","Christian",
"Christopher","Clarence","Clark","Clay","Clayton","Clifford",
"Clinton","Coby","Cody","Cohen","Colby","Cole","Coleman",
"Colin","Collin","Colt","Colten","Colton","Conner","Connor",
"Conor","Conrad","Cooper","Corbin","Corey","Cornelius",
"Cortez","Cory","Craig","Cristian","Cristobal","Cristofer",
"Cristopher","Cruz","Cullen","Curtis","Cyrus","Dakota","Dale",
"Dallas","Dallin","Dalton","Damari","Damarion","Damian",
"Damien","Damion","Damon","Dandre","Dane","Dangelo","Daniel",
"Danny","Dante","Daquan","Darian","Darien","Darin","Dario",
"Darion","Darius","Darnell","Darrell","Darren","Darrius",
"Darryl","Darwin","Daryl","Dashawn","Davian","David","Davin",
"Davion","Davis","Davon","Dawson","Dayton","Deacon","Dean",
"Deandre","Deangelo","Declan","Demarcus","Demarion",
"Demetrius","Dennis","Denzel","Deon","Derek","Derick",
"Derrick","Deshaun","Deshawn","Desmond","Destin","Devan",
"Deven","Devin","Devon","Devonte","Devyn","Dexter","Diego",
"Dillan","Dillon","Dimitri","Dion","Domenic","Dominic",
"Dominick","Dominik","Dominique","Donald","Donavan","Donovan",
"Donte","Dorian","Douglas","Drake","Draven","Drew","Duncan",
"Dustin","Dwayne","Dylan","Dylon","Ean","Earl","Easton",
"Eddie","Edgar","Edison","Eduardo","Edward","Edwin",
"Efrain", "Efren","Eli","Elian", "Elias","Elijah",
"Eliseo","Elisha","Elliot","Elliott",
"Ellis","Elmer","Elvin","Elvis","Emanuel","Emerson",
"Emiliano","Emilio","Emmanuel","Emmett","Enrique","Enzo",
"Eric","Erick","Erik","Ernest","Ernesto","Esteban","Estevan",
"Ethan","Ethen","Eugene","Evan","Everett","Ezekiel",
"Ezequiel","Ezra","Fabian","Felipe","Felix","Fernando",
"Fidel","Finn","Finnegan","Fisher","Francis","Francisco",
"Franco","Frank","Frankie","Franklin","Freddy","Frederick",
"Fredrick","Fredy","Gabriel","Gael","Gage","Gaige","Gannon",
"Garret","Garrett","Garrison","Gary","Gauge","Gaven","Gavin",
"Gavyn","Geoffrey","George","Gerald","Gerardo","German",
"Giancarlo","Gianni","Gideon","Gilbert","Gilberto","Giovani",
"Giovanni","Giovanny","Glenn","Gonzalo","Gordon","Grady",
"Graham","Grant","Grayson","Gregory","Greyson","Griffin",
"Guadalupe","Guillermo","Gunnar","Gunner","Gustavo","Haden",
"Hamza","Harley","Harold","Harrison","Harry","Hassan",
"Hayden","Heath","Hector","Henry","Holden","Houston",
"Howard","Hudson","Hugh","Hugo","Humberto","Hunter","Ian",

```
"Ibrahim","Ignacio","Immanuel","Irvin","Irving","Isaac",
"Isaak","Isai","Isaiah","Isaias","Isiah","Ismael","Israel",
"Issac","Ivan","Izaiah","Jabari","Jace","Jack","Jackson",
"Jacoby","Jaden","Jadon","Jadyn","Jaeden","Jaheim","Jaiden",
"Jaidyn","Jaime","Jair","Jairo","Jake","Jacob","Jakob",
"Jalen","Jamal","Jamar","Jamari","Jamarion","Jamel","James",
"Jameson","Jamie","Jamir","Jamison","Jan","Jaquan","Jared",
"Jaren","Jaron","Jarrett","Jarvis","Jase","Jason","Jasper",
"Javier","Javion","Javon","Jax","Jaxon","Jaxson","Jay",
"Jayce","Jayden","Jaydin","Jaydon","Jaylan","Jaylen",
"Jaylin","Jaylon","Jayson","Jean","Jefferson","Jeffery",
"Jeffrey","Jeramiah","Jeremiah","Jeremy","Jermaine","Jerome",
"Jerry","Jesse","Jessie","Jesus","Jett","Jimmy","Joaquin",
"Joe","Joel","Joey","Johan","John","Johnathan","Johnathon",
"Johnny","Johnpaul","Jon","Jonah","Jonas","Jonathan",
"Jonathon","Jordan","Jorden","Jordon","Jordy","Jordyn",
"Jorge","Jose","Josef","Joseph","Josh","Joshua","Josiah",
"Josue","Jovan","Jovani","Jovanni","Jovanny","Jovany",
"Juan","Judah","Jude","Julian","Julien","Julio","Julius",
"Junior","Justice","Justin","Justus","Kade","Kaden","Kadin",
"Kadyn","Kaeden","Kai","Kaiden","Kale","Kaleb","Kamari",
"Kamden","Kameron","Kamren","Kamron","Kane","Kanye","Kareem",
"Karl","Karson","Karter","Kasey","Kason","Kayden","Keagan",
"Keanu","Keaton","Keegan","Keenan","Keith","Kellen","Kelton",
"Kelvin","Kendall","Kendrick","Kennedy","Kenneth","Kenny",
"Kenyon","Keon","Keshawn","Keven","Kevin","Keyon","Keyshawn",
"Khalil","Kian","Kieran","Kobe","Kody","Kolby","Kole",
"Kolton","Konner","Konnor","Korbin","Korey","Kristian",
"Kristopher","Kurt","Kyan","Kylan","Kyle","Kyler","Lamar",
"Lance","Landen","Landon","Landyn","Lane","Larry","Lawrence",
"Lawson","Layne","Layton","Leandro","Lee","Leland","Leo",
"Leon","Leonard","Leonardo","Leonel","Leroy","Levi","Lewis",
"Liam","Lincoln","Logan","London","Lorenzo","Louis","Luca",
"Lucas","Lucian","Luciano","Luis","Luka","Lukas","Luke",
"Maddox","Makai","Makhi","Malachi","Malakai","Malaki",
"Malcolm","Malik","Manuel","Marc","Marcel","Marcelo","Marco",
"Marcos","Marcus","Mariano","Mario","Mark","Markell",
"Markus","Marlon","Marques","Marquez","Marquis","Marquise",
"Marshall","Martin","Marvin","Mason","Mateo","Mathew",
"Mathias","Matias","Matteo","Matthew","Matthias","Maurice",
"Mauricio","Maverick","Max","Maxim","Maximilian",
"Maximillian","Maximo","Maximus","Maxwell","Mekhi","Melvin",
"Messiah","Micah","Michael","Micheal","Miguel","Mike",
"Mikel","Miles","Milo","Milton","Misael","Mitchell",
```

```
"Mohamed","Mohammad","Mohammed","Moises","Morgan","Moses",
"Moshe","Muhammad","Myles","Nash","Nasir","Nathan",
"Nathanael","Nathanial","Nathaniel","Nathen","Nehemiah",
"Neil","Nelson","Nestor","Nicholas","Nick","Nickolas",
"Nico","Nicolas","Nigel","Nikhil","Nikolas","Noah","Noe",
"Noel","Nolan","Norman","Octavio","Oliver","Omar","Omari",
"Omarion","Orion","Orlando","Oscar","Osvaldo","Oswaldo",
"Owen","Pablo","Parker","Patrick","Paul","Paxton","Payton",
"Pedro","Perry","Peter","Peyton","Philip","Phillip",
"Phoenix","Pierce","Porter","Pranav","Preston","Prince",
"Quentin","Quincy","Quinn","Quinten","Quintin","Quinton",
"Rafael","Ralph","Ramiro","Ramon","Randall","Randy",
"Raphael","Rashad","Raul","Ray","Raymond","Reagan","Reece",
"Reed","Reese","Reginald","Reid","Reilly","Remington","Rene",
"Reuben","Rex","Rey","Reynaldo","Rhett","Rhys","Ricardo",
"Richard","Ricky","Rigoberto","Riley","Rishi","River",
"Robert","Roberto","Rocco","Rocky","Roderick","Rodney",
"Rodolfo","Rodrigo","Rogelio","Roger","Rohan","Roland",
"Rolando","Roman","Romeo","Ronald","Ronaldo","Ronan",
"Ronnie","Rory","Ross","Rowan","Roy","Royce","Ruben",
"Rudy","Russell","Ryan","Ryder","Ryker","Rylan","Ryland",
"Rylee","Sage","Salvador","Salvatore","Sam","Samir",
"Sammy","Samuel","Santiago","Santino","Santos","Saul",
"Savion","Sawyer","Scott","Seamus","Sean","Sebastian",
"Semaj","Sergio","Seth","Shamar","Shane","Shannon","Shaun",
"Shawn","Shayne","Shea","Sheldon","Sidney","Silas","Simeon",
"Simon","Sincere","Skylar","Skyler","Solomon","Sonny",
"Soren","Spencer","Stanley","Stefan","Stephan","Stephen",
"Sterling","Steve","Steven","Stone","Sullivan","Talan",
"Talon","Tanner","Tariq","Tate","Taylor","Tayshaun","Teagan",
"Terrance","Terrell","Terrence","Terry","Thaddeus",
"Theodore","Thomas","Timothy","Titus","Tobias","Toby",
"Todd","Tomas","Tommy","Tony","Trace","Travis","Travon",
"Trent","Trenton","Trevon","Trevor","Trey","Tristan",
"Tristen","Tristian","Tristin","Triston","Troy","Tucker",
"Ty","Tye","Tyler","Tyree","Tyrell","Tyrese","Tyrone",
"Tyshawn","Tyson","Ulises","Ulysses","Uriel","Valentin",
"Van","Vance","Vaughn","Vicente","Victor","Vincent",
"Vincenzo","Wade","Walker","Walter","Warren","Waylon",
"Wayne","Wesley","Weston","Will","William","Willie","Wilson",
"Winston","Wyatt","Xander","Xavier","Xzavier","Yahir",
"Yair","Yosef","Yusuf","Zachariah","Zachary","Zachery",
"Zack","Zackary","Zackery","Zain","Zaire","Zakary","Zander",
"Zane","Zavier","Zechariah","Zion" ];
```

```
    }

    // Dictionary members
    AjaxTutorial.Dictionary.prototype =
    {
      // filter each item
      _matchItem : function( element, index, array)
      {
        if (element.toLowerCase().indexOf(this._prefix.toLowerCase())
    == 0) Array.add(this._results, element);
      },

      // get the matching items for a prefix
      getMatchingItems: function(prefix)
      {
        // return the cached items for the same prefix
        if(this._prefix.toLowerCase() == prefix.toLowerCase())
        {
          return Array.clone(this._results);
        }

        // fetch the new items according to the new prefix
        this._prefix = prefix.toString();
        this._results = [];

        Array.forEach(this._dictionary,
                  Function.createDelegate(this,this._matchItem));
        return Array.clone(this._results);
      }
    };

    // register the Dictionary class
    AjaxTutorial.Dictionary.registerClass("AjaxTutorial.Dictionary");
```

5. Add an **HTML Page** named `EnhancedTest.html`, and update its code as shown in the following code snippet:

```
<!DOCTYPE html PUBLIC "-//W3C//DTD XHTML 1.0 Transitional//EN"
"http://www.w3.org/TR/xhtml1/DTD/xhtml1-transitional.dtd">
<html xmlns="http://www.w3.org/1999/xhtml" >
<head>
  <title>Microsoft AJAX Library Case Study: Creating Custom Client
Components</title>
  <script type="text/javascript" src="Scripts/MicrosoftAjax.js">
  </script>
  <script type="text/javascript" src="Scripts/Timer.js">
  </script>
  <script type="text/javascript" src="Scripts/Dictionary.js">
```

```
    </script>
    <script type="text/javascript" src="Scripts/EnhancedTextBox.js">
    </script>
</head>
<body>
    <h1>Microsoft AJAX Library Case Study: Creating Custom Client
Components</h1>

    <p>Start typing a name:</p>
    <form>
      <input type="text" id="name" />
    </form>

    <script type="text/javascript">
      // add handler for the application init event
      Sys.Application.add_init(pageInit);

      // page init event handler
      function pageInit()
      {
        // create the EnhancedTextBox behavior for the name DOM element
        $create(AjaxTutorial.EnhancedTextBox, {interval:1000}, {},
                null, $get("name"));
      }
    </script>
</body>
</html>
```

6. Execute `EnhancedTest.html`, and type "**Aj**". The text should be
    auto-completed to "Ajax," as shown in Figure 7-5. You can also test the script
    at `http://www.cristiandarie.ro/asp-ajax/EnhancedTest.html`.

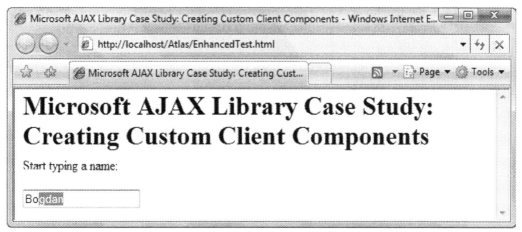

Figure 7-5. Testing EnhancedTextBox

What Just Happened?

The goal of this example was to show how we can create custom client components. We will start the analysis with our custom `Timer` component. Its creation started by registering the `AjaxTutorial` namespace:

```
// Register the AjaxTutorial namespace
Type.registerNamespace("AjaxTutorial");
```

We continued by declaring the component's constructor. Because the `Timer` control derives from `Sys.Component`, the constructor first calls `initializeBase()`, which ensures the base class is created properly:

```
// Timer constructor
AjaxTutorial.Timer = function()
{
    // initialize base class
    AjaxTutorial.Timer.initializeBase(this);
```

Here is where we also define the fields, properties, and handlers for our component:

```
    // set up class members
    this._interval = 1000;
    this._enabled = false;
    this._timer = null;
}
```

The `_interval` and `_enabled` fields store the values for their corresponding properties. `interval` represents the interval of time between two consecutive `tick` events. `enabled` is a Boolean value indicating whether the timer is active or not.

The `tick` event exposed by the timer can be seen as the component's heartbeat. To build the timer we use JavaScript's `setInterval()` and `clearInterval()` methods. The `_timer` private field contains the timeout ID returned by `setInterval()`.

After creating the class constructor, we continued by building its members, starting by overriding the `initialize()` method. This function itself starts by calling the `initialize()` method of the base class, `Sys.Component`, to ensure that is also properly initialized. Also in `initialize()` we call `startTimer()` to start the countdown to the next `tick` event, if the timer is enabled:

```
// Timer members
AjaxTutorial.Timer.prototype =
{
    // initialize the timer
    initialize: function()
    {
```

```
    // initialize base class
    AjaxTutorial.Timer.callBaseMethod(this, "initialize");

    // start the timer if it's enabled
    if(this._enabled) this._startTimer();
},
```

Next, we make sure that the component can be gracefully disposed, by overriding the dispose() method. Here, we only stop the timer and call the dispose() method of the base class in order to let it do its own cleanup.

```
// dispose of the timer
dispose: function()
{
  // make sure the timer is stopped
  this._stopTimer();

  // be sure to call base.dispose()
  AjaxTutorial.Timer.callBaseMethod(this, "dispose");
},
```

Then we declared the setter and getter methods for our properties, interval and enabled. The getters for both properties are quite trivial as they simply return the property values:

```
// interval getter
get_interval: function()
{
  return this._interval;
},

// enabled getter
get_enabled: function()
{
  return this._enabled;
},
```

On the other side, the setters are quite interesting as they implement some custom logic. When setting a new interval for the timer, we raise the inherited propertyChanged event (from Sys.Component) for our interval property by calling the inherited raisePropertyChanged() method (also from Sys.Component). A change of the interval implies restarting the timer, and this can only happen when the component is not during the first phase of the component's creation, when this parameter is passed to the $create() method.

```
// interval setter
set_interval: function(value)
{
  if (this._interval !== value) {
    this._interval = value;
    this.raisePropertyChanged("interval");
    // do not restart the timer during the creation phase
    if (!this.get_isUpdating() && this._timer !== null)
      this._restartTimer();
  }
},
```

The `enabled` property has an equally interesting setter method. It is very similar in terms of functionality to `set_interval()` as it first raises the `propertyChanged` event and then starts or stops the timer if the component is not in its first phrase of creation.

```
// enabled setter
set_enabled: function(value)
{
  if (value !== this._enabled) {
    this._enabled = value;
    this.raisePropertyChanged("enabled");
    // do not enable the timer during the creation phase
    if (!this.get_isUpdating())
      if(this._enabled)
        this._startTimer();
      else
        this._stopTimer();
  }
},
```

The `tick` event's implementation is quite straightforward—no surprises here. What's different from the previous examples is that we don't need the events property with its getter `get_events()` method, as `Sys.Component` has this feature built in.

```
// tick event
add_tick: function(handler)
{
  this.get_events().addHandler("tick", handler);
},

remove_tick: function(handler)
{
  this.get_events().removeHandler("tick", handler);
},
```

The core of the component is represented by the start and stop methods as they control whether the timer is raising events or not. Both of them are quite straightforward as they represent wrappers for JavaScript's `setInterval()` and `clearInterval()` methods.

```
// start the timer
_startTimer: function()
{
  // save timer cookie
  this._timer = window.setInterval(Function.createDelegate(this,
this._onTick), this._interval);
},

// stop the timer
_stopTimer: function()
{
  // prevent multiple calls
  if(this._timer) {
    window.clearInterval(this._timer);
    this._timer = null;
  }
},
```

The component exposes a single public method that allows the timer to be restarted. This method simply calls `_stopTimer()` and `_startTimer()` in order to do its job:

```
// start or restart the timer
restartTimer: function()
{
  this._stopTimer();
  this._startTimer();
},
```

When the timer "ticks", the `_onTick()` function executes, which uses a helper function named `_raiseAjaxEvent()` to raise the `tick` event by executing all its registered event handlers.

After the class implementation is complete, we register the component. With this last step we have successfully created our first custom client component:

```
AjaxTutorial.Timer.registerClass("AjaxTutorial.Timer", Sys.Component);
```

Let's now have a look at `EnhancedTextBox`. When creating this class we started, as usually, by registering its namespace, and creating its constructor. We end up registering the namespace multiple times, to make sure that it exists when we need it for our class declaration without relying on other scripts to register the namespace.

As the behavior has an associated DOM element, we need to pass it to our constructor. In turn the behavior passes it to the base class (`Sys.UI.Behavior`) when calling the `initializeBase()` method, which will add it to the DOM element's list of behaviors.

```
// EnhancedTextBox constructor
AjaxTutorial.EnhancedTextBox = function(element)
{
    // initialize base class
    AjaxTutorial.EnhancedTextBox.initializeBase(this, [element]);
```

Things become more interesting when we meet the fields and properties of the behavior, which hold the component's state. Most of them have self-descriptive names:

```
    // set up the initial behavior state
    this._onKeyUpHandler = null;
    this._onKeyPressHandler = null;
    this._onFocusHandler = null;
    this._dictionary = null;
    this._index = 0;
    this._prefix = "";
    this._timer = null;
    this._interval = 2000;
    this._onTickHandler = null;
    this._wasKeyUpDownPressed = false;
    this._wasAnyKeyPressed = false;
}
```

Things are getting even more interesting as we move on. The overridden `initialize()` method has a bit more logic than simply calling the `initialize()` method of the base class, `Sys.UI.Behavior`. It also creates a new `Dictionary` object, and it registers the `keyup`, `keypress`, and `focus` events of the DOM element associated to the behavior. The `get_element()` method of `Sys.UI.Behavior` is used in the process to retrieve the DOM element associated to the component.

```
    // initialize
    initialize: function()
    {
        // initialize base class
        AjaxTutorial.EnhancedTextBox.callBaseMethod(this, "initialize");

        // create the dictionary
        this._dictionary = new AjaxTutorial.Dictionary();

        // KeyUp
        this._onKeyUpHandler = Function.createDelegate(this, this._onKeyUp);
        $addHandler(this.get_element(), "keyup", this._onKeyUpHandler);
```

```
    // KeyPress
    this._onKeyPressHandler = Function.createDelegate(this, this._
onKeyPress);
    $addHandler(this.get_element(), "keypress", this._onKeyPressHandler);

    // Focus
    this._onFocusHandler = Function.createDelegate(this, this._onFocus);
    $addHandler(this.get_element(), "focus", this._onFocusHandler);
```

Also in `initialize()` we create the timer component, and we set the focus on our element by using the DOM element's `focus()` method:

```
    // Tick
    this._onTickHandler = Function.createDelegate (this, this._onTick);
    this._timer = $create(AjaxTutorial.Timer, {interval:this._
interval, enabled:true}, {tick:this._onTickHandler}, null, null);

    // focus on the DOM element
    this.get_element().focus();
},
```

At the other side of the component's page life cycle we have the `dispose()` method. As we had more work in the `initialize()` method, it is normal to have almost the same amount here. Following the recommendation, we release all the resources and handlers we declared during initialization:

```
    // dispose
    dispose: function()
    {
      // remove the event handlers
      $removeHandler(this.get_element(), "keyup", this._onKeyUpHandler);
      $removeHandler(this.get_element(), "keypress", this._
onKeyPressHandler);
      $removeHandler(this.get_element(), "focus", this._onFocusHandler);

      // make sure the timer is not enabled
      if(this._timer) {
        this._timer.remove_tick(this._onTickHandler);
      }
```

As in any `dispose()` method, the final step consists of calling the base class's `dispose()` method. We don't need to worry about the timer component's cleanup as it has its own `dispose()` method, which is called by `Sys.Application` because it is registered as a disposable object:

```
    // call dispose of the base calss
    AjaxTutorial.EnhancedTextBox.callBaseMethod(this, "dispose");
},
```

We move on to declaring the getter and setter methods for the `interval` property. As was the case for the timer component, the getter method simply returns the internally stored value, and the setter method sets the new value and raises the `propertyChanged` event. It's worth noting that the setter method doesn't do anything if the value you're trying to set is identical to the one that is already stored by the component.

The `_onTick()` event handler verifies if any key different than the up and down arrow keys have been pressed, in which case the current word is auto-completed using the `_getNextMatchingItem()` function:

```
_onTick: function()
{
  if(this._wasAnyKeyPressed && !this._wasKeyUpDownPressed) {
    this._index = -1;
    this._prefix = this.get_element().value;
    this._getNextMatchingItem();
    this._wasAnyKeyPressed = false;
  }
},
```

The `_onKeyPress()` and `_onKeyUp()` functions, and their supporting functions, implement the mechanics of type-ahead auto-completion. As their functionality isn't overly complex and only relies on basic JavaScript functionality, we'll leave analyzing them to you as an exercise.

Using the Components

We have chosen a simple example in order to show how we can create components, register to their events, and see the order in which their events are raised. The custom components are included in the page by referencing their JavaScript source files:

```
<head>
  <title>Microsoft AJAX Library Case Study: Creating Custom Client
Components</title>
  <script type="text/javascript" src="Scripts/MicrosoftAjax.js">
  </script>
  <script type="text/javascript" src="Scripts/Timer.js">
  </script>
  <script type="text/javascript" src="Scripts/Dictionary.js">
  </script>
  <script type="text/javascript" src="Scripts/EnhancedTextBox.js">
  </script>
</head>
```

The user interface has only one textbox that we will enhance using the
EnhancedTextBox behavior. The textbox is defined like this:

```
<form>
  <input type="text" id="name" />
</form>
```

We add the new behavior to this textbox during the init event of the application. In
order to do so, we first register an event handler for Sys.Application's init event:

```
<script type="text/javascript">
  // add handler for the application init event
  Sys.Application.add_init(pageInit);
```

The pageInit() event handler simply uses $create(). As explained in Chapter 6,
$create() is just the short version of Sys.Component.create(). The first parameter
is the type of the behavior (AjaxTutorial.EnhancedTextBox), the second parameter
is used to pass initialization parameters to this class ({interval:1000}), the third
parameter is used to set up events (none in our case), the fourth parameter is used
to set referenced components (none in our case), and the last parameter is the DOM
element on which we're applying the behavior, which we get using $get("name"):

```
// page init event handler
function pageInit()
{
  // create the EnhancedTextBox behavior for the name DOM element
  $create(AjaxTutorial.EnhancedTextBox, {interval:1000}, {},
          null, $get("name"));
}
```

Summary

This chapter completed the tutorial of the world of the Microsoft AJAX Library
by having you create a simple component named Timer, and a behavior named
EnhancedTextBox. Understanding these mechanics will help you be a better
ASP.NET AJAX programmer, which is particularly important when using the
Microsoft AJAX Library in the context of more complex projects. Chapter 8 will
discuss tools and techniques for debugging your Microsoft AJAX code.

8

Debugging Tools and Techniques

Developing AJAX applications that involve complex client-side programming and communication with the server side raises the need for equally complex debugging tools and techniques.

Most of today's AJAX frameworks, including the Microsoft AJAX Library, offer built-in capabilities for debugging and tracing. In this chapter we will learn about the capabilities built in the Microsoft AJAX Library, and we'll also learn about third-party debugging and tracing tools.

More specifically, you will:

- Learn about the debugging and tracing capabilities of Microsoft AJAX Library
- Learn how to enable and use Internet Explorer's debugging capabilities
- Work with Web Development Helper, Developer Toolbar, and other Internet Explorer tools
- Work with Firefox plugins such as FireBug, Venkman JavaScript Debugger, and Web Developer
- Use Fiddler to analyze the traffic between the web server and your web client

AJAX Debugging Overview

Unfortunately, today's tools for client-side debugging and tracing aren't as evolved as their server-side counterparts. For example, things such as capturing ongoing communication traffic between the client and the server, or client-side debugging, aren't usually supported by today's IDEs (Integrated Development Environments) such as Microsoft Visual Studio 2005. The next version of Visual Studio (code-named Orcas at the time of writing) promises a lot of improvements in this area:

- Improved IntelliSense technology with support for JavaScript code, which provides coding hints based on specially-formatted comments in the code
- Breakpoints in inline JavaScript code

These are only the most important new coming features; there are others as well. For more information we suggest that you browse and keep an eye on Scott Guthrie's blog at `http://weblogs.asp.net/scottgu/`, the JScript blog at `http://blogs.msdn.com/jscript/`, Bertrand Le Roy's blog at `http://weblogs.asp.net/bleroy/`, and the other resources mentioned in Chapter 1.

Until this new edition of Visual Studio is released, we can rely on third-party tools that can do a very good job at helping us develop our AJAX applications. As you found out earlier, you'll meet a number of tools for Internet Explorer and Mozilla Firefox.

Debugging and Tracing with Microsoft AJAX Library

The common practices for debugging JavaScript code are:

- Putting alert messages throughout the code to get notified about the values of the variables
- Logging tracing messages in a `<div>` element

While the first option is straightforward, the second option offers a centralized place for storing different messages and could be considered more appropriate. Nevertheless both options can come in quite handy depending on the circumstances.

Microsoft AJAX Library offers the `Sys.Debug` object that has a series of methods that you can use for debugging and tracing. The diagram of this class is presented in Figure 8-1.

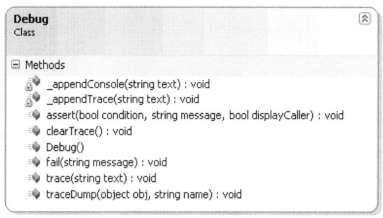

Figure 8-1. The Debug class

As we can easily see in the diagram, `Sys.Debug` offers the most common features that we can find also in other languages: `assert()`, `trace()`, `traceDump()`, `fail()`, and `clearTrace()`.

`assert()`, `trace()`, and `fail()` automatically send the messages to the debugging console of the browser. To see the messages in IE you need to have the Web Development Helper, and for Firefox you need the FireBug plugin. Both of these tools are presented later in this chapter. Internally `assert()` calls `fail()` if the expression evaluates to false. `fail()` simply logs the message passed in by assert to the debugging console.

`trace()` offers an interesting feature beside logging to the debugging console: it offers the possibility to log the trace message in a `<textarea>` element with the ID `TraceConsole`. If such an element is found, `trace()` will log this message in this element too. This feature was demonstrated in the exercises in Chapter 5.

The `clearTrace()` function simply clears the `<TraceConsole>` element, if found.

The `traceDump()` function traces all the information about an object including its properties. Internally this function uses the `trace()` function so that we can have the information logged in the browser's debugging console, and in the `<TraceConsole>` element (if it exists).

MicrosoftAjax.debug.js

You might have wondered why the Microsoft AJAX Library comes with both release and debug version of the JavaScript file. The major features of the debug version of the library files are:

- The script is nicely formatted
- The names of variables are not obfuscated
- The script contains code comments
- Some of the functions have the optional summary data that will be used by Visual Studio "Orcas" for code auto-completion
- The script outputs debugging-friendly information
- Parameters are validated

Once the development stage is finished, you can switch your application to the release version of the script (`MicrosoftAjax.js`), which is smaller and doesn't contain the debugging features presented above.

Perhaps the most interesting features of the debug version are the last two: debugging-friendly information and parameter validation.

Anonymous Functions vs. Pseudo-Named Functions

We will explain these two concepts by taking a look at how different functions are defined in the debug and release version of the library. The debug version of the library contains:

```
function Sys$_Debug$assert(condition, message, displayCaller) {
    ...
}

Sys._Debug.prototype = {
    assert: Sys$_Debug$assert,
    ...
}
```

and:

```
String.format = function String$format(format, args) {...}
```

In the release version of the library we have:

```
Sys._Debug.prototype = {
    assert: function(c, a, b) {
        ...
}
```

and:

```
String.format = function() {...}
```

In the release version, we have methods that are anonymous functions. This means that within a debugger stack trace the method name will read **JScript anonymous function** (as shown in Figure 8-2). This is not very useful for debugging purposes, is it?

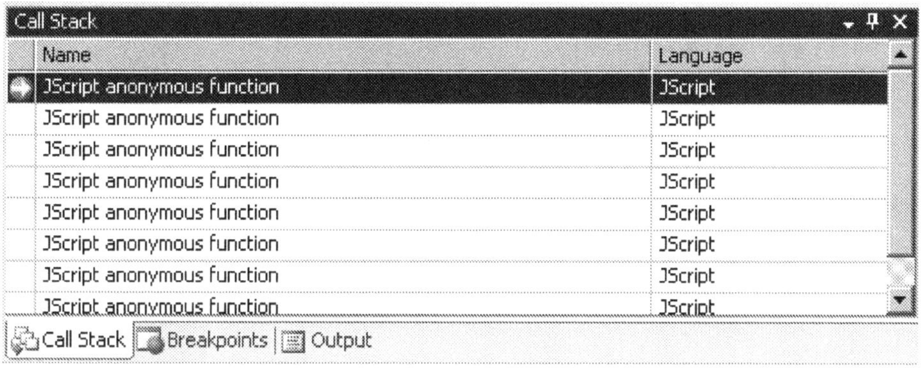

Figure 8-2. Call Stack showing anonymous functions

However, the debug version of the library uses the dollar-syntax to provide alias names for our functions: `String$format()` for `String.format()` and `Sys$Debug$assert()` for `Sys.Debug.assert()`. When using the debug version of the file, the stack trace would look like Figure 8-3.

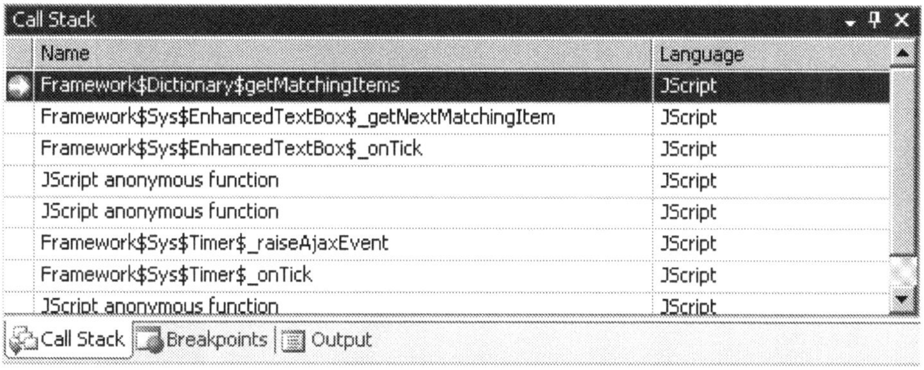

Figure 8-3. Call Stack showing named functions

We can still notice some anonymous functions as they are the result of creating callback or delegate functions. The example shows two different ways of coding:

- In the debug version, the function is declared outside the prototype and then referenced in the prototype declaration.
- In the release version, the declaration is done directly where the function is declared (outside or inside the prototype).

Parameters Validation

Another interesting feature that has not been documented in the Microsoft AJAX Library documentation is that of parameters validation.

Type safety is one of the typical problems when it comes to using JavaScript. Although the dynamic type features are really useful, sometimes we might really want to make sure that a parameter or object is of a certain type. To check the data type of an object, you can try converting the object to the desired type, or using the methods defined by `Type`. Fortunately the Microsoft AJAX Library has a function that does the dirty work for us: `Function._validateParams()`. The class diagram in Figure 8-4 shows the `_validateParameter()` and `_validateParams()` methods of the `Function` class.

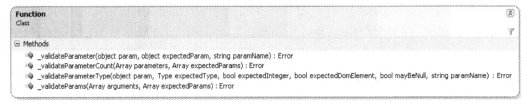

Figure 8-4. The Function class

The `Function._validateParams()` function, even if it is declared as private (by convention, using the leading `underscore`), can be used by our scripts as it is used throughout the debug version of the Microsoft AJAX Library. Here's an example of using this function:

```
function Sys$_Debug$fail(message) {
/// <param name="message" type="String" mayBeNull="true"></param>
    var e = Function._validateParams(arguments,
        [ {name: "message", type: String, mayBeNull: true} ]);
    if (e) throw e;
```

This shows how the parameter for the `fail()` function is validated as a `String`. We can also see the additional code comments inside the function, which are meant to be used by the IntelliSense feature in Visual Studio "Orcas" to check for the correctness of the parameter types.

While the first parameter of `_validateParams()` represents an array of parameters to be checked, the second parameter is an array of JSON objects describing the validation rules for the array of parameters. Each JSON object contains a validation rule for a parameter. The JSON object is a dictionary of keys and values. The list of keys that can be used is described in the table that follows.

Key	Description
name	The name of the parameter
type	The allowed type for this parameter (ex: `String`, `Array`, `Function`, `Sys.Component`, etc.)
mayBeNull	Boolean value indicating whether this parameter can be passed as `null` or not
domElement	Boolean value indicating whether this parameter is a DOM element or not
integer	Boolean value indicating whether this parameter should have an integer value or not
optional	Boolean value indicating whether this parameter is optional or not
parameterArray	Boolean value indicating whether this parameter should be an `Array` or not
elementType	The allowed type for each element of an array (type must be `Array`)
elementMayBeNull	Boolean value indicating whether an array element could have `null` or not (type must be `Array`)
elementDomElement	Boolean value indicating whether each element of an array is a DOM element (type must be `Array`)
elementInteger	Boolean value indicating whether each element of an array should have an integer value (type must be `Array`)

The function returns an error message if the parameters don't validate and the error is typically thrown like this:

```
if (e) throw e;
```

This exception could be caught and the appropriate measures taken programmatically. If the exception is not caught, the error will pop up in the debugging console of the browser.

Debugging in Internet Explorer

By default, JavaScript errors are ignored by Internet Explorer. In order to be able to debug in Internet Explorer, you need to:

1. Start Internet Explorer and go to **Tools | Internet Options | Advanced** and clear the **Disable script debugging (Internet Explorer)** and **Disable script debugging (Other)** checkboxes. If you want a pop-up window to be displayed for each error, you need to check the **Display a notification about every script error** checkbox, as shown in Figure 8-5.

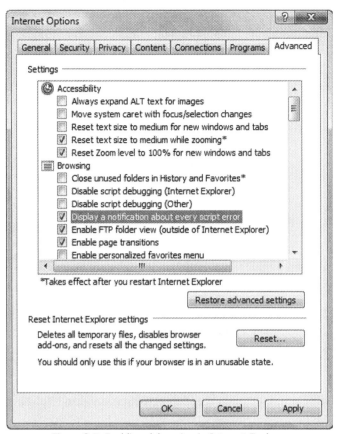

Figure 8-5. Enabling debugging in Internet Explorer

2. Open the solution you want to debug in Visual Studio.

3. Execute the project.

4. After the Internet Explorer window opens, go back to Visual Studio.

5. Open the script explorer by going to **Debug | Windows | Script Explorer**.
    The script explorer will list the available script files that can be debugged (see
    Figure 8-6).

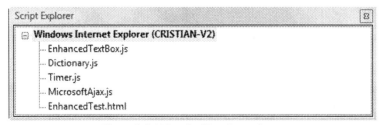

Figure 8-6. Using the IE script explorer

6. Double-clicking a file in the script explorer will open it in the editor. There you can place breakpoints inside JavaScript files, and the feature will work just as it does when debugging server-side code. Figure 8-7 shows Visual Studio while we were debugging the case study from Chapter 7.

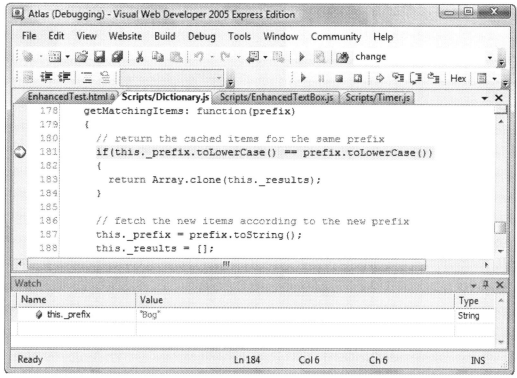

Figure 8-7. Debugging JavaScript code using Visual Studio

Alternatively, if you have Visual Studio, you can attach the debugger to an existing the Internet Explorer process by selecting **Debug | Attach to Process**, and then choosing the Internet Explorer process (**iexplore.exe**).

If Internet Explorer is configured for debugging and a script error is encounted in the browser while no debugger is attached, you're promoted to choose one of the available debuggers:

- Visual Studio and Visual Web Developer 2005
- Microsoft Script Debugger (downloadable from Microsoft's website)
- Microsoft Script Editor (ships with Microsoft Office)

For more about debugging web applications in Visual Studio, see these links:

- `http://msdn2.microsoft.com/en-us/library/sc65sadd(VS.80).aspx`

- `http://www.developerfusion.co.uk/show/5918/`

- `http://msdn2.microsoft.com/en-us/library/k2h50zzs(VS.80).aspx`

Web Development Helper

Web Development Helper is a great tool developed by Nikhil Kothari and should be used by every developer who needs the following development features:

- HTTP(S) traffic monitoring
- DOM inspector
- Script errors and immediate window

Web Development Helper can be downloaded from:
`http://www.nikhilk.net/Project.WebDevHelper.aspx`.

For more documentation about this tool, check the following links:

- `http://projects.nikhilk.net/WebDevHelper/Readme.pdf`

- `http://www.nikhilk.net/WebDevHelperDebuggingTools.aspx`

- `http://weblogs.asp.net/scottgu/archive/2006/11/13/Nikhil_2700_s`
  `-WebDevHelper-Utility-and-ASP.NET-AJAX-Support.aspx`

When it comes to debugging, the tool offers nice features such as showing the trace, catching run-time errors, and showing the full call stack (including script URL, line number, and line of code). The **Script Console** window allows entering custom script that is executed within the document context.

Internet Explorer Developer Toolbar

Microsoft offers the Internet Explorer Developer toolbar as an option for exploring web pages. It is especially useful for working with the page's DOM element, CSS styles, cookies, etc. It can be downloaded Microsoft's website..After it installs, you open it through **Tools | Toolbars | Explorer Bar | IE Developer Toolbar**.

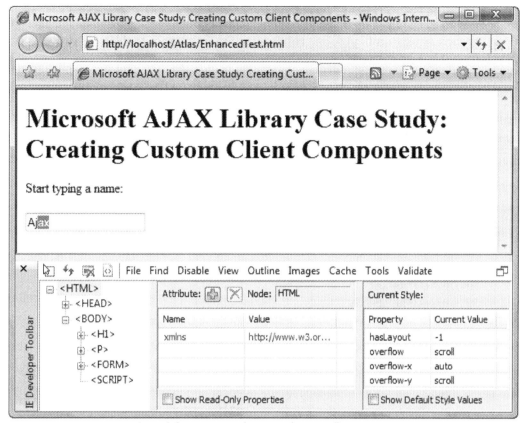

Figure 8-8. Internet Explorer Developer Toolbar in action

It is worth mentioning that it doesn't compete with Nikhil's tool, but it's more like a complementary tool as it doesn't offer JavaScript debugging capabilities or any of the other main features by Web Development Helper.

Other tools

There are other other tools that are worth mentioning and that you should keep an eye on:

- Damian Meher's **TraceJS** is a tool that logs every line of script executed in Internet Explorer. Find it at
  `http://damianblog.com/2006/11/23/tracejs/`.

- Julien Couvreur's **XMLHttpRequest debugging** bookmarklet. See `http://blog.monstuff.com/archives/000291.html` and `http://weblogs.asp.net/bleroy/archive/2006/05/15/446532.aspx`.

Debugging in Firefox

With the increasing number of users of Firefox, the number of tools used for web development has grown as well.

First of all, Firefox offers an **Error Console** accessible from the **Tools** menu, where all the JavaScript errors, warnings, and messages are logged. It also has a built-in script evaluator within the document context, and the DOM Inspector tool, which can be selected at installation time, so we can say that the features packaged into Firefox are quite advanced in comparison with the default features of Internet Explorer. Figure 8-9 shows the Error Console signalling a typo in our code.

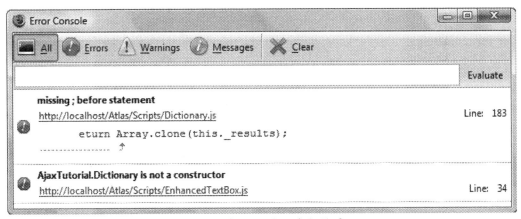

Figure 8-9. The Error Console in Firefox

Firebug

Firebug (`http://www.getfirebug.com/`) is a Firefox plugin that offers almost anything a web developer could want from a debugging tool:

- Debugging and profiling script
- Monitoring HTTP traffic
- Examining HTTP headers
- Inspecting and editing the DOM
- Inspecting and editing CSS
- Quick search for filtering errors and messages

Delivering such a powerful set of tools in one free product makes Firebug the perfect choice for debugging applications in Firefox. Figure 8-10 shows Firebug in action.

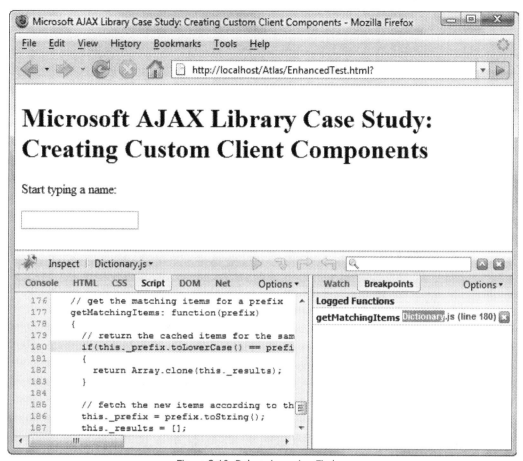

Figure 8-10. Debugging using Firebug

Venkman JavaScript Debugger

The Venkman JavaScript debugger (http://www.mozilla.org/projects/ venkman/) is a powerful tool for debugging in Mozilla-based browsers (Firefox, Netscape, and Seamonkey).

Like Firebug, Venkman JavaScript Debugger offers debugging and profiling, full call stack, breakpoints, local variables, and watches, all within an interface that is very similar to Visual Studio. Figure 8-11 shows this tool in action.

Figure 8-11. Debugging using Venkman JavaScript Debugger

You can find a few excellent online articles for using Venkman JavaScript Debugger:

- `http://www.svendtofte.com/code/learning_venkman/`
- `http://www.hacksrus.com/~ginda/venkman/`
- `http://www.webreference.com/programming/javascript/venkman/`

Web Developer

Similar to what Firebug and Internet Explorer Developer Toolbar offer, Web Developer plugin (`https://addons.mozilla.org/en-US/firefox/addon/60`), provides a most comprehensive set of tools for:

- DOM information and inspection
- Outlining different elements (frames, headings, tables, links, etc.)
- HTTP headers, JavaScript, images information
- Cookies
- CSS
- Page validation (CSS, HTML, WAI, links, Section 508)

All in all, this extension is a very good companion for developing websites. The homepage for this extension and some documentation can be found at `http://chrispederick.com/work/webdeveloper/`.

Fiddler

When it comes to inspecting and tampering with the HTTP(S) traffic from our computer and the Internet, the most popular tool you can find is Fiddler. This is a freeware tool that allows inspecting all HTTP and HTTPS traffic and tampering it, setting breakpoints, making it an ideal candidate for debugging applications.

It also offers an event-based subscription system offering the capability to easily extend it. Install Fiddler from `http://www.fiddler2.com/Fiddler2/`. You can find a quick introduction to Fiddler on MSDN, and in the following resources:

- Fiddler tutorial `http://www.developer.com/lang/jscript/article.php/3631066`
- Fiddler2 demonstration videos `http://www.fiddler2.com/fiddler/help/video/default.asp`
- Fiddler2 extensions development `http://www.fiddlertool.com/fiddler2/extensions.asp`
- Fiddler2 user interface `http://www.fiddler2.com/Fiddler/help/ui.asp`

Testing

There are a lot of testing tools available today, but only few of them allow for automatic testing of AJAX applications. Dan Wahlin has put together a list of automated testing and debugging tools on his weblog at `http://weblogs.asp.net/dwahlin/` on 2007/02/16.

In his article we can find some of the tools that we presented so far, and also a comprehensive list of tools that we can use for automatic testing.

A less documented feature of Fiddler is that it can generate Visual Studio WebTest files that can be using in Visual Studio. Why is this necessary? Visual Studio doesn't record AJAX requests based on XMLHttpRequest, but only full postbacks.

In order to create a Visual Studio WebTest file, you need to follow these steps:

1. Open Fiddler.
2. Start capturing the traffic by pressing *F12* or by selecting **File | Capture Traffic**.
3. Browse the AJAX application and Fiddler will register the requests.
4. After having finished the steps save the session by going to **File | Save | Session(s) | as Visual Studio Web Test**.
5. Now you can import the generated file in Visual Studio and use it for automatic testing.

Summary

Debugging and testing are quite complex tasks and they could be the subject of an entire book. The goal of this chapter was to introduce the common tools and techniques for debugging and also to offer a glimpse into the world of automated testing tools for AJAX applications. With the continuous growth of AJAX applications, the need for more complex tools will generate new products so that it's worth keeping an eye on what's new in this domain.

We hope you enjoyed reading this book, and that it helps you create better ASP.NET AJAX applications!

A
Microsoft AJAX Library Reference

This appendix has been designed to be a quick reference and visual guideline to the Microsoft AJAX Library namespaces and classes that have been mentioned in this book. This reference attempts to supplement the official library documentation available at `http://ajax.asp.net/docs/ClientReference/`. In the following pages, you will find:

- Description of the conventions used in the class diagrams
- Function reference
- JavaScript base type extensions reference
- `Sys` namespace reference
- `Sys.UI` namespace reference
- `Sys.Net` namespace reference
- `Sys.Serialization` namespace reference

Conventions

In this book, you were first introduced to class diagrams in Chapter 5. There you learned that unlike in C#, several conventions need to be used in order to implement typical OOP concepts using JavaScript code. Class diagrams use different conventions for the different types of items they describe, such as class fields, properties, methods, and events.

Fields are variables of primitive types and can be accessed directly using a class instance. **Properties** are mechanisms where the values of class fields can be accessed or altered only through getter and setter functions. This restriction is by convention only; the fields that store property values can be accessed directly, but the convention requires using the getter and setter methods.

The property's field that internally store its value is declared with a leading underscore (_). The getter and setter methods are prefixed with "get_" and "set_" followed by the property name. For example, a property called name would be implemented using JavaScript code like this:

```
this._name = myvalue;
...
get_name: function()
{
    return this._name;
},

set_name: function(value)
{
    .   this._name = value;
}
```

Methods are functions inside a class. The term comes from the OOP world, but in the case of JavaScript, *method* and *function* can often be used interchangeably.

Events represent notifications that an action has occurred. The implementation for events in JavaScript is very similar to the one chosen on the server-side .NET platform.

The JavaScript implementation for an event named change looks like this:

```
this._events = new Sys.EventHandlerList();
...

// register a change event handler
add_change: function(handler) {
  this.get_events().addHandler("change", handler);
},

// unregister a change event handler
remove_change: function(handler) {
  this.get_events().removeHandler("change", handler);
}
```

When an event is raised, one or more functions, called handlers, can be invoked in response. Handlers can be registered and deregistered from an event. Each event handler would typically have a signature like the following:

```
function MyHandler(source, eventArgs)
```

Here, `source` represents the object that raised the event, and `eventArgs` contains an object derived from `Sys.EventArgs` which contains the parameters sent to our event. This strongly resembles the .NET style of event handlers.

The diagrams in this book have been created using the Class Diagram feature of Visual Studio 2005 Team System Edition. Note, however, that this feature doesn't actually work with JavaScript—to create class diagrams, we created C# classes that correspond to the Microsoft AJAX Library functions. The mentioned conventions were used to port the JavaScript code to C#. Here are a few examples:

- Unlike public methods, private (by convention) JavaScript methods are named with a leading underscore. See Figure A-1.

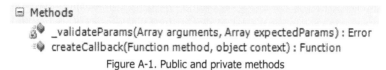

Figure A-1. Public and private methods

- JavaScript properties (by convention) are declared as C# properties (see Figure A-2); read-only JavaScript properties are represented as C# properties having only a getter (see Figure A-3).

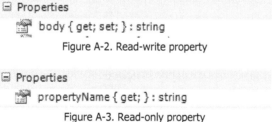

Figure A-2. Read-write property

Figure A-3. Read-only property

- Private (by convention) JavaScript fields are represented as C# fields with leading underscore(s)—see Figure A-4; all public Javascript fields are mapped to public C# fields (see Figure A-5).

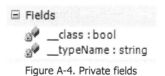

Figure A-4. Private fields

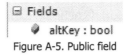
Figure A-5. Public field

- All the events (by convention) exposed by JavaScript objects are mapped to C# events; the classic `EventHandler` in C# is replaced by convention by `Function` (see Figure A-6).

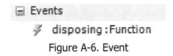
Figure A-6. Event

Function Class

The `Function` class (Figure A-7) provides basic features for functions and it is used throughout the library.

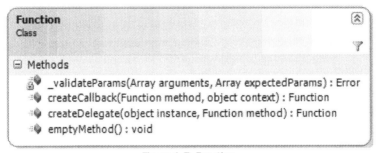
Figure A-7. Function

emptyMethod() Method

Static method that represents an empty function.

_validateParams() Method

Static method that validates a list of parameters against of list of JSON objects representing the validation rules.

Parameters

arguments – Array of parameters to be validated.

expectedParams – Array of JSON objects describing the validation rules for the arguments.

Returns

The method return an `Error` message if the arguments do not validate.

Remarks

Each JSON object contains a validation rule for a parameter. The JSON object is a dictionary of keys and values.

The list of keys that can be used is given in the following table:

Key	Description
name	The name of the parameter
type	The allowed type for this parameter (examples: `String`, `Array`, `Function`, `Sys.Component`, etc.)
mayBeNull	Boolean value indicating whether this parameter can be passed as `null` or not
domElement	Boolean value indicating whether this parameter is a DOM element or not
integer	Boolean value indicating whether this parameter should have an integer value or not
optional	Boolean value indicating whether this parameter is optional or not
parameterArray	Boolean value indicating whether this parameter should be an `Array` or not
elementType	The allowed type for each element of an array (type must be `Array`)
elementMayBeNull	Boolean value indicating whether an array element could have `null` or not (type must be `Array`)
elementDomElement	Boolean value indicating whether each element of an array is a DOM element (type must be `Array`)
elementInteger	Boolean value indicating whether each element of an array should have an integer value (type must be `Array`)

The function returns an `Error` message if the parameters don't validate and this error is typically thrown as shown below.

```
if (e) throw e;
```

This error could be caught and the appropriate measures can be taken programmatically. If not caught, the error will pop up in the debugging console of the browser.

Example

```
function Sys$_Debug$fail(message) {
/// <param name="message" type="String" mayBeNull="true"></param>
  var e = Function._validateParams(arguments, [
    {name: "message", type: String, mayBeNull: true}
    ]);
    if (e) throw e;
```

The above example is extracted from the debug version of the library.

createDelegate() Method

Static method that creates a delegate for a given function and instance object.

Parameters

instance – the referenced object inside the method.

method – the method for which the delegate is created.

Returns

The method returns a delegate function.

Remarks

When the handler is an instance method and uses the `this` word in its body, we need to attach it as an event handler. We can use this method so that in the returned function `this` means the same thing as in the original instance context.

Example

```
myObject = function(){
   var handler = Function.createDelegate(this,this.myMethod);
}

myObject.prototype = {
  myMethod: function() { …
   }
}
```

createCallback() Method

Static method that creates a callback function for a given method and an optional context.

Parameters

method – the method for which the callback is created.

context – the arbitrary context for calling the callback function.

Returns

The method returns a callback function.

Remarks

The context parameter is optional, but if it is omitted the callback function simply represents the original method with an additional level of indirection.

Even if the callback function is called without any parameters, the initial context will still be remembered.

Example

```
var myCallback = Function.createCallback(myMethod, "test");
function myMethod(message){
    alert(message);
}
myCallback();
```

The output of the above mentioned code snipped is an alert message with the **test** message.

Type Class

The Type class (Figure A-8) provides useful static methods for type-handling and type reflection, which helps implementing OOP features with JavaScript. It represent an alias for Function.

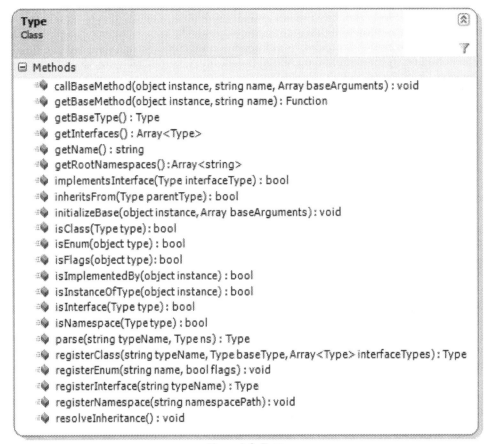

Figure A-8. Type

JavaScript Base Type Extensions

The ECMAScript (JavaScript) objects have been enriched with some new methods in order to make the programmer's transition from using the .NET Framework's classes to JavaScript's objects much easier.

Array Class

The Array class (Figure A-9) represents an extension of the built-in JavaScript `Array` object. It provides reflection information about the type and the type name of an object and also additional *static* methods offered by the .NET environment for arrays.

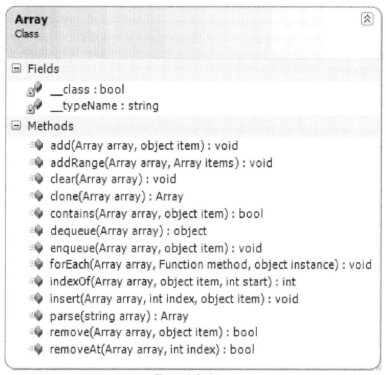

Figure A-9. Array

All the methods in this class are *static* methods.

```
var a = ["1", "2", "3"];
var b = ["11", "12", "13"];
// Add an element to an array
Array.add(a, "4");
Sys.Debug.trace(a);
// Output: 1,2,3,4

// Add a range of elements to an array
Array.addRange(a, ["5", "6"]);
Sys.Debug.trace(a);
 // Output: 1,2,3,4,5,6

// Clone an array
var c = Array.clone(a);
Sys.Debug.trace(a);
```

```
// Output: 1,2,3,4,5,6

// Clear an array
Array.clear(c);
Sys.Debug.trace(c);
// Output:

// Check to see if an array has an element
        Sys.Debug.trace(Array.contains(a,"3"));
// Output: true

// Dequeue the last element from an array
Sys.Debug.trace(Array.dequeue(a));
// Output:  1

// Apply a function to all the elements of an array
Array.forEach(a,function(element, i, array){
Sys.Debug.trace("Array[" + i + "]=" + element);
});
// Output: Array[0]=2
Array[1]=3
Array[2]=4
Array[3]=5
Array[4]=6
// Search an element in an array
Sys.Debug.trace(Array.indexOf(a,"5",2));
// Output:  3

// Insert an element in an array at a specified position
Array.insert(a,3,"8");
Sys.Debug.trace(a);
// Output: 2, 3, 4, 8, 5, 6

// Parse a string and return an array
Sys.Debug.trace(Array.parse('["0","1","2"]'));
// Output : 0, 1, 2

// Remove an element from an array
Array.remove(a, "1");
Sys.Debug.trace(a);
// Output : 2, 3, 4, 8, 5, 6

// Remove an element at a specified position from an array
Array.removeAt(a,2);
Sys.Debug.trace(a);
// Output : 2, 3, 8, 5, 6
```

Boolean Class

The `Boolean` class (Figure A-10) represents an extension of the built-in JavaScript `Boolean` object. It provides reflection information about the type and the type name of an object and also an additional method offered by the .NET environment.

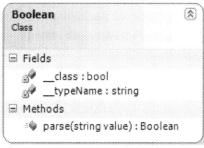

Figure A-10. Boolean

```
var bool = Boolean.parse("true");
        Sys.Debug.trace(bool);
// Output: true
```

Date Class

The `Date` class (Figure A-11) represents an extension of the built-in JavaScript `Date` object. It provides reflection information about the type and the type name of an object and also additional methods offered by the .NET environment for creating and formatting a date.

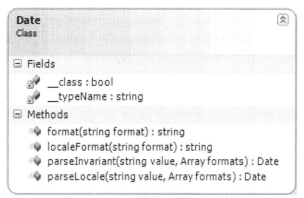

Figure A-11. Date

Please refer to `Sys.CultureInfo` for more information about the localization features.

`Date` and `Number` JavaScript variables can be formatted to their corresponding locale.

Predefined string patterns	Description
d	Short date pattern :`MM/dd/yyyy`
D	Long date pattern : `dddd, dd MMMM yyyy`
t	Short time pattern : `HH:mm`
T	Long time pattern : `HH:mm:ss`
F	Full date time pattern : `dddd, dd MMMM yyyy HH:mm:ss`
M or m	Month day pattern : `MMMM dd`
s	Sortable date time pattern : `yyyy'-'MM'-'dd'T'HH':'mm':'ss`
Y or y	Year month pattern : `yyyy MMMM`

The above table represents the predefined string patterns for the `InvariantCulture`. As we can see each predefined pattern translates into a series of format specifier characters. Below we can find the complete list of format specifier characters:

Format specifier character	Description
dddd	Full day name (Sunday, Monday, etc.)
ddd	Abbreviated day name (Sun, Mon, etc.)
dd	Day of the month, 2 digits (00…31)
d	Day of the month (0…31)
MMMM	Full month name (January, February, etc.)
MMM	Abbreviated month name (Jan, Feb, etc.)
MM	Month of the year, 2 digits (01…12)
M	Month of the year (1…12)
yyyy	Year, 4 digits (2006)
yy	Year, 2 digits (06, 00, 99)
y	Year (6, 0, 99)
hh	Hour (1…12)
h	Hour (0…23)
HH	Hour, 2 digits (00…23)
H	Hour (0…23)
mm	Minutes, 2 digits (00…59)
m	Minutes (0…59)

Format specifier character	Description
ss	Seconds, 2 digits (00…59)
s	Seconds (0…59)
tt	AM or PM
t	A or P (short for AM and PM)
f	Hundreds of milliseconds, 1 digit (0…9)
ff	Hundreds and tens of milliseconds, 2 digits (00…99)
fff	Milliseconds (000…999)
z	Time zone offset in hours (+7, -2)
zz	Time zone offset in hours, 2 digits (+ 07, -02)
zzz	Time zone offset in hours and minutes (+07:00, -02:00)

 The string passed to the format() or localeFormat() methods should have a single character if it is a predefined pattern, or at least two characters if it has format specifier characters.

```
// Displays the current date using the InvariantCulture object
Sys.Debug.trace ((new Date()).format("F"));
// Output: Friday, May 18, 2007 4:58:36 PM

// Displays the current date using the CurrentCulture object set for
French
Sys.Debug.trace((new Date()).localeFormat("F"));
// Output: vendredi 18 mai 2007 17:03:47

// Parse a string date using two date formats from InvariantCulture
object. The first format is skipped and the second one is choosed
Sys.Debug.trace(Date.parseInvariant("05/17/2007","MM-dd-yyyy","MM/dd/
yyyy"));
// Output: Thu May 17 00:00:00 UTC+0300 2007

// Parse a string date using the predefined short date format from
French CurrentCulture object. The short date pattern is dd/MM/yyyy
Sys.Debug.trace(Date.parseLocale("17/05/2007","d"));
// Output: Thu May 17 00:00:00 UTC+0300 2007
```

Error Class

The Error extension class (Figure A-12) contains a series of *static* methods that return Error objects.

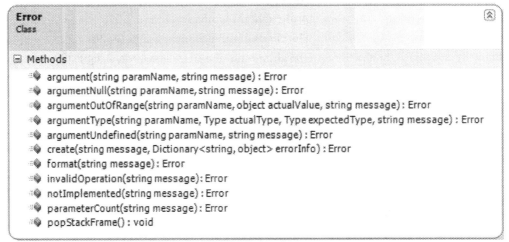

Error
Class

⊟ Methods
- ◆ argument(string paramName, string message) : Error
- ◆ argumentNull(string paramName, string message) : Error
- ◆ argumentOutOfRange(string paramName, object actualValue, string message) : Error
- ◆ argumentType(string paramName, Type actualType, Type expectedType, string message) : Error
- ◆ argumentUndefined(string paramName, string message) : Error
- ◆ create(string message, Dictionary<string, object> errorInfo) : Error
- ◆ format(string message) : Error
- ◆ invalidOperation(string message) : Error
- ◆ notImplemented(string message) : Error
- ◆ parameterCount(string message) : Error
- ◆ popStackFrame() : void

Figure A-12. Error

create() Method

Static method that creates and returns an Error object.

Parameters

message – the optional message to be displayed in the error.

errorInfo – a JSON object containing a collection of keys and their values.

Returns

The method returns the created Error object.

Remarks

The method creates and returns an Error object. It can receive an optional message and JSON object containing an additional collection of keys and their values. This collection will be added to the error message where the keys will represent additional attributes and the values would represent their values. The message parameter is mapped as the message attribute of the Error object.

Example

```
var e = Error.create(displayMessage, { name: "Sys.ArgumentException",
paramName: paramName });
```

The preceding example is extracted from the debug version of the library in the `Error.argument()` method.

Following are few other examples for `Error`:

```
// Create and throw and argument error
var err = Error.argument("valueParameter", "Invalid parameter");
throw err;
/* Output: Sys.ArgumentException: Invalid parameter
Parameter name: valueParameter */


// Create and throw a null argument error
var err = Error.argumentNull("nullParameter", "The parameter does not
accept null values");
throw err;
/* Output: Sys.ArgumentNullException: The parameter does not accept
null values
Parameter name: nullParameter */


// Create and throw an argument out of range error
var err = Error.argumentOutOfRange("valueParameter", 11, "The
parameter accepts values between 1 and 10");
throw err;
/* Output: Sys.ArgumentOutOfRangeException: The parameter accepts
values between 1 and 10
Parameter name: valueParameter
Actual value was 11. */


// Create and throw an argument type error
var err = Error.argumentType("valueParameter", Date, Number, "The
parameter is not the expected type");
throw err;
/* Output Sys.ArgumentTypeException: The parameter is not the expected
type
Parameter name: valueParameter */


// Create and throw an undefined argument error
if(typeof(parameter) === 'undefined')
```

```
{
  var err = Error.argumentUndefined("parameter", "The parameter type
is undefined");
  throw err;
}
//Output Sys.ArgumentUndefinedException: The parameter type is
undefined
Parameter name: parameter


// Create and throw an invalid operation error
var err= Error.invalidOperation("An invalid operation has been
detected");
throw err;
// Output: Sys.InvalidOperationException: An invalid operation has
been detected


function test()
{
  // Create and throw a not implemented error
  var err= Error.notImplemented("Method not implemented");
  throw err;
}
test();
// Output: Sys.NotImplementedException: Method not implemented


function testParams()
{
  if(arguments.length>0)
  {
    // Create and throw a parameter count error
    var err= Error.parameterCount("Too many parameters");
    throw err;
  }
}
testParams("test");
// Output: Sys.ParameterCountException: Too many parameters


var err = Error.format("Bad format specified ");
throw err;
// Output: Sys.FormatException: Bad format specified
```

Number Class

This class represents an extension of the built-in JavaScript Number object. It provides reflection information about the type and the type name of an object, and also additional methods offered by the .NET environment for creating and formatting a number.

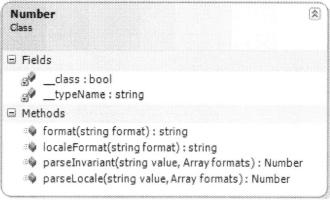

Figure A-13. Number

 Please refer to Sys.CultureInfo for more information about the localized features.

The patterns for the Number object are:

Format specifier character	Description
d or D	Decimal format
c or C	Currency format
n or N	Number format
p or P	Percentage

Please check the link below for more info:

http://msdn2.microsoft.com/en-us/library/44e531aa-1383-48ad-887b-fa15d81566c3.aspx

```
// This example shows how the same value is parsed using the
InvariantCulture and the French CurrentCulture.
var a = Number.parseInvariant("2.55");
var b = Number.parseLocale("2,55");
Sys.Debug.trace(a + b);
// Output: 5.1
```

Object Class

This class represents an extension of the built-in JavaScript `Object` object and it provides reflection information about the type and the type name of an object.

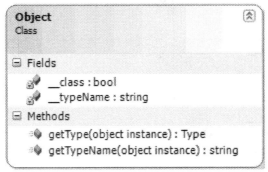

Figure A-14. Object

```
var array = ["1","2"];
Sys.Debug.trace (Object.getTypeName(array));
// Output: Array
```

RegExp Class

This class represents an extension of the built-in JavaScript `RegExp` object and it provides reflection information about the type and the type name of a regular expression.

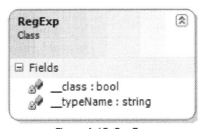

Figure A-15. RegExp

Without adding any additional functions, it offers the same functionality that is provided by JavaScript by default.

String Class

This class represents an extension of the built-in JavaScript `String` object. It provides reflection information about the type and the type name of an object and also additional methods offered by the .NET environment for arrays.

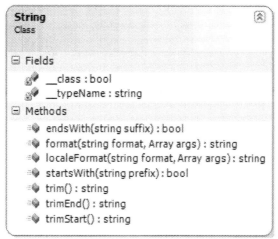

Figure A-16. String

```
// Trim a string
        var str = " My text ";
        Sys.Debug.trace(str.trim());
// Output:My text

        // Left trim a string
        var str = " My text ";
        Sys.Debug.trace(str.trimStart());
// Output:My text

        // Right trim a string
        var str = " My text ";
        Sys.Debug.trace(str.trimEnd());
// Output: My text

        // Test to see if a string starts with another string
        var str = "test string";
        Sys.Debug.trace(str.startsWith("tes"));
// Output:true

        // Test to see if a string ends with another string
        var str = "test string";
        Sys.Debug.trace(str.endsWith("tes"));
// Output:false

        // Format a string based on the arguments using the
            InvariantCulture object
        Sys.Debug.trace(String.format("On {0:F} the market share is
                                      {1:p}",new Date(),23.24));
```

```
// Output:On Friday, 18 May 2007 20:35:33 the market share is 23.24 %
        // Format a string based on the arguments using the
           CurrentCulture object
        Sys.Debug.trace(String.localeFormat("On {0:F} the market
                                share is {1:p}",new Date(),23.24));
// Output: On vendredi 18 mai 2007 20:35:33 the market share is
   23,24 %
```

Sys Namespace

The following members of the Sys namespace are covered here:

- Sys.Application
- Sys.ApplicationLoadEventArgs
- Sys.Browser
- Sys.CancelEventArgs
- Sys.Component
- Sys.CultureInfo
- Sys.Debug
- Sys.EventArgs
- Sys.EventHandlerList
- Sys.IContainer Interface
- Sys.IDisposable Interface
- Sys.INotifyDisposing Interface
- Sys.INotifyPropertyChange Interface
- Sys.PropertyChangedEventArgs
- Sys.ScriptLoader
- Sys.ScriptLoaderTask
- Sys.StringBuilder

Sys.Application Class

The Sys.Application object (Figure A-17) object represents the central point for handling client components registered in the application and it is also the one that exposes the main page life cycle events. It works with the Sys.ScriptLoader object to load the scripts in the page.

Figure A-17. Sys.Application

Sys.ApplicationLoadEventArgs Class

Sys.ApplicationLoadEventArgs (Figure A-18) extends Sys.EventArgs and stores the information passed by the load event of Sys.Application.

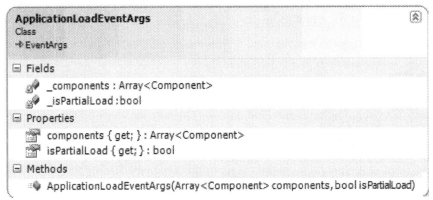

Figure A-18. Sys.ApplicationLoadEventArgs

Sys.Browser Class

Sys.Browser (Figure A-19) contains contains information based on browser detection and is used throughout the library to solve compatibility issues.

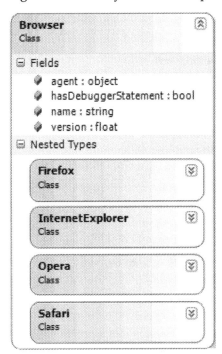

Figure A-19. Sys.Browser

Sys.CancelEventArgs Class

Sys.CancelEventArgs (Figure A-20) extends the Sys.EventArgs class and offers a base class for all the canceled event arguments.

Figure A-20. Sys.CancelEventArgs

Sys.Component Class

Sys.Component (Figure A-21) is the base class for all the components, controls, and behaviors. It is used so that the objects' lifetime is managed by Microsoft AJAX Library.

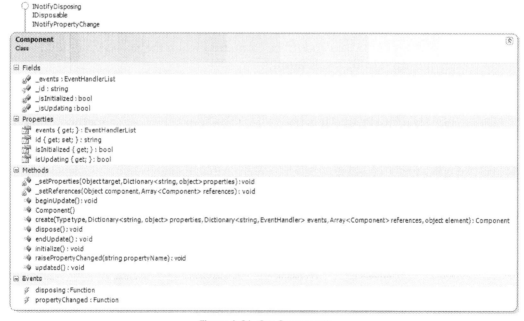

Figure A-21. Sys.Component

Sys.CultureInfo Class

`Sys.CultureInfo` (Figure A-22) represents the base class for objects storing culture-related information.

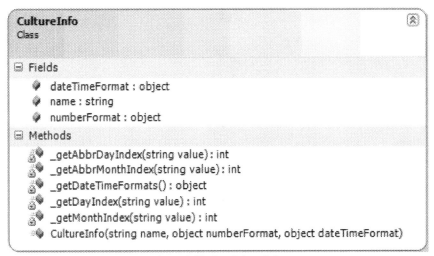

Figure A-22. Sys.CultureInfo

Based on this class we also have two additional objects:

- `Sys.CultureInfo.InvariantCulture`, which is a `CultureInfo` object having a culture that does not belong to any language or locale. It specifies how dates and numbers should be formatted when the `format` method is used, thus no specific locale applies

- `Sys.CultureInfo.CurrentCulture`, which is also a `CultureInfo` object having the current culture and thus a specific locale. If no locale is specified, it defaults to `en-US` and it is used when the `localeFormat()` method is used.

Sys.Debug Class

`Sys.Debug` (Figure A-23) provides methods that can be used for debugging and tracing functionality.

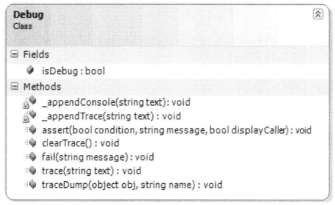

Figure A-23. Sys.Debug

Sys.EventArgs Class

Sys.EventArgs (Figure A-24) represents the base class for all the event arguments objects passed by event sources. Sys.EventArgs.Empty represents such an object and is defined in Microsoft AJAX Library.

Figure A-24. Sys.EventArgs

Sys.EventHandlerList Class

Sys.EventHandlerList class (Figure A-25) is used for storing event handlers for different events. The events' names represent the keys and a list of event handlers the values in an internal dictionary.

Figure A-25. Sys.EventHandlerList

Sys.IContainer Interface

The Sys.IContainer interface (Figure A-26) defines methods for all components that contain other components. It is implemented by Sys.Application.

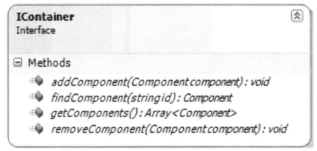

Figure A-26. Sys.IContainer

Sys.IDisposable Interface

The Sys.INotifyDisposing interface (Figure A-27) represents a common interface for closing and releasing resources held by objects registered using Microsoft AJAX Library.

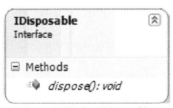

Figure A-27. Sys.IDisposable

Sys.INotifyDisposing Interface

The Sys.INotifyPropertyChange interface (Figure A-28) defines the disposing event. When implemented, it notifies other objects when it is about to release resources. It is implemented by Sys.Component and thus by all components, behaviors, and controls.

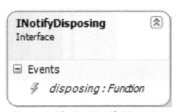

Figure A-28. Sys.INotifyDisposing

Sys.INotifyPropertyChange Interface

The Sys.INotifyPropertyChange interface (Figure A-29) defines the propertyChanged event. It is implemented by Sys.Component and thus by all components, behaviors, and controls.

Figure A-29. Sys.INotifyPropertyChange

Sys.PropertyChangedEventArgs Class

Sys.PropertyChangedEventArgs (Figure A-30) extends Sys.EventArgs class and is used as an event argument by the propertyChanged event.

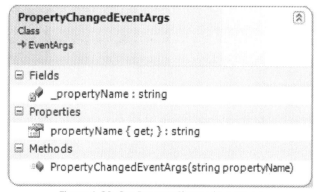

Figure A-30. Sys.PropertyChangedEventArgs

Sys.ScriptLoader Class

Sys.ScriptLoader (Figure A-31) offers a centralized mechanism for loading script files.

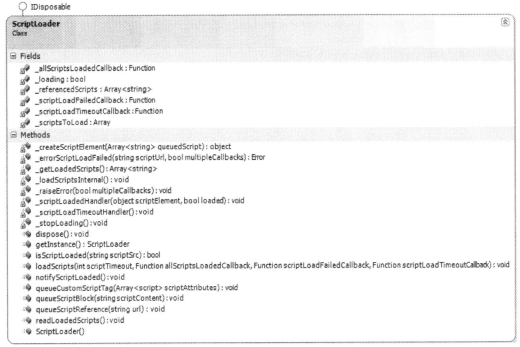

Figure A-31. Sys.ScriptLoader

Sys.ScriptLoaderTask Class

Sys.ScriptLoaderTask (Figure A-32) is used by Sys.ScripLoader to load a particular script file.

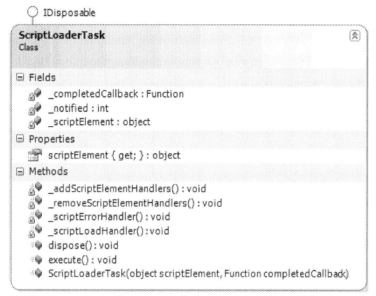

Figure A-32. Sys.ScriptLoaderTask

Sys.StringBuilder Class

Sys.StringBuilder class (Figure A-33) offers a mechanism for concatenating strings.

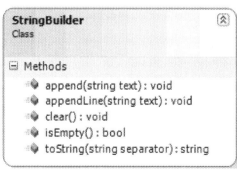

Figure A-33. Sys.StringBuilder

Sys.UI Namespace

We cover the following members of Sys.UI:

- Sys.UI.Behavior
- Sys.UI.Bounds
- Sys.UI.DomElement
- Sys.UI.DomEvent
- Sys.UI.Key
- Sys.UI.MouseButton
- Sys.UI.Point
- Sys.UI.VisibilityMode

Sys.UI.Behavior Class

Sys.UI.Behavior class (Figure A-34) extends Sys.Component and represents the base class for all behaviors.

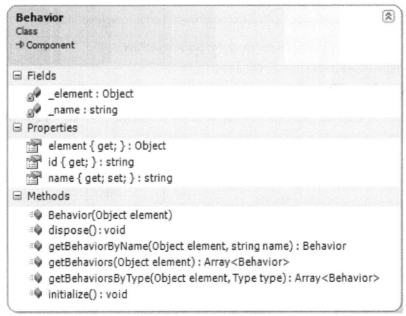

Figure A-34. Sys.UI.Behavior

Sys.UI.Bounds Class

`Sys.UI.Bounds` (Figure A-35) contains information about a point's position, a width, and a height.

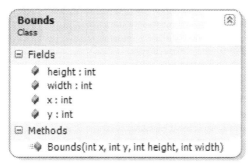

Figure A-35. Sys.UI.Bounds

Sys.UI.Control Class

`Sys.UI.Bounds` class (Figure A-36) extends `Sys.Component` and represents the base class for all controls.

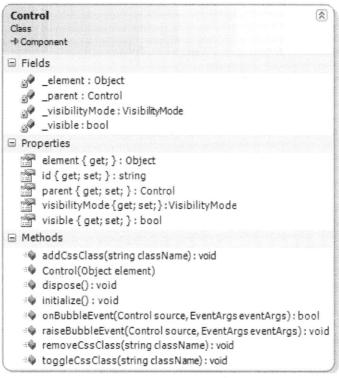

Figure A-36. Sys.UI.Bounds

Sys.UI.DomElement Class

`Sys.UI.Bounds` class (Figure A-37) a set of methods for operating on a DOM element.

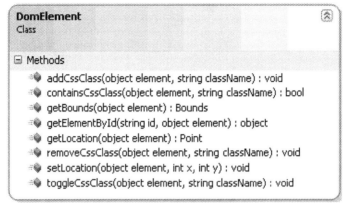

Figure A-37. Sys.UI.Bounds

getElementById() Method ($get)

Static method that searches a DOM element by its ID.

Parameters

id – the ID of the DOM element to be searched for.

element – optional DOM element that specifies parent element to search in.

Remarks

If the DOM element to search in is not specified, the `document` element is presumed by default.

Example

```
//Get a DOM element
var elm=$get('log');
```

addCssClass() Method

Static method that add a CSS class to a DOM element.

Parameters

element – the DOM element.

className – the name of the CSS class.

Example

```
//Add a CSS class
Sys.UI.DomElement.addCssClass($get('log'),'newClass');
```

containsCssClass() Method

Static method that checks to see if a DOM element has a specified CSS class.

Parameters

element – the DOM element.

className – the name of the CSS class.

Returns

The method returns `true` if the DOM element has the specified CSS class or `false` otherwise.

Example

```
//Check to see if a DOM element has a CSS class
Sys.Debug.trace(Sys.UI.DomElement.containsCssClass($get('log'),
'class'));
```

removeCssClass() Method

Static method that removes a CSS class from a DOM element.

Parameters

element – the DOM element.

className – the name of the CSS class.

Example

```
//Remove a CSS class from a DOM element
Sys.UI.DomElement.removeCssClass($get('log'),'class');
```

toggleCssClass() Method

Static method that toggles a CSS class for a DOM element.

Parameters

element – the DOM element.

className – the name of the CSS class.

Example

```
//Toggle a CSS class
Sys.UI.DomElement.toggleCssClass($get('log'),'class');
```

getLocation() Method

Static method that gets the position of the upper left corner for a DOM element.

Parameters

element – the DOM element.

Returns

The method returns a `Sys.UI.Point` object containing the upper left corner's position.

getBounds() Method

Static method that gets the bounds for a DOM element.

Parameters

element – The DOM element.

Returns

The method returns a `Sys.UI.Bounds` object containing the position and dimensions of the DOM element.

Remarks

The method internally uses `Sys.UI.DomElement.getLocation()` for the x and y fields of the `Sys.UI.Bounds` object and the `offsetWidth` and `offsetHeight` attributes of the DOM element for the `width` and `height` fields of the same `Sys.UI.Bounds` object.

For more information about the boxing model please check:

`http://www.w3.org/TR/CSS21/box.html`

Example

```
//Toggle a CSS class
Sys.UI.DomElement.toggleCssClass($get('log'),'class');
```

setLocation() Method

Static method that sets the absolute position for a DOM element.

Parameters

element – the DOM element.

x – number of horizontal pixels from the top left corner.

y – number of vertical pixels from the top left upper corner.

Remarks

The method internally sets the `position` CSS attribute to `absolute` and the `left` and `top` attributes to x and y.

Example

```
//Set the location for a DOM element
Sys.UI.DomElement.setLocation($get('log'),10,20);
```

Sys.UI.DomEvent Class

`Sys.UI.DomEvent` (Figure A-38) stores all the information that is passed to a handler registered to a DOM event and also provides methods for registering to a DOM event.

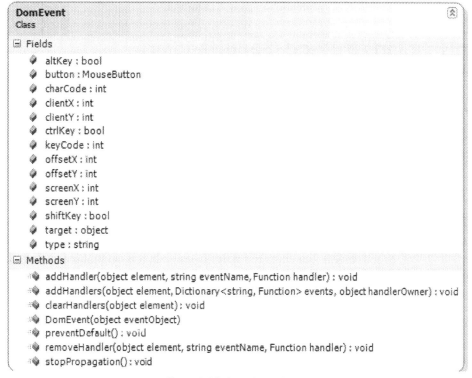

DomEvent
Class

- Fields
  - altKey : bool
  - button : MouseButton
  - charCode : int
  - clientX : int
  - clientY : int
  - ctrlKey : bool
  - keyCode : int
  - offsetX : int
  - offsetY : int
  - screenX : int
  - screenY : int
  - shiftKey : bool
  - target : object
  - type : string
- Methods
  - addHandler(object element, string eventName, Function handler) : void
  - addHandlers(object element, Dictionary<string, Function> events, object handlerOwner) : void
  - clearHandlers(object element) : void
  - DomEvent(object eventObject)
  - preventDefault() : void
  - removeHandler(object element, string eventName, Function handler) : void
  - stopPropagation() : void

Figure A-38. Sys.UI.DomEvent

Sys.UI.Key Class

This enumeration contains the key codes.

Figure A-39. Sys.UI.DomEvent

addHandler() Method ($addHandler)

Static method that adds a handler to an event of a DOM element.

Parameters

element – the DOM element.

eventName – the name of the event the handler is being attached to.

handler – the handler to be attached to the DOM element's event.

Remarks

In the event handler, the `this` keyword refers to the DOM element. Use `Function. createDelegate()` to create handler delegates inside objects so that this refers the object and not the DOM element.

Example

```
// Add a handler for the keypress event
// Version 1
    this._onKeyPressHandler = Function.createDelegate(this, this._
onKeyPress);
```

```
    $addHandler(this.get_element(),'keypress',this._
onKeyPressHandler);
// Same as Sys.DomEvent.addHandler
...
_onKeyPress: function(e){..}

// Version 2
$addHandler(element, 'keypress', handler);
function handler(e){..}
```

addHandlers() Method ($addHandlers)

Static method that adds a series of handlers to different events of a DOM element.

Parameters

element – the DOM element.

events – a JSON object containing pairs of event names and their handlers.

handlerOwner – if specified, `this` will point to it inside event handlers.

Remarks

There is no need to create delegates for the event handlers as with the `addHandler()`. This method internally uses `Function.createDelegate()` if `handlerOwner` is specified.

This method could be used inside the `initialize()` method of a component when a series of event handlers need to be attached.

Example

```
//Add a series of handlers in a control or behavior
$addHandlers(this.get_element(),{'mousedown' : this._
onMouseDown,'mouseup' : this._onMouseUp} , this);
_onMouseDown: function(e){...},
_onMouseUp: function(e){...}
```

clearHandlers() Method ($clearHandlers)

Static method that removes all the event handlers attached to a DOM element.

Parameters

element – the DOM element.

Remarks

This method should be used in the `dispose()` method of a component in order to remove the attached event handlers.

Example

```
//Clear all handlers attached to a element
$clearHandlers(this.get_element());
```

preventDefault() Method

Method that prevents the default event action from taking place.

Example

```
function myEvent(e)
{
   e.preventDefault();
}
```

removeHandler() Method

Static method that removes an event handler from the DOM element it is attached to.

Parameters

element – the DOM element.

eventName – the name of the event the handler is being removed from.

handler – the handler to be removed from the DOM element's event.

Example

```
//Remove an event handler
Sys.UI.DomEvent.removeHandler(this.get_element(),'mousedown',handler);
```

stopPropagation() Method

Method that prevents the event from bubbling up the hierarchy.

Example

```
function myEvent(e)
{
   e.stopPropagation();
}
```

Sys.UI.MouseButton Enumeration

Sys.UI.MouseButton (Figure A-40) contains elements that represent the mouse buttons.

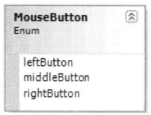

Figure A-40. Sys.UI.MouseButton

Sys.UI.Point Class

Sys.UI.Point (Figure A-41) contains information about a point's position.

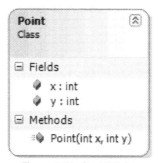

Figure A-41. Sys.UI.Point

Sys.UI.VisibilityMode Enumeration

Sys.UI.VisibilityMode (Figure A-42) contains two values for the visibility CSS property of a DOM element.

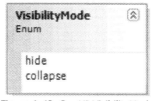

Figure A-42. Sys.UI.VisibilityMode

Sys.Net Namespace

We cover the following classes of Sys.Net:

- Sys.Net.NetworkRequestEventArgs

- Sys.Net.WebRequest

- Sys.Net.WebRequestExecutor

- Sys.Net.WebRequestManager

- Sys.Net.XmlHttpExecutor

Sys.Net.NetworkRequestEventArgs Class

Sys.Net.NetworkRequestEventArgs (Figure A-43) stores the underlying Sys.Net.WebRequest and is passed as an argument object for the invokingRequest event.

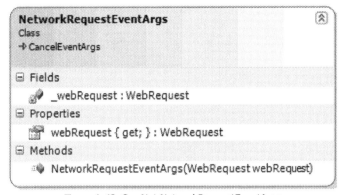

Figure A-43. Sys.Net.NetworkRequestEventArgs

Sys.Net.WebRequest Class

`Sys.WebRequest` (Figure A-44) encapsulates the necessary functionality in order to make web requests from the client side. It uses an underlying `Sys.Net.WebRequestExecutor` (`Sys.Net.XmlHttpExecutor` by default) to actually make a request. It exposes properties, methods, and events in order to easily make a request.

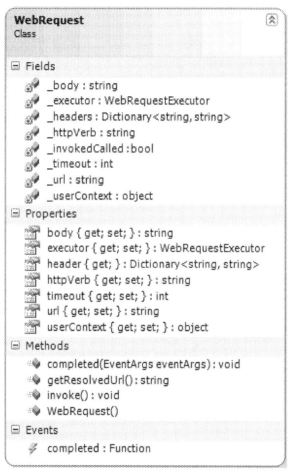

Figure A-44. Sys.WebRequest

Sys.Net.WebRequestExecutor Class

Sys.Net.WebRequestExecutor (Figure A-45) represents an "abstract" class (by convention as some of the methods throw an Error.notImplemented() error) and it is the base class for different implementation of executor classes for web requests. Currently, only the Sys.Net.XmlHttpExecutor class based on the XMLHttp object is available.

Figure A-45. Sys.Net.WebRequestExecutor

Sys.Net.WebRequestManager Class

`Sys.Net.WebRequestManager` (Figure A-46) coordinates all the web requests initiated from the browser exposing two additional events for more control.

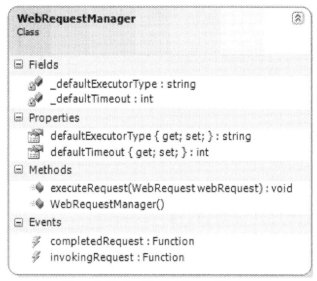

Figure A-46. Sys.Net.WebRequestManager

Sys.Net.XmlHttpExecutor Class

`Sys.Net.XmlHttpExecutor` (Figure A-47) extends `Sys.Net.WebRequestExecutor` and represents an executor for web requests based on the `XMLHttp` browser object.

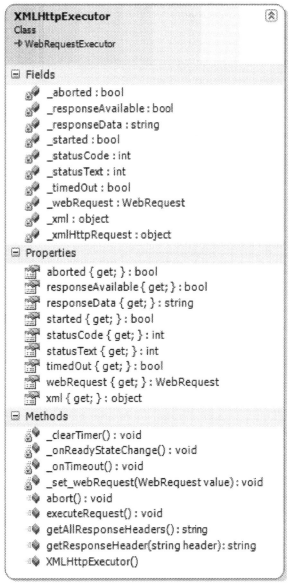

Figure A-47. Sys.Net.XmlHttpExecutor

Sys.Serialization Namespace

This namespace contains a single class: Sys.Serialization.JavaScriptSerializer.

Sys.Serialization.JavaScriptSerializer Class

Sys.Serialization.JavaScriptSerializer (Figure A-48) provides two static methods for serializing types into JSON formatted data strings and for deserializing JSON formatted data strings into JavaScript types.

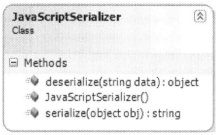

Figure A-48. Sys.Serialization.JavaScriptSerializer

serialize() Method

Static method that serializes a JavaScript object into a string representation of the corresponding JSON object.

Parameters

obj – the JavaScript object to be serialized.

Returns

The method returns the string representation of the JSON object representing the JavaScript object.

Remarks

Date objects are serialized as \/Date(milliseconds from the 1st January 1970)\/.

Properties that start with $ are skipped.

Non-finite numbers are not serialized. The isFinite() JavaScript function is used to determine whether a number is finite or not.

Special characters are escaped using a \ and Unicode characters by using \u00.

deserialize() Method

Static method that deserializes a JSON object and returns a JavaScript object.

Parameters

data – the string representation of the JSON object to be deserialized.

Returns

The method returns the JavaScript object corresponding to the JSON object.

Remarks

Date objects are serialized as \/Date(milliseconds from the 1st January 1970)\/ so that they can be correctly deserialized.

The JavaScript object is constructed by calling eval() on the JSON string.

Index

A

AJAX
  about 15
  advantages 19
  application building, ASP.NET used 28
  ASP.NET AJAX 20
  disadvantages 19
  DOM 17
  examples 17
  for validations 16
  need for 15
  resources 21
  technologies used 17, 18
  tools 21
  Web 2.0 10
  XMLHttpRequest 17
anonymous function
  versus pseudo-named functions 222
application, building
  ASP.NET, using 28
array, sorting
  Bubble Sort algorithm used 137
array class 243
ASP.NET AJAX
  about 20
  ASP.NET AJAX control toolkit 21
  ASP.NET AJAX extensions 20
  Microsoft AJAX library 20
  Quickstart 28
  technologies used 21
asynchronous communication
  about 116
  client side 117, 118
  server side 118, 119
  uses 116

Asynchronous JavaScript and XML. *See* **AJAX**

B

behaviors
  about 181
  Sys.UI.Behavior 188
boolean class 245
Bubble Sort algorithm
  about 137
  array, sorting 137-139
  working 140-142

C

Cascading Style Sheets. *See* **CSS**
classes
  about 82
  behavior 82
  events 142
  features, Type class 143
  fields and properties 142
  member types 142
  methods 142
  state 82
  Type class 143
classes, JavaScript
  about 90
  C# classes 93-95
  class diagram 93
  constructor 90
  external functions, referencing 96
  object members, creating 98
  objects, as associate arrays 96-98
  private members 99, 100
  prototypes 100, 101

client-side web technologies
  about 14
  JavaScript 14
client components
  creating 177, 191, 192
client page events 184
client side synchronous communication
  about 117
  conversion layer 117
  core communication layer 117
  layers 117
  proxies layer 117
closures
  about 89
  for inheritance 105
components
  about 180
  creating 182, 183
  disposing 183
  timer component 193
  using 216, 217
controls
  about 181
  Sys.UI.Control 190
conventions, Microsoft AJAX Library
  events 236
  fields 236
  JavaScript properties 237
  methods 236
  private 237
  properties 236
  public 237
CSS 61

D

date class
  about 245
  format specifier character 246, 247
  string patterns 246
debugging
  Firefox 230
  Internet Explorer 225-227
  MicrosoftAjax.debug.js 222
  Microsoft AJAX Library, using 220-225
  overview 220
  parameters, validating 224, 225

Document Object Model. *See* **DOM**
DOM
  about 17
  CSS 61
  events 177-180
  HTML, manipulating 46
  HTML structure, creating 56
  JavaScript events 51
  placeholders 51

E

encapsulation 83
EnhancedTextBox behavior
  about 194
  creating 196
enumerations 165
environment, setting up
  Atlas, for Windows Vista 26
  Atlas, for Windows XP 27
  IIS, installing 22-25
  project folder, creating 25-27
  Visual Web Developer, installing 25
error class
  about 248
  create() method 248
events
  DOM elements 177
  load 186
  pageLoad() method 187
  pageUnload() method 188
  unload 188
execution context. *See* **JavaScript execution
    context**

F

Fiddler
  about 233
  resources 233
FireBug 230
Firefox, debugging
  about 230
  FireBug 230, 231
  Venkman JavaScript debugger 231, 232
  web developer 233

functions, JavaScript
  about 85
  anonymous functions 88, 89
  as variables 86-88
  closures 89
  inner functions 89
functions, Microsoft AJAX Library
  _validateParams 238
  createCallback 241
  createDelegate 240
  emptyMethod 238
  type class 242

H

HTML 11

I

inheritance
  about 83
  closures, using 105-108
  implementing, Microsoft AJAX Library
      used 156-160
  prototyping 105-110
  register method 154
  tight coupling 84
inner functions 89
interfaces
  about 166
  implementing 167-172
Internet Explorer, debugging
  about 225
  IE Developer toolbar 228, 229
  tools 229
  Web Developer Helper 228

J

JavaScript
  about 45
  adding content in HTML page, write
      method used 46, 47
  CSS 61
  events 51
  functions 85
  HTML manipulating, DOM used 46-51
  HTML structure, creating 52

  object detection 68
  objects 84
  placeholders 51
  websites, for learning 46
  XMLHttpRequest object, for asynchronous
      HTTP server requests 65
JavaScript base classes extensions
  about 136
  date, as Array class 136
  date, as Date class 137
  objects, creating 136
JavaScript base type extensions
  about 242
  array class 243, 244
  date class 246, 247
  error class 248
  number class 251
  object class 252
  RegExp class 252
  string class 252
JavaScript execution context
  about 101
  choosing 103-105
  eval() execution context 101
  function execution context 101
  global execution context 101
  this.x 102
  types 101
  var x 102
  x 102
JavaScript Object Notation 110
JSON 110

M

Microsoft AJAX Library
  about 113
  classes 142
  client components, creating 177
  components 113
  conventions 235
  debugging 220
  enumerations 165
  features 114, 115, 136
  functions 238
  inheritance 154
  inheritance, implementing 156-160

interfaces 166
JavaScript base classes extensions 136
layered architecture 115
references 235
WebRequest class 119

N

namaspaces 143
number class 251

O

object class 252
Object Oriented Programming. *See* OOP
objects 82
objects, JavaScript
  creating 84, 85
  features 85
OOP
  about 81
  classes 82
  concept 81
  encapsulation 83
  events 82
  inheritance 83
  methods 82
  objects 82
  polymorphism 84

P

parameters
  validating 224, 225
placeholders 51
polymorphism 84
prototyping
  for inheritance 108-110
pseudo-named functions
  versus anonymous functions 222

Q

Quickstart
  about 28
  files included 29
  working 30

R

RegExp class 252

S

server-side web technologies
  about 13
  ASP.NET 13
server side synchronous communication 118
string class 252
Sys.Application 184
Sys.Net namespace
  Sys.Net.NetworkRequestEventArgs 274
  Sys.Net.WebRequest 275
  Sys.Net.WebRequestExecutor 276
  Sys.Net.WebRequestManager 277
  Sys.Net.XmlHttpExecutor 278
Sys.Serialization namespace
  Sys.Serialization.JavaScriptSerializer 279
Sys.UI namespace
  Sys.UI.Behavior class 264
  Sys.UI.Bounds class 265
  Sys.UI.Control class 265
  Sys.UI.DomElement class 266
  Sys.UI.DomEvent class 269
  Sys.UI.Key class 270
  Sys.UI.MouseButton class 273
  Sys.UI.Point class 273
  Sys.UI.VisibilityMode class 273
Sys namespace
  Sys.Application class 255
  Sys.ApplicationLoadEventArgs class 256
  Sys.Browser class 256
  Sys.CancelEventArgs class 257
  Sys.CultureInfo class 258
  Sys.Debug class 258
  Sys.EventArgs class 259
  Sys.EventHandlerList class 259
  Sys.IContainer interface 260
  Sys.IDisposable interface 260
  Sys.INotifyingDisposing interface 260
  Sys.INotifyingPropertyChange interface 261
  Sys.PropertyChangedEventArgs class 261
  Sys.ScriptLoader class 262
  Sys.ScriptLoaderTask class 263
  Sys.StringBuilder class 263

T

testing
  Visual Studio Web Test files 234
tight coupling 84
timer component
  about 193
  creating 196
tracing
  Microsoft AJAX Library, using 220
Type class
  about 143
  creating 145-147
  features 143
  namaspaces 143
  working 148-154

V

validation
  AJAX, using 16
  types 16
Venkman JavaScript debugger
  about 231
  Firefox, debugging in 231

W

Web 2.0 10
WebRequest class
  working with 119-129
web technologies
  about 11
  ASP.NET 13
  client-side technologies 14
  HTML 11
  HTTP 11
  JavaScript 14
  server-side technologies 13

X

XMLHttpRequest object
  about 17, 65
  call stack 67
  creating 65-69
  for asynchronous HTTP server requests 65
  object detection 68
  server requests, initiating 69-72
  server response, handling 72-79

Building Websites with VB.NET and DotNetNuke 4

ISBN: 978-1-904811-99-2   Paperback: 336 pages

A practical guide to creating and maintaining your own DotNetNuke website, and developing new modules and skins

1. Specially revised and updated version of this acclaimed DotNetNuke book

2. Create and manage your own website with DotNetNuke

3. Customize and enhance your site with skins and custom modules

4. Extensive coverage of the DAL and DAL+ for custom module development

5. Complete coverage of setup, administration, and development

Community Server Quickly

ISBN: 978-1-847190-87-1   Paperback: 304 pages

A Concise and Practical Guide to Installation, Administration, and Customization

1. Get Community Server Express Edition set up and running fast

2. Learn to manage blogs, users, forums, and file and photo galleries

3. How to customize, market, and monetize your site

Please check **www.PacktPub.com** for information on our titles

Programming Windows Workflow Foundation

ISBN: 978-1-904811-21-3   Paperback: 252 pages

A C# developer's guide to the features and programming interfaces of Windows Workflow Foundation

1. Add event-driven workflow capabilities to your .NET applications.

2. Highlights the libraries, services and internals programmers need to know

3. Builds a practical "bug reporting" workflow solution example app

ODP.NET Developer's Guide

ISBN: 978-1-847191-96-0   Paperback: 328 pages

A practical guide for developers working with the Oracle Data Provider for .NET and the Oracle Developer Tools for Visual Studio 2005

1. Application development with ODP.NET

2. Dealing with XML DB using ODP.NET

3. Oracle Developer Tools for Visual Studio .NET

Please check **www.PacktPub.com** for information on our titles